Chasing Tales

STUDIA IMAGOLOGICA
AMSTERDAM STUDIES ON CULTURAL IDENTITY

12

Serie editors
Hugo Dyserinck
Joep Leerssen

Imagology, the study of cross-national perceptions and images as expressed in literary discourse, has for many decades been one of the more challenging and promising branches of Comparative Literature.
In recent years, the shape both of literary studies and of international relations (in the political as well as the cultural sphere) has taken a turn which makes imagology more topical and urgent than before. Increasingly, the attitudes, stereotypes and prejudices which govern literary activity and international relations are perceived in their full importance; their nature as textual (frequently literary) constructs is more clearly apprehended; and the necessity for a textual and historical analysis of their typology, their discursive expression and dissemination, is being recognized by historians and literary scholars.

The series STUDIA IMAGOLOGICA, which will accommodate scholarly monographs in English, French or German, provides a forum for this literary-historical specialism.

Chasing Tales
Travel Writing, Journalism and the History of British Ideas about Afghanistan

Corinne Fowler

Amsterdam - New York, NY 2007

Cover image: *Save Me From My Friends*, Nov. 30, 1878.
Reproduced with permission of Punch Ltd., www.punch.co.uk

Cover Design: Erick de Jong

The paper on which this book is printed meets the requirements of "ISO
9706:1994, Information and documentation - Paper for documents -
Requirements for permanence".

ISBN: 978-90-420-2262-1
©Editions Rodopi B.V., Amsterdam - New York, NY 2007
Printed in the Netherlands

Chasing Tales is dedicated to the memory of all the Afghans who have lost their lives, or livelihoods, in other people's wars. I offer this book as a small contribution towards understanding the cultural forces that have shaped British ideas about Afghanistan in the hope that the history of Anglo-Afghan contact will have a slightly reduced power to shape further misunderstandings.

Contents

Acknowledgements

Written with thanks for assistance, friendship and support of a number of people who deserve special thanks. To Angela Smith, who offered wise and constructive advice throughout the writing of this book. Most particularly I wish to thank Bethan Benwell, Fiona Chalamander, Fiona Darroch, Timothy Fitzgerald, Adrian Hunter, Michelle Keown, Brian MacNair and Mark Nixon for offering to read drafts or discuss ideas despite their busy schedules. Also to James Procter, for continual generosity and encouragement. I am also grateful to David Richards, Manuel Hernandez, Mohammed Naguib, Shuruq Naguib, Sahar Saba and Payam Shalchi for their willingness to discuss ideas with me. I am also extremely thankful to those who have provided valuable feedback to my conference papers, particularly Charles Forsdick, John Eade, Ludmilla Kostova, Garry Marvin, Alasdair Pettinger, Kristi Siegel, and Tim Youngs. This book would not have been possible without the financial support of the Arts and Humanities Research Board, which included an additional grant for a study trip to the British Film Institute. The study would also have been impossible to complete without the generous cooperation of the Glasgow Media Group, particularly Greg Philo, who provided access to the Group's extensive archives for weeks on end. Finally, I am deeply grateful for the sustained support and interest of my close friends David Harley, Jane Baron, Steve Baron and my family Yvonne, Malcolm, Naomi and Jairo.

Note: An earlier, shorter version of Part Two appeared as 'Where ethnographers fear to tread: the counter-influence of ethnography on Christopher Kremmer's *The Carpet Wars* (2002) and Christina Lamb's *The Sewing Circles of Herat* (2002)' in *Journeys* 4:1, 2003.

Preface

Several years ago I noticed a woman engrossed in a book on a train. She was reading Jason Elliot's *An Unexpected Light. Travels in Afghanistan*. It was late September 2001 and, for the first time since the Soviet retreat in 1989, Afghanistan had become the focus of international media attention. It has since been shunted back into the limelight.

For that journey's duration at least, the woman had elected to read a travel book instead of a newspaper. Perhaps she craved an experiential narrative, tales of adventure in Afghanistan, or she may even have wanted an anthropologically-inspired account of cross-cultural encounter. After all, travel narratives have amply demonstrated their ability to perform either or both functions. Very possibly she sought to understand *The Places In Between*, as Rory Stewart was later to name his 'post-Taliban'[1] travel book about Afghanistan. Certainly, as it seemed to me then, drawing intimate cultural portraits was not the natural territory of the newspaper I had set down on the table in front of me.

Later that week I overheard a remark that the British public was in the process of being 'familiarised' with Afghanistan. The comment led me to revisit the scene of reading on the train the day before. Did the reader consult Elliot to supplement news media coverage of Afghanistan in the light of the forthcoming military attacks? What, to her mind, was the book's relationship to the production of knowledge about Afghanistan? Specifically, what was its role in the development of British ideas about Afghans? How sceptical was she about the insights Elliot's travel narrative had to offer? I did not then go so far as to ask her what she hoped to derive from the book. Her motives therefore remain undisclosed, but now that Afghanistan's troubles have flared up again, these larger questions deserve further investigation.

Introduction

This study is not about Afghanistan. The country's diverse, mobile population militates against the conception of Afghanistan as a bounded socio-cultural entity knowable by an enquiry such as mine. More than this, its history of contested borders, ongoing disputes over *Pashtunistan* and dispersed systems of governance problematise its delineation as a culturally or geo-politically sealed object of study, or indeed of writing. The following discussion therefore explores those notional Afghanistans that have prevailed in the popular British imagination from the early nineteenth century to the present. In tracing this historical and imaginative trajectory, I follow a well-established tradition of scholarship, namely that of imagology, or image studies. Hugo Dyserinck, who played a leading role in the development of this tradition, has noted the 'striking vitality and longevity' of 'imagotypical structures' (2003: 6).[2] Given the character and tone of very recent reporting on Afghanistan's ongoing troubles, my study of this pivotal moment of news media coverage certainly bears that out.

Patrick Holland and Graham Huggan suggest that scholars might usefully divide sites of travel into 'zones of repetition' (such as the liminal, the exotic, the Oriental and the tropics) (1998:67 & 68). Such an approach is not adopted here. While, as George E. Marcus argues, it is desirable to scrutinise the 'fiction of the whole' on which many 'place-focused' discussions are premised (1998:45), Afghanistan's past and present geo-political significance requires close attention to the powerful historical and cultural significance of Afghan borders for the British. Of course, as I shall discuss, travel writing is by no means unresponsive to notions that bear no direct relation to Afghanistan, such as *The 1001 Nights*-inspired depictions of excessive brutality. Even so, for a number of compelling reasons related to the Great Game[3] (or Victorian Cold War) and the First Anglo-Afghan War (1839-1842), British conceptions of Afghanistan tend to be particularly insular and self-referential. These conceptions are, to a surprising degree, contained within and even created by, Afghanistan's borders. To categorise Afghanistan as broadly 'Oriental' would therefore do scant justice to the specific histories of Afghan-British contact within those borders. British notions of 'warlike Afghans' are not primarily derived from generalised notions of Islamic militancy but rather flow from traumatic colonial memories of actual military encounters. For the British at least, broader notions of Islam tend to play a secondary role in confirming and supporting these impressions.

Ideally, attention to place should be considered alongside radical shifts in that place's relationship to a range of geo-political contexts. This study considers how, why and when shifting political climates and geo-strategic issues at home and abroad do and do not register in travel writing about Afghanistan. With the significant exception of the early nineteenth and twenty-first centuries, it is not possible to offer close scrutiny of historical specificities unique to particular decades.[4] The study's site-specific approach instead allows close attention to persistent patterns of representation, some of which have withstood considerable social and political upheaval.

Reinhold Schiffer claims that the writings of European travellers about non-European countries have had a bad press from critics, whose observations about travel writing are, he claims, 'shot through with fervent ideological loyalties' (1999:1). This study does not answer to the description of 'fervent'. Even so, it makes no apology for its ethical dimension, which is made transparent. While I agree with Schiffer that Britain does not have a monopoly on 'cultural arrogance' (1), travel writing about Afghanistan nevertheless raises a number of compelling questions. Of central interest is the reliance of travel narratives on heavily fictionalised and mythologised notions of Afghanistan that are chiefly the legacy of the First Anglo-Afghan War. While this need not automatically raise ethical concerns, travel narratives have played a formative role in the development of British ideas about Afghanistan, many of which resurfaced in reporting on the 2001 conflict. Also examined, therefore, is the prevalence of nineteenth-century conceptions of Afghanistan in British news media coverage of Operation Enduring Freedom. Casting its net deep into the nineteenth century, the study investigates how British travellers and journalists continue to inherit the paranoias and prejudices of their nineteenth-century predecessors and why, in British imaginations, Afghans tend to remain warlike, medieval, murderous and unruly.

A brief history of British travel through Afghanistan since the early nineteenth century

Although, by the nineteenth century, travellers had for over four hundred years passed through Afghanistan on trans-Asian trade routes (a network of ancient roads later termed, and indeed mythologised, as 'the Silk Road'), the dawn of the century saw an influx of European travellers, especially to Afghanistan's 'lesser-known' north-eastern regions.[5] In the early to mid-nineteenth century, explorers such as John Wood of the East India Company (whose 1836-1838 expedition is recorded in *A Journey to the Source of the River Oxus*) were charged with making geographical discoveries and gathering cartographic and topographic information. Probably the last archetypal explorer figure was Sir Aurel Stein, who entered the Little Pamir in 1906 on an archaeological and geographical expedition and later conducted a survey of the Amu Darya valley in 1915. There were other categories of traveller. Throughout the nineteenth century, military, political and commercial reconnaissance personnel travelled through Afghanistan to further the economic and strategic interests of Britain and, by the twentieth century, a tradition of hunting and adventuring was well established. Wealthy trophy-hunters from both Afghanistan and the United States revived the tradition in the 1960s when shooting of *ovis ovuli*, or Marco Polo sheep, was actively promoted as a leisurely pastime (Shahrani 2002:28-44).

An identifiably British tradition of travel writing emerged around the time of the 1839 British invasion of Afghanistan. This traumatic encounter inspired a great deal of travel, literary and historical writings since it culminated in a disastrous retreat during the First Anglo-Afghan War between 1841 and 1842, an episode that General Sir Michael Rose has called 'one of the darkest chapters in British military history' (in Macrory 2002:i). Commencing at the beginning of the British retreat in 1841, Lady Florentia Sale's *Journal of the First Afghan War* (1841-2) is an indictment of Britain's military and political tactics during, and immediately preceding, the retreat. Her damning yet patriotic *Journal* communicated to an alarmed Victorian audience the horror of the massacre, when nearly sixteen thousand soldiers and camp followers were killed on their retreat from Kabul. Sale's *Journal* was an important source for definitive historical accounts of this war, notably Sir John Kaye's *History of the War in Afghanistan* (1851), and influential writers such as Rudyard Kipling would have been familiar with it. Sale's narrative was undoubtedly a source of inspiration for Kipling's writing about Afghanistan since her husband, soldiers' hero 'Fighting Bob Sale', is a figure to whom Kipling repeatedly returns in his Afghan-inspired stories and *Barrack-Room Ballads* (1892).

Part One takes its title from a passage in Jason Elliot's *An Unexpected Light* (1999), which interrogates the tendency of travel writers to hang 'old stories on the necks of new characters' (337). The first section deals with the thematic imprint of First Anglo-Afghan War contexts on recent travel writing about Afghanistan. Instrumental to the development of British ideas about that country is the writing of Kipling, which represents the single biggest literary influence on subsequent travel narratives. As the following section explores, of particular relevance is Kipling's story 'The Man Who Would Be King' (1888), which features Nuristan (a province of Afghanistan known in Kipling's day as 'Kafirstan') and his novel *Kim* (1901), that heightens an already well-established sense of colonial foreboding at the prospect of crossing the North-West Frontier. This frontier was for many decades the most vulnerable of British India's borders and the symbolic point of entry into uncolonised, and uncolonisable, Afghan terrain. Part One investigates the role played by these literary pieces, resonant as they are with the memory of British incursions into precise locations, in reviving and perpetuating those memories.

Probably the best-known British narrative written before the First Anglo-Afghan War was Mountstuart Elphinstone's *An Account of the Kingdom of Caubul*, written twenty-four years before British India commenced its invasion of Afghanistan in 1839. Elphinstone led an 1808 British Mission to Shah Shujah, the then beleaguered King of Afghanistan, with the purpose of drawing up a treaty to quieten British fears of any alliance forming between Afghanistan and Napoleon, which might have led to an invasion of British India from the north

(Macrory: 33). Elphinstone's Mission failed when, later that year, the Shah was forced to flee the throne and take refuge in British India. Nevertheless, Elphinstone's proto-ethnographic description of Afghanistan has been described in Sir Olaf Caroe's preface as 'the greatest and most readable volume we possess on the Afghan country and the Afghan people' (Caroe in Elphinstone 1972edn: x). Though the Mission did not venture much beyond the environs of the North-West Frontier, Caroe states that Elphinstone 'knows of every tribe, its ways and its location' (Xx-xxi). Elphinstone's narrative scarcely makes such bold claims of omniscience. On the contrary, as Elphinstone admits: 'I have seen but part of the countries which I am about to describe' (xxix). As Part One (iii) examines, however, attributed to Elphinstone's account is a form of absentee authority (by which is meant the authority accorded to narratives whose authors never visited Afghanistan) that established a precedent for later writers such as Kipling. The section considers the ethical implications of absentee authority since nineteenth-century travel to Afghanistan generated a body of narratives by writers who never set foot in the regions about which they claim to have knowledge. Heavy reliance on the absentee authority of anterior writings has ramifications for those recent travel narratives that aspire to a degree of informational status; recent texts tend to inherit this trait of 'absenteeism'. Part One goes on to argue that Kipling's writing was instrumental to British news audiences' (re)familiarisation[6] with Afghanistan during the early stages of Operation Enduring Freedom in 2001. Despite the problematic association of Kipling with the tradition of absentee authority, newspaper articles in particular were littered with references to the canonical writer.

Among the most influential twentieth-century British travellers to Afghanistan is Robert Byron, whose *The Road to Oxiana* (first published in 1937) has undergone several reprintings, as has Eric Newby's 1955 classic, *A Short Walk in the Hindu Kush*. More recent travel writing comes from Freya Stark (*The Minaret of Djam*), first published in 1970, Peter Levi (*The Light Garden of the Angel King*), first published in 1972, and Bruce Chatwin ('A Lament For Afghanistan'), written in 1980. Part One deals with only one writer from the United States, Jean Bowie-Shor, whose version of Afghanistan tends not to conform to the British renderings. Certain details of Bowie-Shor's 1955 travel account place her at odds with her British counterparts. For example, her narrative attributes blue-eyed and fair-haired children in north-eastern Afghanistan to the intermingling of Afghan and Russian blood (151), while the explanation favoured (or at least consistently raised) by generations of writers from the British tradition derives from an ancient legend popularised by Kipling's 'The Man Who Would Be King'[7], that people from the province of Nuristan are distantly related to the soldiers of Alexander the Great, who passed through the region twenty-five centuries before.

A major theme of this study is the legacy of nineteenth-century contexts and ideas to late twentieth and early twenty-first-century British travel writing and journalism about Afghanistan. As with most travel writers, British travellers to Afghanistan routinely pay homage to their forebears. Of Marco Polo's *Travels*, John Wood writes '[it is] a work illustrated by copious and most erudite notes [...that] first impressed me with a conviction of the authenticity of the narrative' (149). Chatwin writes of Byron's *The Road to Oxiana*: 'My own copy – now spineless and flood stained after four journeys to Central Asia – has been with me since the age of fifteen'. He describes how he 'aped both his [Byron's] itinerary and – as if that were possible – his style' (1998: 287-288). More recently, in the 'Acknowledgements' section of *An Unexpected Light*, Jason Elliot pays tribute 'to former travellers from whose works I have drawn strength'. Importantly, he discovers that he is not alone in his liking for British writing about the region; the head man of an Afghan village where Elliot stays keeps a copy of Lawrence's *Seven Pillars of Wisdom* on his shelves (1999: 103).

Not only are travel writers inspired by, and stylistically indebted to, their predecessors, but they also literally follow in their footsteps. Jean Bowie-Shor's book is named *After You, Marco Polo* while Victoria Finlay's handbag contains a photocopied chapter of John Wood's account of an identical journey made by him in 1851 (335). Contemporary British accounts are therefore infused with the ideas and feelings of their predecessors about Afghanistan. The intrusion of nineteenth-century phraseology or even single vocabulary items betrays a particular historical and literary indebtedness to writing from that period. Contemporary travel writers habitually substitute the name 'Nuristan' for the province's pre-1896 name 'Kafirstan', and certain turns of phrase contain the linguistic remnants of British India, such as the Hindu appellation 'Pathan' (rather than its modern variant, 'Pashtun') to describe the people associated with a region straddling the North-West Frontier. As Part One discusses, borrowing vocabulary items from the nineteenth-century is symptomatic of processes taking place at a deeper structural and ideological level. Of central interest to this study is the habit of superimposing geographically and historically disparate memories onto contemporary Afghan scenes and settings, an idea that Eva Sallis explores in relation to *The Thousand and One Nights* by noting that the *Nights* were 'cut loose from one history and insecurely attached to another' by Victorian readers (1999: 58). In historically imprecise twentieth and twenty-first century imaginations, I will argue, these traumatic memories have become partially dislodged from their original context of attempted British conquest and displaced onto contemporary Afghanistan in the form of generalised myths about warlike Afghans. More than this, the horror and intrigue associated with precise geographical locations (particularly Nuristan, sites of massacre on the road to Jalalabad and the dreaded North-West Frontier) have become imaginatively dispersed throughout the country so that Afghanistan's diverse range of cultural and geographical locations tends increasingly to be tarred with the same sinister brush.

Despite travel writers' inevitable sense of belatedness, and while, as Holland and Huggan argue, regions 'accrue ever denser layers of textuality' as time goes on, Afghanistan is a less-visited region than, for example, India or Turkey. Unlike travel to more popular locations, its geographically hostile and primarily rural terrain and (in recent decades) persistent experience of warfare mean that travel through the country is by no means, in the words of Holland and Huggan, 'stripped of immediate pioneering thrill' (1998: 67). To this day, Afghanistan remains an 'adventurous' location for the British. The literal inaccessibility of Afghanistan means that travel writing about Afghanistan is less troubled by the problem of cliché and not as subject to the same imperatives to parody or refute the discoveries and insights of earlier travellers as has been suggested is generally the case (Holland and Huggan: 67). With the exception of Eric Newby's self-parody, which represents a response to shifting masculinities and a

consciousness of the impossibility of adopting an explorer's stance
after empire, travel writing about Afghanistan has a tendency to defer
more readily to the portrayals of earlier writings, adopting a more
corroborative tenor than generalised theories about travel writing
might lead us to expect. Rather than offering what Holland and
Huggan describe as a 'highly personal vision' (10) (or even, as Jason
Elliot puts it, 'some private hallucination' (17)) of Afghanistan,
British travel writers inherit from their predecessors a peculiarly
mythologised sense of the country as lawless and brutal.

Part One (v) ends by exploring the conceptualisation of Afghanistan
as being contemporaneous with medieval Europe.[8] While the practice
of medievalising a country is not unique to writing about Afghanistan,
its prevalence in British travel writing makes it worthy of attention in
its own right. The section that follows examines Afghanistan's
persistent medievalisation in news media coverage of Operation
Enduring Freedom, asserting that the medieval comparison bespeaks
the anxieties, desires and self-perpetuating agendas of 'modernity'
itself.

Genres and sub-genres

Joan Pau Rubies argues that the category descriptor 'genre' is best
'defined in its plurality' in order to convey the breadth and variety of
the writing it encompasses (in Hulme and Youngs 2003:244). This is
certainly the case with travel writing about Afghanistan, which can be
broadly divided into sub-genres according to the varying
circumstances and purposes of travel during different historical
periods and changing political circumstances, to which travel
narratives necessarily respond. Although it would be tidy-minded to
suggest that these sub-genres do not, at certain junctures, impinge on
one another's territory (they clearly do) some form of sub-
classification nevertheless proves useful purely because ongoing
warfare encroaches on certain of these sub-genres.

Mountstuart Elphinstone's 1815 *An Account of the Kingdom of
Caubul* is a pillar of the British tradition. His narrative is primarily
informational and proto-ethnographic. To an extent, Elphinstone's
writing finds its contemporary counterpart in the travel writing of war

correspondents such as Christina Lamb, whose work is discussed in Part Two. As the study's second part explores, the increasing trend of correspondents to produce travel narratives as an accompaniment to, or by-product of, their professional work has created a semi-professionalised sub-genre that I have described (perhaps unflatteringly) as pseudo-ethnographic journalism. A military sub-genre emerged during the First Anglo-Afghan War, with the *Journal* of Lady Florentia Sale, Vincent Eyre's *The Military Operations at Kabul* (1843) and Lieutenant-General Colin Mackenzie's *Storms and Sunshine of a Soldier's Life*, which was published years after the massacre in 1886. A tradition of exploration extends from the years immediately preceding the First Anglo-Afghan War encompassing the discovery-led writing of John Wood and, straddling the nineteenth and twentieth centuries, the more archaeologically focused writing of Sir Aurel Stein, whom Michael Wood describes as 'the greatest archaeologist-explorer of all'.[9] A tradition of archaeological and aesthetic writing was established by Byron (1937) and taken up by Levi and Stark (1972). In D. Talbot Rice's introduction to the 1950 edition of Byron's travel account, he coins a somewhat broader term - 'art-travel' - for writing primarily concerned with 'buildings, paintings and works of art' (1950:vi). However, as I discuss, this sub-genre was relatively short-lived since the onset of war meant that 'art-travellers' found their quests literally interrupted or, occasionally, ethically unsustainable due to their bourgeois associations. Running in thematic, if belated, parallel to the explorer tradition of writing is that of the twentieth-century adventurer journeying through Afghanistan's north-eastern regions. In a sense, the adventurer figure endures to the present, finding its twenty-first century counterpart in the war correspondent. Newby's *A Short Walk in the Hindu Kush* falls broadly into this sub-category. Later examples are Dervla Murphy's *Full Tilt* (1965)[10] and, more recently, Jonny Bealby's *For a Pagan Song* (1999).

Within each sub-category is found a wide variety of styles and approaches, ranging from the formal and densely-referenced to 'low-brow' narratives that make only very limited overt reference to their literary forebears. Self-confessed reliance on a single source, as is the case with Jonny Bealby's in-the-footsteps narrative inspired by 'The Man Who Would Be King', means that his account is also shaped by nineteenth-century texts that have been refracted through Kipling's story. Bealby writes: '[Nuristan] appeared as mysterious and foreboding in reality as it had in fiction' (20), and comments such as these seem to confirm Said's notion that '[t]ravel throws one back on what one has read about it' (1978: 93). However, as this study argues, the process cannot be accurately described as one of straightforward influence. The process is more complex and multi-faceted than Said's statement allows. In other cases there is a conspicuous, even deliberate, lack of referentiality, as can be seen with Dervla Murphy's *Full Tilt*, whose narrative style and content tend to militate against the adoption of an informational stance. However, as I shall discuss, because nineteenth-century accounts do not merely transmit themselves through direct perusal of their pages by any single travel writer, texts that are not self-evidently 'writerly' are rarely at variance with the salient features of the British tradition.

Part Two, entitled 'Where ethnographers fear to tread', maintains the focus on genre by considering the crucial relationship between British anthropology, travel writing and journalism about Afghanistan. First it examines the recent travel narratives of two journalists, Christopher Kremmer and Christina Lamb, to consider the significance of travel writing's generic overlap with ethnography. As is the case with the study's inclusion of writing by Jean Bowie-Shor, the choice of Kremmer, an Australian, signals a temporary departure from an exclusive focus on the British tradition. However, this is justified by the sustained focus on generic overlap and the pressing need to avoid enslavement to my own system of classification, which is intended to assist and order the discussion rather than to impose fixed and inflexible boundaries.

Since travel writing predates ethnography, research has so far concentrated on the influence of the former on the latter (Pratt 1986; Pau-Rubies 2002). Less attention has been paid to the question of counter-influence: the presence of pre-crisis modes of ethnography in recent travel narratives. Part Two argues that travel writing by journalists such as Kremmer and Lamb is subject to imperatives to transmit a degree of authority, credibility and insight that the traditionally low-status genre of travel writing generally struggles to accomplish. Part Two deals with the pseudo-ethnographic content of

British news media coverage towards the end of 2001. Taken into account in these discussions, however, will be recent interventions in the anthropological 'crisis' debate by feminist ethnographers who regret the determinism associated with the postmodern turn in ethnography and who, like feminist critics in the parallel field of literary criticism, do not wish to rule out the possibility of agency.

Women travellers and their critics: debating nineteenth-century travel narratives

My discussion of the significance of gender is not relegated to a sub-section but rather integrated into the study as a whole. In their recently published anthology of women's travel writing, Shirley Foster and Sara Mills appear to recommend that theirs be the last collection of its kind. 'Ideally', they argue, 'we would like to see anthologies of travel writing and critical essays on travel writing which do not make any essentialist assumptions, which refer equally to men's and women's work' (2002: 5). This study takes up that suggestion. Mapping power's multiple trajectories requires that gender is placed in the context of a range of factors that have a bearing on travel writers' constructions of Afghanistan, such as the ongoing impact of nineteenth-century colonial writing on the history of British ideas about the Anglo-Afghan encounter. As Indira Ghose points out, while it is critically important to consider the significance of gender, it is best to avoid becoming obsessed with it 'to the exclusion of all other relations of power' (1998: 159). Sidonie Smith also suggests that, since '[c]entres and margins shift against various horizons of power' (432), there is a pressing need to explore where, when and why such shifts occur. Throughout this study, gender is theorised as one of several variables that have a significant influence on British travel writing and news media coverage.[11]

Despite its concentration on relatively recent travel writing and news media coverage about Afghanistan, my discussion is written with an eye on critical debates about the relationship of nineteenth-century women's travel narratives to colonialism, partly because the thematic fingerprints of the nineteenth-century can be detected all over recent accounts of Afghan-British encounters. This last point is important to take into consideration when establishing whether travel narratives and journalism by women has a different relationship to the history of ideas about Afghanistan. As scholars such as Mills and Ghose have discussed, a significant body of feminist criticism has asserted that nineteenth-century women's travel writing is qualitatively different from that of its male counterpart. Indeed, Elleke Boehmer argues that nineteenth-century travel writing by women is necessarily 'inflected by the speaking positions allowed within colonial culture' (1998: xxxi). Implicit in Boehmer's statement is an explanation of difference that is based on gendered positionality, as opposed to gendered interiority. My findings support the contention that positionality is critically important since, as I will argue, it remains significant in late twentieth and early twenty-first-century accounts.[12] Complicating this claim, however, is the view finally adopted by this study, namely that it is neither possible nor desirable simply to confirm or deny that men and women have different relationships to the history of ideas about Afghanistan. ⌊Rather I explore the extent to which it is possible to determine the precise causes of subversions of, or deviations from, dominant representational tendencies.⌋ If we allow that colonial women travellers sometimes represented the colonised in 'more nuanced and identified' ways (Boehmer xxviii), the growing body of criticism on women's travel writing highlights the dangers of making such claims unreservedly, and without qualification (Ghose 1998; Mills and Foster 2002). Aside from the difficulties associated with categorisations based on gender alone,[13] close scrutiny of the diverse elements that act on *all* travel writing about Afghanistan tempers any suggestion that women's travel writing is 'generically distinct' from that of men, a claim that Mills has convincingly rejected (6).

Importantly, the study's discussion of British men and women's representations of the Afghan-British encounter is removed from the arena of value judgment. As critics of nineteenth-century travel writing have discovered, valorising women travellers runs the risk of viewing them as transcendent individuals, thereby ignoring the colonial context from which their narratives emerge.[14] Apportioning blame risks analysing them in terms of individual morality rather than being sensitive to the pathology of colonialism, or indeed of imperialism, itself.[15] Mills, for example, has argued that conflicting demands on nineteenth-century women travellers to be feminine and yet to make confident pro-imperialist assertions 'pulled' their writing 'in different textual directions', thereby 'expos[ing]' imperialism's 'unsteady foundations' (1992:3). The implications of this claim for recent writing about Afghanistan are investigated throughout this study.

Publications such as Mary Russell's *The Blessings of a Good Thick Skirt* (1986) and Mary Morris and Larry O Connor's *The Virago Book of Women Travellers* (1994) are indicative of an earlier tendency, supported from the late nineteen-seventies by publishing initiatives such as Virago's Reprint Library and, more recently, its Travellers series to celebrate nineteenth-century women's travel writing as proto-feminist.[16] Of ongoing concern to my discussion is the contention, often implicit in discussions of colonial women's travel writing, that women's transgression of gender boundaries predisposes them to breach racial boundaries. As Smith has argued, this secondary breach is by no means an inevitable consequence of the first (in Smith and Watson 1992:420). Of interest to critics such as Mills, Ghose and Cheryl McEwan has been the way in which earlier scholars and anthologists dealt with the 'colonial' content of women's travel writing. Travel writing by women reflects the fact that colonial women, for whom travel to the colonies often served a liberatory function, were both 'acted upon and acting' (Anne McClintock in McEwan 2000:11). In this study, the relationship of contemporary women's travel writing to nineteenth-century notions of Afghanistan is understood in terms of both halves of McClintock's equation. As earlier generations of feminist scholars have advised, it is productive to return men's and women's travel writing - and indeed their journalism - to the specific contexts of historical and ideological processes, generic convention, editorial intervention and critical reception.[17]

Central to my understanding of women's potentially different relationship to the history of ideas about Afghanistan is the question of authorial intent, again indicating the important critical legacy of studies about colonial women's travel writing. Persistent disagreement among scholars of nineteenth-century women's travel writing over the 'anti-imperialist' or 'proto-feminist' content of writings by figures such as Mary Kingsley arises partly from the diverse range of reading strategies employed. It is my belief that critical debates about colonial women's travel writing centre on authorial intent. Despite this, only Mills (and, to a lesser degree, Ghose) dwell on the relevance of intentionality.[18] Meanwhile celebratory critics have consistently failed to address this issue, partly because they tend to pursue biographical readings (Mills 1992) that rely upon notions of autonomous authorship. Mills observes that many critics of women's travel writing persist in producing 'partial and coherent readings' that at least implicitly embrace authorial intent (5). By so doing, they enable themselves to make confident assertions about a writer's political intent (usually proto-feminist or anti-colonial). This study problematises the notion that subversions of dominant patterns of representation can always be said to arise from conscious intent. As Mills has observed, scholars will ideally attend not so much to ways in which narratives express the feelings or opinions of an individual, but to their 'relationship to other discourses'. Rather than seeking a text's unity, she argues, the critic should trace 'the different voices discursively produced' within each travel narrative (9). Mills's statement encapsulates the aim of this site-specific study.

Any refusal to privilege political intent carries the attendant risk of prematurely discounting women's agency as writers. While it is desirable to exorcise lingering notions of essentialist authorship (Ghose 1998), my discussion incorporates the interventions of feminist ethnographers in order to forestall a deterministic approach to men's and women's travel writing about Afghanistan. It is thus necessary to straddle two positions: first, negating the idea that discursive structures can be transcended and, second, understanding how these structures may be altered through persistent, possibly strategic, subversions and negotiations[19] of those existing structures. Of special interest is that which Judith Butler has described as 'variations on the repetition' of certain 'rule-bound discourses' (in Smith and Watson: xx).[20] This feature is most readily identifiable in postmodern travel narratives.

One further aspect of nineteenth-century travel narratives by women is pertinent to this study. Scholarly work does not always lay sufficient store by the fact that textual ambiguity is not the preserve of writing by colonial women.[21] Indeed, all empire writing tends to trail ambiguity in its wake. The instability of imperial rhetoric is itself a recurrent source of narrative tension. Mills's contention that men's writing is more 'straightforwardly colonial' than women's is problematic in the sense that there is nothing 'straightforward' about the colonial. There are two main reasons for this. One has to do with political opposition to empire, ranging from agnosticism about the colonial project (doubts about its moral justification) to radical dissent both from the metropole and, more importantly, from within the colonies themselves. The other relates to the 'discursive polyphony' (Pratt 1986:140) of imperial discourse. As Boehmer suggests, analyses of empire writing are ideally informed by a 'perception of the multiplicity and instability at the very heart of the colonial project' (xvi & xvii).[22] Correspondingly, terms such as *anti-colonial* imply strategic opposition when subversions of colonialism can often be traced back to the flawed logic, tensions and contradictions at the core of imperialism itself. When Mills argues that women 'constitute counter-hegemonic voices within colonialist discourse' (23), therefore, it is unlikely she meant to suggest that men replicate imperialist discourses in uncomplicated ways. Elsewhere she stresses the importance of attending to evidence of 'personal conflict' and textual ambiguity in *all* colonial writing. As she advises, travel narratives can be read 'less as simply replications or reaffirmations of colonial rule, but rather as symptoms of contradictions inherent in that power relation' (3). Once again, this study closely follows her advice.

Men and women reporting Afghanistan

My study of news media coverage is similarly informed by an investigation of the relationship between journalists' gender and two related questions. First, it asks whether gender had any bearing on the relationship between the 2001 British news coverage and the history of British ideas about Afghanistan or indeed the degree to which it is possible to adequately answer such questions. Second, it considers the extent to which news reports by men and women facilitated an understanding of Afghans, particularly Afghan women, as actors in, and commentators upon, Operation Enduring Freedom.

In her introduction to *The Bookseller of Kabul*, the Norwegian journalist Asne Sierstad points out that she has unique access to her sources: '[h]ad I been a man I would never have been able to live so close to the women of the household' (2004: 5). This said, she also raises the issue of her curious 'bi-gendered' status (5), which implies a degree of privilege and autonomy that troubles any sense that cross-cultural solidarity is a straightforward affair.[23] Jennifer Cuff's report for 'From Our Own Correspondent' similarly conveys a sense of 'bi-gendered' or 'honorary manhood' status when she describes entering a room of Afghan men seated according to social importance only to find herself being 'perched on a high chair' beside her host ('Challenging prize for Afghan poll winner', 'From Our Own Correspondent', BBC *Radio 4*, 26 June 2004). This tangible sign of privilege is likely to be predicated on Cuff's perceived closeness to centres of political power, or at least on her ability to deliver reports to global media networks. The potential benefits of greater access to local women are clearly tempered by female correspondents' access to the realm of mainstream news reporting. To give as much weight to Afghans' various perceptions of the status of journalists as to the self-images of women such as Lamb, Sierstad and Sebba, is to return to the principle described by Smith that '[c]entres and margins shift against various horizons of power' (432).

As feminists from various scholarly quarters have pointed out, it is important not to discount the issue of agency, intentional or otherwise.[24] Nevertheless, considerations of agency on the part of individual journalists need to be placed in the context of established journalistic conventions, reporting conditions (especially political, practical and time constraints), stringent editorial processes, market forces, the cultural norms of newsrooms, and so on. Established practices of war reporting are also central to the study's discussion. Of particular relevance is the persistent tendency of war correspondents to under-represent unofficial actors of global conflicts. Augusta C. DelZotto's study of news media coverage of the Kosovan conflict found that the loudest voice was granted to male 'key players' and 'elite figures' of war (2002). Also crucial is the ideological backdrop of the War on Terror to the reporting of Operation Enduring Freedom. Weighing up the relative influence of these factors can be difficult. As with analyses of nineteenth-century women's travel writing, it is not always possible to make definitive statements about the significance of gender because of the number of factors in play. Nevertheless, its ongoing significance requires striking a balance between being open to the possibility of gendered agency on the one hand while resisting the temptation to homogenise reporting as either 'female' or 'male' on the other. As I argue in Part Two, reporting by men is sometimes more self-reflexive than caricatures of men's journalism allow. There is, for example, evidence that male journalists are participating in a sustained critique of what U.S. journalist Robert D. Kaplan characterises as the 'foreign male in the war zone, who s[ees] himself as a character in a movie' (2001: 75).

Other analytical difficulties pertain to the gendered division of labour, of which reporting on Operation Enduring Freedom was fairly typical. Although there were some high-profile women news anchors such as Kirsty Wark and Fiona Bruce, only a handful of television news reports were by women correspondents.[25] This gender imbalance was not always the case in documentary-making about Afghanistan. Saira Shah's documentary 'Beneath the Veil', for example, was instrumental in raising awareness both of women's experiences living under Taliban rule and of the post-war humanitarian crisis.[26] More generally however, women journalists tended to produce articles for newspapers or reports for radio. This gender-related differentiation of generic output accounts for the study's inclusion of transcripts of radio reports from BBC *Radio 4's* 'From Our Own Correspondent' in the survey of news media coverage in 2001. The division of labour hampers any straightforward comparative approach to journalistic productions by men and women since it is not possible to compare like with like. As I discuss in Part Three, however, reporting by men and women in 2001 shared a salient theme, the 'plight' of Afghan women, which I trace through radio and television reports and newspaper articles. The theme's prominence was related to the pseudo-feminist content of coalition leaders' rhetoric of liberation. Female and male journalists' treatment of Afghan women thus provides the best opportunity for a rigorous comparative focus.

Some of the claims made by British journalists about reporting by women parallel those theories of women's travel writing that are partially founded on assumptions of gendered interiority.[27] A common claim, advanced by Lamb, Anne Sebba and others, is that female war correspondents are less focused on the machinery of war than men (Lamb: appendix six; Sebba in Allan 2003: 77). Sebba even goes so

far as to say that concentration on the apparatus of war is symptomatic
of men's tendency to take the 'soft option', since war machinery is
'less taxing to one's emotional being' (77). In an interview carried out
by the author of this study, however, Lamb blames the overemphasis
on scenes of actual combat on male editors rather than on the war
correspondents themselves:

> A difficulty for women reporters, too, is that all the news editors [...] in
> British newspapers are male, what they often want from the correspondents
> on the ground is sort of 'bang bang' and battles [...] so it's quite difficult
> sometimes to be trying to write stuff from behind the scenes, because to
> them that's not the story, the story is the fighting on the ground [...] I think
> that happens for male and female correspondents (December 2003,
> appendix six).

Women news professionals commonly cast doubt on the idea that their
work is significantly different from that of their male counterparts.
Hannerz notes that, while women journalists frequently comment on
the *machismo* of male colleagues, they tend to believe that the
constraints and conditions of reporting mean that there is little
difference in outcome (2004: 94). Furthermore, Stuart Allan suggests
that women reporters are under intense pressure to comply with
'masculinised norms of reporting', although he fails to specify what
such an approach or style might entail (2004: 128). Once again, the
question of access to women interviewees is of paramount importance.
Cecilia Udden's suggestion that women reporters have greater
opportunity to meet local women than their male colleagues is entirely
justified (Hannerz 2004: 95).[28] More problematic claims of gender-
related differences in reporting pertain to cross-cultural solidarities
between women. Sylvia Poggioli suggests that, during the Bosnian
war, the increase in numbers of women correspondents meant that
rape was foregrounded as a serious issue (Hannerz: 95). Complicating
this claim is DelZotto's focus on news coverage of rape during the
Kosovo conflict. She found that women's role as commentators on the
experience of living through conflict tended to be restricted to that of
'the rape survivor' in ways that did little to challenge women's
portrayal as passive victims, or '[w]eeping women' (2002: 146). Allen
also points out that news accounts consistently sideline women's
voices or represent them as 'passive reactors' to events or as
representatives of the uninformed public (2004: 129). Part Three

problematises narratives of cross-cultural solidarity among women by examining some of the faultlines between Afghan women and British journalists.

British news media coverage of Operation Enduring Freedom

Part Three is exclusively devoted to recent British news media coverage of Operation Enduring Freedom and its title, 'retailing insight', foregrounds the economic dimension of news production. The discussion is based on a survey of British news media coverage of these military operations between September and December 2001. This included BBC1 and ITV television news reports broadcast during this period together with a survey of newspaper articles. Also studied were over one hundred BBC *Radio Four* reports for 'From Our Own Correspondent' and a number of television documentaries broadcast before, during and after the specified period. The first section considers how the absence of geo-political contexts to conflict fought on Afghan soil is implicated in historically amnesiac political rhetoric about the need for military intervention on the part of the coalition. Following this, I examine the resurrection of nineteenth-century themes in British news media coverage. In particular, the study interrogates the way in which nineteenth-century conceptions of Afghan warfare (again based on the traumatic 1842 massacre) tended to detract from the uncomfortable military realities of operations such as Operation Enduring Freedom. The final section of Part Three concentrates on the theme of Afghan women's 'plight' by concentrating on journalists' reporting of the *burqua* and their response to the prevalence of 'women's liberation' as a central feature of coalition rhetoric.

As far as Afghanistan is concerned, it is entirely necessary to study news media coverage alongside travel writing. To separate travel writing and journalism would be an artificial exercise, since sustained news media coverage during Operation Enduring Freedom promotes increasing generic interdependence. Travel writing published since 2001 cannot now be removed, nor can it remove itself, from the context of recent international media attention. Equally, as I have suggested, when British correspondents found themselves barred from Afghan territory during the early weeks of Operation Enduring

Freedom, many turned to travel narratives and histories of those early
nineteenth-century Anglo-Afghan encounters as a means of
(re)familiarising British news audiences with the region. [Close
scrutiny of this coverage enables this study to chart the course of
nineteenth-century notions from genre to genre and from context to
context.]

[Any sustained focus on persistent patterns of representation risks
incurring the charge of rehearsing Saidian debates and duplicating an
associated tendency to pursue over-homogenised 'readings' of travel
writing and news media coverage.] It seems justified to ask whether
my discussion reaches beyond the bounds of identifying and
categorising these patterns, or whether this process is a justifiable end
in itself. This is a valid question that deserves a well-considered
response. Until now, no extensive survey of tropes associated with
Afghanistan has been carried out. There is a pressing need to sketch
the history of British ideas about Afghanistan so that news stories'
(largely unacknowledged) nineteenth-century legacy may be properly
understood for the first time. However, this is not the alpha and omega
of my study. Representational *dis*continuities are scrutinised
throughout the discussion, however atypical they may be. Attending to
significant disruptions of, or interventions in, representational norms
about Afghanistan re-opens the question of authorial agency and
contributes usefully to debates about the ethics of reporting and
associated ethnographic dilemmas of representation. Part Three
considers the extent to which certain strategies might be adopted by
individual journalists (if not by news organisations themselves) to
disrupt or even transform the powerful drift of ideas about
Afghanistan. With this end in mind, close attention is paid to instances
where news reports or newspaper articles successfully bring a degree
of equity to the scene of the Afghan-British encounter, thereby
facilitating a shift from *consumption* on the part of news audiences to
interaction.[29]

Great care has been taken throughout not to homogenise British news
media coverage. This has been accomplished in two ways, firstly by
attending to a range of news media and secondly, by adopting as
flexible and nuanced a 'reading' strategy as possible. When inherited
ideas migrate to various forms of news media, they do not enter some

creative vacuum where they continue to exist intact and unaltered. Of course, there is a great deal of mileage in Said's contention that the constant reiteration of certain ideas means that the subject of representation 'stands charged and convicted without the need for supporting arguments or modulating qualifications' (1997: xviii). Even so, inherited notions of Afghanistan undergo considerable transformation simply because they are affected by a range of variables. Journalistic agency is merely one factor that has an impact on news media coverage. It is thus important to distinguish between ideas' *substance* (those inherited tropes and dominant themes) and the varying modes of their *representation*. While 2001 news media coverage did not necessarily differ markedly in substance from the salient themes of travel writing and anthropology about Afghanistan, specific imperatives (to reduce complexity, to avoid controversy, to accept the frame of the War on Terror, to conform to styles commonly heralded as good journalism, and so on) mean that these ideas undergo specific revisions as they are subjected to conflicting pressures and consequently reshaped to serve a variety of purposes. Meanings are notoriously unstable; it is not possible to claim that an idea has survived intact simply because it is traceable to a nineteenth-century travel narrative or to a poem by Kipling. It would be misleading, for example, to exaggerate the significance of a phrase about 'unruly Afghans' in a single news report. Despite its strong association with Sir Alfred Lyall's notion of uncolonisable Afghans in 'The Amir's Soliloquy' (Azoy 2003:21),[30] the phrase's significance is most effectively assessed in relation to the report's entirety. This enables a more measured assessment of the extent to which the report's analytical content (together with the images it contains) tends to sustain or contradict the notion of 'unruliness' as a fixed Afghan trait. Only when the phrase is prevalent in a sizeable proportion of news reports does the assertion of Afghan unruliness accrue significance.

Chasing Tales

The title of this study, 'Chasing Tales', is intended to convey the circulation, and indeed the circularity, of ideas commonly found in travel writing and journalism about Afghanistan. However, since the study avoids over-homogenised readings, it is important to stress that this title relates primarily to ideas' substance rather than to their representation. The 'tales' component of the title stresses the derivation of these ideas from fictionalised sources, particularly the writing of Kipling. Although direct experience of travel plays an important, though by no means straightforward, part in the modification of ideas, Afghanistan's continued status as a seldom-visited country[31] accounts for the degree to which self-evidently fictionalised tales have tended, since the nineteenth century, to be privileged over eye-witness accounts. Although the image of 'chasing' in perpetual circles risks incurring the charge of deterministic analysis, the unusually high degree of inter-referentiality between and among texts and news reports fully justifies the study's title.

I return to Schiffer's critique of 'fervent' ideological investment. In many senses, his accusation lacks historical depth. Dyserinck provides a useful overview of the usefulness of the imagological tradition which, in his words, 'promise[s] to form a bridge to other human sciences, in order to solve problems the importance of which indeed "dépasse la seule littérature"' (2003:3). In the 1950s, for example, imagological studies made important contributions to 'research on the psychological background of the in[t]er-European nationality conflicts' (3). My work testifies to the longevity and usefulness of that discipline, which began so long ago with the study of 'Germanophobia' (Dyserinck: 6) has here extended its reach to examine the historical roots of phenomena such as 'Afghanophobia' in British imaginations. Such an approach has been described by Robert Escarpit (in Dyserinck 2003) and, more recently by Philip Schlesinger (2006), as the sociology of literature. In this respect, as Dyserinck himself argues, this scholarly venture is 'of great extraliterary promise' (5). Ethical commitment therefore need not be tied to 'ideological loyalties' as Schiffer suggests. Ideally, however, a study that raises ethical concerns will also offer constructive conclusions. Investigated throughout, therefore, is the potential for travel narratives and news media coverage to subvert, negotiate and strategically revise popular British notions of Afghanistan. The study ends by combining its insights with an assessment of the viability and relevance of proposals by anthropologists and media professionals for more experimental, responsible and self-reflexive practices.

Part One
Hanging old stories on the necks of new characters: the legacy of nineteenth-century Afghan-British encounters.

'[They] have seen the Afghan ghost and have never lost the impression' (Lord Salisbury in Heathcote 1980: 91).[32]

The psychological impact of the First Anglo-Afghan War on British imaginations cannot be underestimated. The political consequences, too, were grave: British power had been destabilised in Central and South Asia, and British unpopularity reached new heights in Afghanistan even while Russia was increasing its influence in the region (Heathcote: 82). The First Anglo-Afghan War was significant for Victorians for other reasons, not least because it served as a warning of the potential for successful insurrection in British India. As Macrory points out, the significance of Britain's tarnished military reputation was not lost on the 'Mutineers'[33] fifteen years later (2002: 15). As a result, Victorian historical accounts of the War were imbued with a sense of its significance for the internal stability of British India. Published just six years before the 1857 'Mutiny', Sir John Keay's *History of the War In Afghanistan* (1851), seems plagued by its shadow-story; the future possibility of a major uprising in India. Written as it was at a fraught moment in British India's history, Keay's recounting of this Anglo-Afghan tale of woe would have seemed profoundly relevant to British India's ongoing survival. The fear that plagues Keay's historical account reveals itself in numerous ways, not least in his discussion of the early nineteenth-century ambitions of the former Afghan Amir, Zehman Shah, to invade British India. In this discussion, a telling vocabulary item, *hordes*, invites a meditation on the rise and fall of earlier empires such as the Mongol empire, thereby bearing historicised testimony to the probable future collapse of British India, a notion that was profoundly disturbing to another recurrent assertion in Keay's history, that of British India's 'settled tranquillity' (3). Indeed, Keay's frequent deployment of the word 'tranquillity' makes an implicit, but telling, connection between past Afghan and future Indian uprisings. Though his introduction might be straightforwardly read as one of confidence in British invincibility ('[w]e [...] in these times trustingly contemplate the settled tranquillity of the north-western provinces of India' (3)) it carries a coded warning against colonial complacency. Significantly, the reader is reminded that a key actor and victim of the First Anglo-Afghan War, Sir William McNaughten, suffered because '[n]othing disturbed his faith in the general tranquillity of [Afghanistan]' (629). Keay's *History* did not merely address the threat to the security of British India within its very borders, but also the threat, real or imagined, from countries to the north. From the early nineteenth century, Afghanistan was considered, in Keay's words, 'the high-road from Europe to the heart of our Indian Empire' (7). Before 1809 there prevailed the perceived threat, largely unfounded, that Napoleon would invade British India via Afghanistan. This threat soon took a different shape: by the 1830s the fear, which this time had some grounds, was that Afghanistan and Iran might collaborate with Tsarist Russia against British India.[34]

I return to the military and psychological significance of Afghan borders, especially the North-West Frontier, as potential points of entry to (and exit from) the relative security of British India. The frontier's significance for the Great Game (largely fought between Tsarist Russia and Victorian Britain) is summarised as follows by historian James Morris in *Pax Britannica. The Climax of An Empire*:

> Much of Victorian imperial history had depended upon the fear of Russian intentions [...] The most vulnerable frontier point of all lay in the north-west corner of India, in the tangled country around Afghanistan - Alexander's gateway to India. It was a double anxiety. Afghanistan itself was a very unreliable neighbour, and the frontier was inhabited by lawless Muslim tribes owing no very definite allegiance to anybody, and making it exceedingly difficult to establish a firm line of defence. This was the country of the Great Game (1968: 276).

As a result of these political circumstances, the North-West Frontier and, by extension, Afghanistan, were envisaged as uncolonisable spaces and ever-present reminders of the limit to British authority and influence. Correspondingly, imperial self-assurance faltered at the

North-West Frontier due to the perception that, once in Afghan territory, British travellers' personal safety was no longer guaranteed. During the build-up of tension between British India and Afghanistan immediately preceding the First Anglo-Afghan War, Alexander Burnes's 1832 journey beyond the Pass through Afghanistan's north-eastern Kunduz province led him to write: '[t]he name of Englishman, which had carried us safely through all other places, was here replete with danger' (1839: 30). Similar sentiments were expressed in 1877 by Lord Lytton, quoted here in the 1991 travel narrative of Peter Somerville-Large: 'I know of no other spot where, after twenty-five years of occupation [of British India] a great civilised power has obtained so little knowledge of [...the Pathans] that the country within a day's ride of its most important garrison is an absolute terra incognita, that there is absolutely no security for British life a mile or two beyond our [Indian] border' (31).

Even when not directly alluded to, the First Anglo-Afghan War haunts travel accounts right up to the present. Though the failure of the British was due to a series of spectacular tactical and political errors of judgement rather than ferocious Afghan resistance (Heathcote: 209), and, despite the fact that, by the War's close, Britain restored supremacy of arms by recapturing Ghazni and Kabul, the massacre of nearly 16,000 troops, wives and servants of British India's army as it retreated from Kabul to Jalalabad fostered a belief in Afghan brutality that became embedded in the popular memory thereafter.[35]

Afghanistan in the writing of Rudyard Kipling, and Kipling in travel writing about Afghanistan

The colonial legacy of wariness at crossing the North-West Frontier is inherited and sustained by Kipling, who visited the frontier only once in his life as a young journalist, to report on the meeting between the new Viceroy, Lord Dufferin, and the Amir, Abdul Rahman, in Rawalpindi, 1885. According to Harold Orel, Kipling 'walk[ed] over the frontier to the mouth of the Pass at Jumrud' and was there shot at by a Pashtun tribesman' (1990: 15). This incident, of profound significance to Kipling's later writing about Afghanistan, is described as follows in Angus Wilson's 1979 biography *The Strange Ride of Rudyard Kipling*: 'While at Peshawar, he made a journey to Fort

Jumrood at the mouth of the Khyber Pass [...] Here, he believed, he
was shot at by Pathans, and it seems more than likely, for even today
the tribes of the neighbouring Kohat Passes have found their only
peaceful preoccupation in turning out replica guns of all times and
places for tourists' (147). The incident seems to have acquired
mythological status, however, since the accuracy of this version of
Kipling's visit to the frontier (recounted in his 1937 autobiography
Something of Myself. For My Friends Known and Unknown) is
disputed by biographer David Gilmour: 'Kipling went up to Peshawar
and had a glimpse of the Khyber pass, his sole experience of the
frontier that later featured in several of his stories. In his memoirs he
recalled that he had been shot at in the Khyber, but this must have
been a trick of memory; a contemporary letter reveals that he was
threatened by an Afghan with a knife' (27). Whatever did or did not
happen to Kipling at the frontier, his account is consistent with British
notions of Afghanistan as a 'lawless' zone beyond the reach of
colonial authority.[36] The narrator of Kipling's 'The Man Who Would
Be King' echoes the warnings of earlier travellers by reacting harshly
to the plan of Peachey Carnehan and Daniel Dravot to cross the
border: '"You *are* two fools," I answered. "You'll be turned back at
the Frontier or cut up the minute you set foot in Afghanistan"' (254).
As the following section explores, much of Kipling's writing retains
and perpetuates this sense of danger, which recent travel writing
clearly inherits.

For Victorians, the importance of the First Anglo-Afghan War to
Kipling's fiction would have been self-evident. Kipling's frequent,
coded allusions to the War mean that the significance of details such
as dead and dying camels in his stories and poems would have relied
upon public memories of the disastrous invasion. To a Victorian
audience it would very likely have been clear from the outset that the
mission of Dravot and Peachey to rule 'Kafirstan' in 'The Man Who
Would Be King' is doomed when Dravot announces: '"every rupee
we could beg, borrow, or steal – are [sic] invested on these two
camels"' (257). Such a detail was imbued with an historical resonance
not immediately apparent to a twenty-first century readership. For
most nineteenth-century readers therefore, Peachey's subsequent
revelation would have come as little surprise: 'our camels couldn't go
along any more because of the mountains [...] then these camels were

no use, and Peachey said to Dravot - "For the Lord's sake let's get out of this before our heads are chopped off," and with that they killed the camels' (260). Peachey and Dravot share the retrospective discovery of the invading Army of the Indus that mules, not camels, are the answer to travelling through Afghanistan's mountainous regions (260). Considered alongside other details in the story, such as the Welleslian[37] description of Afghanistan as 'all snow and ice and mountainous' (263), Peachey and Dravot's ill-fated attempt to conquer the region becomes an almost parodic replay of the First Anglo-Afghan War.

There can be little doubt that the retreat's psychological legacy colours subsequent British travel accounts of Afghanistan. This is doubtless due in part to the scale and violence of the massacre, from which only one European and a small group of Indian sepoys escaped with their lives. Nevertheless, popular works of art and literature kept the memory alive in the British popular imagination. Dr William Brydon's solitary arrival at Jalalabad was immortalised by the late Victorian oil painting of Lady Elizabeth Butler, popularly known as 'The Last Survivor from Kabul' (Heathcote 1980:63).[38] Famous works such as these combined with accounts of the retreat by writers like Lady Florentia Sale, who described in graphic detail the 'murderous knives of the Affghans [sic]' and 'dead bodies, many of them Europeans; the whole naked, covered with large gaping wounds' while others 'had been stripped of all they possessed; and few could crawl more than a few yards, being frost-bitten in the feet' (127). Afghan knives feature prominently in four chilling lines from Kipling's poem 'The Young British Soldier', which, judging from the regularity with which it was and is cited, helped to entrench a British belief in merciless Afghan brutality. The ongoing significance of these lines to the British tradition of travel writing and journalism about Afghanistan is returned to in due course:

> When you're wounded and left on Afghanistan's plains,
> And the women come out to cut up what remains,
> Jest roll to your rifle and blow out your brains
> An' go to your Gawd like a soldier.
> (*The Complete Barrack Room Ballads* lines 97-100).

Importantly, these four lines promote an essentialised notion of a ferocious Afghan spirit, a theme that survives in contemporary British travel writing, although not generally in relation to Afghan women. Indeed, the poem's depiction of female depravity is an isolated one: Afghan violence is more commonly understood by British writers and journalists as originating in *male*, rather than female ferocity. During the Victorian era Kipling's stories and poems, which are steeped in historical accounts of the retreat, combined with prominent histories of the war, such as that by Sir John Keay, to make Afghanistan synonymous with horror in the minds of generations to come.

In contemporary British travel writing, scenes of travellers' first arrivals in Afghanistan are frequently embellished with traumatic descriptions of the 1841-2 retreat. Heightening a sense of danger is almost a contractual obligation for travel writers, and Peter Somerville-Large's 1991 account is typical in its recourse to memories of the retreat to describe his first entry into Afghanistan:

> We managed to hitch a lift in a lorry. Soon the road was a river of ice banked onto both sides by great drifts of snow [...] We crept slowly forward over the Lataband. I thought of the retreat in 1840 [sic] and Lady Florentia Sale reading Hohenlinden before she set out [...] 'Few, few shall part, while many meet/The snow shall be their winding sheet' (127).

Exhibiting a similar reluctance to relinquish nineteenth-century wariness of entering 'hostile' Afghan territory, British-born Saira Shah (*The Storyteller's Daughter* 2003) raises the spectre of the massacre immediately upon describing her first ever crossing into Afghanistan: 'In 1842, nearly 5,000 fighting men – the whole Kabul force of the British army – were hacked to pieces by an Afghan horde' (17). Such a statement reinforces a historically familiar sense of entering enemy territory. Despite this, Shah's recollection is unusually ambivalent since the retreat's memory is accompanied by an unconventional confession that, because her father is Afghan, her 'Afghan side [...] grew up applauding a massacre that, if it happened today, I would surely condemn as an atrocity' (17). Although Shah's narrative conforms to the British tradition by raising the issue of the massacre at a strategic moment, the narrator's identity as both British and Afghan locates her at a point of 'divergent positionings'

(Lowenhaupt Tsing 1993: 9); the massacre is not, on this occasion, presented as straightforward evidence of Afghan treachery. While conforming to the British convention of trawling up the massacre's memory, the narrative exists in tension with the narrator's deviant stance in relation to the massacre; her 'Afghan side' resists any straightforward portrayal of Afghanistan as 'enemy territory'.

Despite narratives' obvious variety, however, contemporary travel accounts inherit a sense of Afghan sedition, which is sometimes (in post-nineteenth-century narratives) disguised with a sense of humour that is perhaps legitimated by many decades of historical remove. This sense of treachery is invariably linked to allusions, covert or otherwise, to the First Anglo-Afghan War. In Peter Levi's *The Light Garden of the Angel King*, two Afghan men (significantly, from the region of the North-West Frontier) discover that the protagonist and his companions are English. These Afghans proceed to relive their predecessors' triumph over the British failure to achieve their nineteenth-century war aims: 'they looked at one another with a reminiscent glimmer in their eyes, and then touched their guns and caught our eyes and roared with laughter. They asked why we ever left, and laughed even louder in their beards' (80). This passage is menacing in the sense that the 'reminiscent glimmer' suggests that the memory is a source of pleasure, or gloating. Moreover, although no actual shooting takes place, the gesture of touching guns suggests an instinctive violence that does little to counter the nineteenth-century sense of latent treachery.

Contemporary travel narratives invariably promote a sense of continuity between Afghans' putatively ruthless past and Afghans' pathological predisposition towards violence. In another arrival scene, this time from Christina Lamb's 2002 *The Sewing Circles of Herat*, memories of the retreat and its attendant anxieties become dislodged from the context of the Great Game and instead attached to contemporary settings. In Herat, she is greeted by Ayubi, who is head of military logistics for commander Ismael Khan:

> [He] exuded so much power that all the men with guns, who had been circling us, rather too interested in our bags, slunk away at once [...] I smiled, enjoying the idea of being escorted by this impressive man to whom

> everyone seemed to bow, and feeling like one of those British envoys in the
> Great Game whose accounts I had read about being conducted to the courts
> of Afghan chieftains (in some cases to be horribly stabbed to death) (142).

The protagonist's feelings here lurch from enjoyment of her elevated social status by privilege of association with her historical forbears to a hint of fear (albeit contained in parentheses) at the possible re-enactment of fabled Afghan sedition. This fear is lent legitimacy by her unwritten appeals to the historical foundations of this sense of imminent threat. It is difficult to establish, however, how serious is the passage's tone; phrases such as 'horribly stabbed to death' fulfil the travel narrative's remit to be exciting, yet it may have a more humorous tone than this analysis allows. Jonny Bealby's sighting of an Afghan horseman is one of countless other examples of this phenomenon: 'we [...] saw a lone horseman charging across the plain [...] Just for a moment I expected him to draw an unseen scimitar and cut us to ribbons' (1999: 100). The nature of the weapon and the description of its imaginary deployment is highly significant since both details lend the scene historically verifiable depth. Although the rider carries a gun, the sense of peril is attached to the 'unseen scimitar', which is reminiscent of the famed long knives of Afghans that were supposedly put to work on 16,000 victims of the 1842 massacre, even though *jezails* were the primary weapons during the conflict. Conjuring up unpleasant images of the massacre as the scimitar does, the reference to 'plains' locates the rider in a more ancient Mongol scene, thereby locating the supposed origin of Afghan brutality (here depicted as a stable characteristic) still further back in history so as to pre-date the 1842 massacre. Jonny Bealby soon concludes there is 'thankfully [...] nothing to fear' from the rider, who merely wishes to rent a horse (101), while Christina Lamb's protagonist also remains safe from harm. In both cases, a heightened sense of drama associated with the sub-genre of adventure-travel combines with subtle and repeated recourse to the anxieties of earlier travellers. In both Lamb and Bealby's accounts, therefore, a sense of impending danger is retained while the provision of key details (the stabbing of British envoys and the wielding of scimitars) provides an historical alibi to acquit the protagonist of the charge of irrational paranoia should the anticipated harm fail to be inflicted.

Before the First Anglo-Afghan War, Richard, Marquis Wellesley famously warned against occupying a land of 'rocks, sands, deserts, ice and snow' (Keay 1951: 363) and Wellesley's words have been almost routinely quoted by travel writers ever since. However grounded in Afghanistan's topological features, its 'forbidding' landscapes are imbued with a sense of psychological dread that is, as I have argued, a legacy of the First Anglo-Afghan War. In contemporary narratives of travel, descriptions of Afghanistan's menacing landscapes are typically accompanied by warnings against crossing the frontier from nineteenth-century figures such as Alexander Burnes, John Wood, Lord Lytton and Rudyard Kipling. The instant the protagonist crosses into Afghanistan, the landscape tends to assume a sinister aspect. In travel narratives, Afghanistan's mountain ranges frequently resemble implements of harm: they become saws, jagged blades and gaping jaws waiting to devour the unfortunate traveller. Particularly recurrent in the British tradition is the vision of Afghanistan as a sharp cutting edge, captured by Sir Aurel Stein's 'boldly serrated' mountain ranges (1929:1). Lamb describes the skyline as 'dark with a serrated mountain range' (2) while, in Dervla Murphy's account, mountain peaks resemble 'broken swords' (62). Metaphors of teeth abound, particularly when the landscape is conflated with the fabled hostility of Afghans to the British. Interestingly, these descriptions are not confined to the mountains around the North-West Frontier but are transposed to mountainous regions elsewhere in Afghanistan. In *An Unexpected Light*, Jason Elliot cites Lowell-Thomas's 1920's description of the mountain range that encircles Kabul: 'you could find no men more worthy of the title "desperado" than the Pashtuns who live among these jagged, saw-tooth mountains of the Afghan Frontier' (51). The metaphor resurfaces elsewhere in Elliot's narrative, when the Hindu Kush is described as a 'white-toothed blade' (463). Saira Shah writes of the 'shark-tooth peaks of north-eastern Afghanistan (100), while, in a yet more sinister image that suggests treachery in waiting, Somerville-Large watches 'peaks like shark's teeth vanish into darkness' (8).

When contemplating the Hindu Kush range in *A Short Walk in the Hindu Kush*, Eric Newby fuses both sets of images outlined above, investing them with the same ominous sense as Christina Lamb's and

Jason Elliot's ranges located farther south: '[b]etween [...] two ridges there seemed to the entrance to a deep valley, the far side rising in a fiendish-looking unscaleable ridge serrated with sharp pinnacles, like a mouth full of filed teeth' (1955: 144). In Newby's narrative, Afghan mountain ranges do not merely lacerate the traveller, but set up barriers and even put out barbs to impale him: 'In front of us the mountain that divided us from Nuristan rose up like a wall topped with spikes' (187). Of course, warning against entering forbidden territories or heightening a sense of danger, even folly at the protagonist's desire to climb a mountain or enter an unsafe location, is an integral part of travel writing's adventure component. Nevertheless, contemporary descriptions are undeniably tainted with the Victorian dread of Afghan hostility against British travellers. In their depictions of landscapes at least, contemporary travel writers tend to confirm rather than challenge the impression that Afghanistan was and is a 'place of [...] slaughter' with the 'constant threat of violence' (Somerville-Large 36).⏋

The collective focus of these writings on implements of dismemberment suggests that, not only have these writers inherited their colonial predecessors' dread of being literally torn limb from limb, but, at a deeper level, their now obsolete fears that the British empire itself will be dismantled.[39] It may be that displaced anxieties over the inevitable loss of empire help to explain the tendency of recent travel writings to superimpose historically disparate memories onto contemporary Afghan scenes and settings.

The problem of absentee authority: the case of Nuristan

'I could never make up my mind whether Kipling had modelled his characters accurately in the image of Anglo-Indian society or whether we were moulding our characters accurately in the image of a Kipling story' (Leonard Woolf in Abrams 2000:1863).

Known before Abdur Rahman's 1896 conquest of the region as 'Kafirstan',[40] Nuristan is described by travellers as a mountainous region remote from any urban centre. Geographically hostile regions continue to have a magnetic pull for contemporary travel writers, as the mounting pile of narratives about travel to 'extreme' locations such as Antarctica readily testifies. In the context of mass tourism, the survival, even revival, of this trend towards journeying through hostile regions is related to an ongoing anti-touristic struggle to recapture authentic spaces of encounter and lost eras of exploration (Buzard 1992). Nuristan's relative inaccessibility by means of mechanised transport does nothing to diminish its reputation as an anti-touristic location and, in this sense, it is particularly suited to the explorer-derived tradition of twentieth-century adventuring and the sub-genre of adventure-travel to which I now turn my attention. Nevertheless, travel writers' fascination with this region is nothing new. For Victorians, 'Kafirstan' was imbued with the same mystique as the Upper Nile because it was considered as virgin territory ripe for exploration (Marx 1999:44). For male travel writers too, Nuristan is a site upon which dominant modes of masculinity are displayed, tested and found wanting. Nuristani guides are deemed mastered or masterful, cigars are smoked or remain unsmoked and the region's mountain ranges are conquered or else considered unconquerable. Regardless of travellers' gendered relationship to the explorer stance, however, almost all travellers note that high passes and heavy snowfall force them to travel in much the same discomfort as their explorer predecessors. In a scene involving a broken-down jeep that necessitates a typically arduous walk along narrow paths, Victoria Finlay embarks on a journey on foot with some guides, a donkey and a photocopy of 'a chapter written by a traveller called John Wood' in her bag (*Colour. Travels Through the Paintbox* 2002: 335). Such a scene is familiar to many travel narratives about Afghanistan. Contemporary travellers emphasise the discomfort of travelling on foot or horseback through the region and refer regularly to their explorer predecessors, often in terms reminiscent of the era of exploration in a way that clearly evokes rather than renounces the 'pioneering thrill' (Holland and Huggan 67) of explorer narratives. The following examples are taken from Jean Bowie-Shor (1955), Eric Newby (1955) and Jonny Bealby (1998) respectively. The gendered nature of the terminology is apparent in the first and third extracts ('penetrated'; 'penetrate'):

…we penetrated deeper and deeper into the rocky wilderness (195).

…the means of getting into it [Nuristan] have not become any easier; neither the aeroplane nor the motor car has made the slightest difference. To get there you still have to walk (84).

…The number of Westerners to penetrate Nuristan in the past twenty years can practically be counted on the fingers of one hand (118).

Nuristan provides a useful point of focus for two related investigations. The first establishes the degree of cross-referentiality and identifies key textual sources for travel writing about Nuristan, including earlier travel writing and the fictional work of Kipling. For the most part, emphasis is placed on the contexts in which influential narratives were written, together with the implications of their ongoing influence on contemporary writing. A related line of enquiry concerns the self-sustaining nature of key tropes and discourses about the region, which has accumulated layer upon layer of rumour and intrigue.

Since the writing of Kipling exerts so much influence over contemporary travel writing about Afghanistan, I begin with an investigation of Kipling's sources for his 1888 story about 'Kafirstan', 'The Man Who Would Be King'.[41] In this story, two former soldiers of Robert Sale's regiment ignore repeated warnings from the narrator not to travel to the region on a quest to become kings. The narrator's warnings turn out to be justified since only one of the men (Dravot) survives to tell the tale of his friend Peachey's death at the hands of 'Kafirs'. In his 1891 review entitled 'Mr. Kipling's Stories', J.M. Barrie prefaced his praise of the story with a statement about authorial originality that might bring a smile to the lips of a contemporary theorist: '[Kipling] owes nothing to any other writer. No one has helped to form him […] He began by being original, and probably when at school learned calligraphy from the copy lines of his own invention' (in Lancelyn-Green 1971: 81). However, Peter Hopkirk and others have effectively demonstrated Kipling's predilection for adapting to his stories details from news reports he encountered as a young journalist, and 'The Man Who Would Be King' is no exception.[42] A key historical figure behind the story is likely to have been William Watts McNair, who disregarded governmental prohibitions on entry to Afghanistan and entered 'Kafirstan' disguised as a *hakim* shortly before the publication of Kipling's story. Edward Marx argues that Kipling was bound to have read McNair's account since the paper he worked for (*The Pioneer*) published McNair's obituary in 1889 and makes reference to MacNair's account of 'Kafirstan' (1999: 53). Significantly, another reviewer of 1891 praised the story as 'an imaginatively brilliant effort brilliantly [sic] sustained through a detailed succession of events' (Gosse in Lancelyn-Green 1971: 119). As I will discuss, those details that 'sustai[n]' the story derive from four of Kipling's sources: Bellew, Raverty, Wood and Yule, all of which are named in the narrative itself (253-4).

An examination of Kipling's sources immediately suggests the ramifications of the story's influence on contemporary travel writing, particularly in relation to the issue of absentee authority for which, as I argued in the Introduction, Elphinstone's *Account* established an important precedent (although, as we might expect, the tradition of absentee authority predates the *Account* by far).[43] However, Elphinstone's widely-respected proto-ethnographic *Account* is mentioned in Sir Henry Yule's 1881 *Encyclopaedia Britannica* entry on 'Kafirstan', to which the narrator of Kipling's story directs Dravot and Peachey in their last minute researches. The *Account* provided some small details about 'Kafirs' although, as I have mentioned, Elphinstone did not himself journey beyond the North-West Frontier Province. In his commentary on Elphinstone's account, Yule implicitly tackles the problem of authenticity and reliability: 'the Afghans believed, with some justification, that he [Elphinstone] had a telescope with which he could see what passed on the other side of a mountain' (821). Significantly, of the travel accounts and reports at Kipling's disposal, none was written by any traveller who had set foot in the region for the simple reason that, up to the time in which the story was set (two years earlier than its 1888 publication – Marx 1999: 56)[44], no European had travelled through 'Kafirstan'. Nevertheless, as with Elphinstone's narrative, scholars often regarded European accounts as legitimate authorities on the region and its inhabitants. Also mentioned in Yule's entry is the 1603 account of Jesuit traveller Benedict Goes, which was based on his meeting with a hermit on the road from Peshawar to Kabul (Levi: 233).[45]

Yule's entry amalgamates a number of sources, which depict the region as a 'land of lofty mountains, dizzy paths, and hair-rope bridges swinging over torrents' (in Marx 1999: 52). Yule's entry names a number of other authorities, among them John Wood, whom Kipling's narrator also commends to the would-be kings of 'Kafirstan'. Wood is another influential writer about Nuristan who never visited the region and instead based his commentary on a meeting with a Nuristani in northern Afghanistan (Marx 1999: 48). Concentrating on the legend that 'Kafirs' are distantly related to Alexander the Great's soldiers, Wood reported that '[Kafirs] resemble Europeans in being possessed of great intelligence and [...] pride themselves on being, to use their own words, brothers of the Firingi [foreigners, generally British]' (1872: 187). The paucity of reports from travellers who had actually passed through the region (and upon whose testimony the British were then prepared to rely) was addressed in an 1883 lecture given by Sir William Thompson, the then president of the Royal Geographic Society. He suggested that the lack of available reports about a region (by then of strategic interest)[46] was '[becoming a subject of] reproach to English geographers' since 'the only accounts of Kafirstan had been obtained through Orientals themselves, whose statements had never been tested by the actual visit of Europeans to the country' (Marx: 53). Indeed, Sir Henry Yule was among those who had never visited the region. However, as with Sir Olaf Caroe's claim that Elphinstone 'knows of every tribe, its ways and its location' (xx-xxi), Yule's entry lends similar legitimacy to the contribution of Major Biddulph, another absentee traveller. Yule draws on Biddulph's account even as he draws attention to Biddulph's absence: '[I]nvitations were brought to Major Biddulph in Chitral in 1878. This officer was unable to avail himself of these, but he had unusual opportunities of seeing and gaining information about the people, and his chapter on the *Siah-posh* is the most authentic account yet available' (821). Bellew, one of the four sources mentioned by Kipling's narrator, compiled his report for the United Services Institute (253) by collating the accounts of travellers and, unusually, by consulting 'the works of different native historians' (in Marx: 49). The briefest examination of Kipling's sources, then, show that, by selecting 'Kafirstan' as his subject, Kipling enters a long tradition of absentee authority that has implications for travel writing which aspires to a degree of informational status, particularly pseudo-ethnographic writing by journalists, a phenomenon I explore in Part Two.

Commentators have already noted the importance of the historical and political context of Kipling's story, which was written in the wake of the Second Anglo-Afghan War (1878-1880). Louis Cornell points out that the story addresses itself, in the broadest sense, to 'public themes of conquest and rule, authority and justice' through its 'transgressive simulation of an earlier period of colonial conquest' (1987: xxxii & 57). However, literary commentaries mention the contexts of the First and Second Anglo-Afghan Wars infrequently despite the fact that the story reworks actual historical events (Marx: 47). Dravot and Peachey had participated in the First War ('we was there with Robert's [Sale] army' (253)) and key details (such as the camels) suggest that the two characters relive the First War while in 'Kafiristan'. For example, Peachey and Dravot enact a parodic reversal of the strategic advantage enjoyed by Afghan fighters posted high in the hills by 'pick[ing] them ["Kafirs"] off at all ranges, up and down the valley' (1877). However, as Marx argues, it is the Second Anglo-Afghan War that provides the 'critical context of the story', since it was written in the aftermath of the British withdrawal from Afghanistan, which determined British policy in the region for some decades (51). For the most part, the Anglo-Indian community hoped for a reversal of the non-interference policy that resulted from the failure of the Second War's aims, and continued to apply pressure on the British government to recognise the country's strategic importance. Anglo-Indians tended to regard the waning of interest in British dealings with Afghanistan both as a tactical mistake in the light of the continuing threat posed by Russia and as an insult to the memory of those who died in the Second Anglo-Afghan War (Marx 51 & 61).

To what extent, therefore, has Kipling's story contributed to the history of ideas about Nuristan? Which of its preoccupations have taken root in contemporary British imaginations? By which means are Kipling's story and its sources disseminated to contemporary travel writers? As this section goes on to explore, there are three assertions in Kipling's story to which contemporary travel writing invariably alludes (and often subscribes). These assertions are as follows: that Nuristani villages are engaged in constant feuding, that Nuristani landscapes are suicidal and perilous to enter (a notion often symbolised by precarious rope bridges) and that Nuristanis are related to the soldiers of Alexander the Great. However, in investigating the prevalence of these three themes, the idea that contemporary narratives about Afghanistan are first and foremost the sum of their intertexts is resisted by examining instances where narratives deviate from prevalent patterns of representation.

I begin with contemporary travel writers' preoccupation with the rope bridges featured in Kipling's story. In the story, outraged 'Kafirs' cause Peachey to fall to his death from a rope bridge that, in keeping with Yule's 'torrents', hangs over 'a ravine with a river at the bottom' (277).[47] In the story Dravot tells Kipling's narrator: 'we tumbled from one of those damned rope-bridges' (262). Since Dravot did not himself fall from the bridge, the claim that 'we tumbled' is clearly inaccurate, raising the possibility that he speaks of a symbolic as much as actual fall from power (268). This interpretation is consistent with traditional assessments of the tale as a cautionary warning against losing the moral authority to rule India, which, Marx argues, the tale 'both is, and is not' (47).[48]

In contemporary travel writing, Nuristani bridges get frequent mention (Eric Newby writes of 'a suicide bridge' (131) and 'five suicidal bridges' (205)) and, for the most part, these are represented as synonymous with the peril of journeying through the region. It is Peter Levi's bridge-crossing scene, however, that best illustrates the bridges' imaginative association with the perils and traumas of the Great Game era:

> As we approached eight thousand feet we passed through swarms of butterflies and small moths of many kinds. For lunch the porters baked bread on a stove. We walked ahead of them for some time till we came to a bridge. As we started to cross to the left bank we saw a party of men with guns sitting in the open like a group for a Victorian photograph and watching us. Bruce [Chatwin] became nervous. Elizabeth was in front as we balanced our way across the bridge and I was behind her; when we were halfway across the rifles came down suddenly to shoulders to point at our heads, and there was an unhurried clicking of bolts as bullets went into barrels. Bruce said, 'Elizabeth, for God's sake stop [...]' [...] but the stream was noisy and I doubt if she heard [...] We walked through a dead silence to

a tree and sat down and I opened a packet of cigarettes and wandered across
as casually as I could to offer them round. The rifles lowered, and fingers
came off triggers (180).

The scene begins innocently enough, indulging in the aesthetic
pleasures of the region's fauna ('swarms of butterflies and moths').
The detail of butterflies is untypical, invested though it is with slightly
sinister connotations ('swarms')[49], since, in travel narratives, an
imminent sense of threat generally dominates the descriptive mode.
However, the utopian scene quickly fades at the looming threat of
gunmen, whose appearance coincides with the bridge's first sighting.
Most noticeable about this passage, however, is the way in which, at
the first sign of danger, the scene is provided with a nineteenth-
century frame, thereby acquiring a particular historical atmosphere.
The men with guns are not forgotten by time, but rather frozen ('like a
group for a Victorian photograph') at a very significant moment in
Afghan-British relations. Even if the symbolic reference to bridges is
overlooked, the scene's historical transferral to a nineteenth-century
context with traumatic associations has a particular analytical
consequence: even though the danger passes, historically verifiable
weight is given to the possibility of harm, or even murder. This
tendency was noted in earlier with the imminent sense of threat in the
narratives of Christina Lamb and Jonny Bealby.

Prominent in Kipling's story is the assertion of Nuristanis'
predilection for inter-village feuding. Marx notes that McNair (the
explorer whose obituary was published in *The Pioneer*) described
Nuristanis as being 'incessantly engaged in petty warfare with the
Mohammedans' (on 55). Wood reported that 'the Kaffirs' had repaid
on the faithful [Muslim invaders] with a tenfold vengeance the injuries
their forefathers suffered when idol temples were razed to make room
for [...a] mosque' (1872: 194). Significantly, both McNair's and
Woods' assessments do not relate to local disputes between villages
but to region-wide resistance against conquest and forcible conversion
to Islam by Amir Abdur Rahman (which later took place in 1896).
According to Kipling's story, Dravot's impression of incessant
fighting is derived from Wood, which the narrator has just handed to
him: "'They're a mixed lot", said Dravot reflectively; "and it won't
help us to know the names of their tribes. The more tribes the more

they'll fight"' (253). This impression is confirmed by Dravot's later
experience of 'Kafirs': '[a]lways fighting they are, and don't let you
sleep at night' (253). In Kipling's story, then, 'Kafir' fighting is set
adrift from its context of social struggle against the prospect of forced
conversion to Islam by the Amir Abdul Rahman and instead redefined
as petty feuding, a redefinition justified in the story by a solitary
investigation of the feuding's cause, which turns out to be a woman's
abduction from a village (262).

The following discussion of Nuristani fighting by Jonny Bealby is
clearly shaped by the emphasis of Kipling's story on local feuding, as
opposed to region-wide dispute, with women or the theft of goats as
the principal cause:

> ...did every village in Nuristan have a murderous quarrel? [...] [M]urder, it
> would seem, is still very often the order of the day. Families still fight
> families, villages fight villages and valleys fight valleys. They continue to
> steal each other's goats, seduce each other's women and kill each other as a
> consequence (179-80).

Before commenting on this passage in detail, it is worth dwelling for a
moment on its potential contribution to wider theoretical discussions
about the tension between travel writers' vicarious, textually-derived
expectations and their (highly mediated) experience of actual place.
As Billie Melman has already noted, travel writing's 'excessively
citationary' nature makes it fertile ground for the sowing and reaping
of inherited notions (in Hulme and Youngs 2002: 117). Travel writing
about Afghanistan tends to bear out the truth of this. The dense
network of referencing can be usefully understood as a literary version
of the biological feeding cycle: travel writers reproduce aspects of
Biddulph, Woods and Yule without ever having consulted their works
simply because Kipling and others have already ingested and
disseminated them. A detailed focus on the various renderings of
Nuristan testifies to this process. At the same time, however, travel
narratives are not merely the sum of their intertexts. As Neil
Whitehead argues, travel narratives are more accurately described as
the 'hybrid result of the negotiations between the writer's expectations
and experiences' (in Hulme and Youngs: 136) Close reading of
Bealby's passage on feuding reveals that these 'negotiations' prove

difficult to map. In Bealby's extract above, then, a Kiplingesque assertion of petty feuding is maintained in the face of evidence to the contrary, later provided by a Red Cross doctor who reports that the nearby Parun valley is characterised by cooperation rather than strife ('the whole valley was responsible for the welfare of each village' (182)). The doctor's evidence is supported in the same chapter by further details of inter-village cooperation over electricity, harvesting, bridge-building and repairs. The feuding Nuristani study is maintained even when the narrative investigates instances of conflict in the valley and finds the cause to be a diverted irrigation channel (179). Despite attending to regional specificities, then, Bealby's summative statement complies with the assessment made in Kipling's story ('They continue to steal each other's goats, seduce each other's women and kill each other as a consequence'). Furthermore, the chapter from which the extract is taken is prefaced by an epigraph taken from Kipling's story: '"Now what is the trouble between your two villages?" And the people points [sic] to a woman' (on 160). Regardless of the chapter's provision of evidence to the contrary, this epigraph occupies a privileged position, offering an analytical summary of the conflict's causes. Furthermore, when Bealby asks a villager what the problem is, the reply tallies with the epigraph, thereby confirming the accuracy of Kipling's analysis: '"It has to do with a woman", he said slowly' (Bealby: 173). In another sentence, the conclusion is reached that feuds, rather than cooperation, epitomise 'the Nuristani way' (181). Bealby's chapter on feuding suggests that, despite providing details elsewhere of the relatively complex picture on the ground, experience neither over-rides, nor even acts as a simple counter-weight, to Kiplingesque expectation. Indeed, it is important to maintain a focus on the inextricability of experience and expectation, which are tightly interwoven, as opposed to polar opposites in perpetual conflict in a manner perhaps conveyed by Rod Edmond's notion of the 'civil war [...] between eye and mind' (1997: 108). However, as Edmond repeatedly argues in relation to writing about the South Pacific, while Bealby's assertions are shaped by Kipling's story, it would not be accurate to claim that the nuances of actual experience completely fail to modify expectations: the mere presence of evidence to contradict the women-and-goats study clearly facilitates a critical reading of the narrative's over-riding conclusions.

Despite the complex interaction between expectation and experience, contemporary narratives rarely dissent from the over-riding conclusion that petty feuding is, as Bealby's narrator put it, 'the Nuristani way'; decontextualised assertions of inter-village feuding are commonplace. As can be seen in the following example, taken from Sheila Paine's *The Afghan Amulet* (1995), past and present inter-village relations (in this case just over the Afghan border) are characterised in a decidedly Kiplingesque manner: 'As they [the inhabitants of the Chitral, Swat and Indus valleys] were perpetually at war with each other, Britain left them well alone [...] anarchy reigned and still does' (35). The narrator here asserts significant continuity between past and present without providing either detailed context or substantiating evidence. Another reference to village feuding (again just over the border), this time by Peter Somerville-Large, is prefaced by a standard reference to hostile landscape: 'I watched the peaks like shark's teeth vanish into darkness and thought of Hunza's cruel history, largely a story of feuding with neighbouring Nagar. In their hatred people would hurl carcasses of cats across the deep ravine [...]; at other times they killed each other for sport' (8). The latent threat posed by the landscape and, by extension, the villagers is heightened by the image of shark's teeth and yet, as is often the way, the source of the rather humorous assertion about cats remains unacknowledged while fighting is presented, in a de-historicised manner, as inevitable and self-perpetuating.

The 'Alexander romance' (Levi: 166) has set the agenda of many travel writers from the British tradition. Several contemporary writers identify interest in, or even a desire to investigate the legend as among their chief motives for travelling to Nuristan. Eric Newby embraces the 'popular legend' (86) by claiming '[t]he admixture of Greek blood [...] gives many of the inhabitants of Nuristan today a startlingly South European look' (87). Both Levi and Bealby state that the legend is a primary reason for visiting. Sheila Paine's journey to Nuristan and its neighbouring regions is fuelled by a 'quest' to find contemporary wearers of an antique garment of clothing: 'Could such a costume possibly be a hangover from Alexander's campaigns' (xiv)? The legend seems closely connected to the Aryan myth and its associated attempts to portray Greece as an ancestor of modern Europe. It dates back to the thirteenth century but interest in, and speculation over, the question was revived in the nineteenth century when Nuristan became a renewed focus of interest for exploration. Peter Levi, one of the more 'writerly' travellers and commentators on Afghanistan, summarises the legend in useful detail:

> There is a persistent rumour that the fine-looking village people of Nuristan are the descendents of Alexander's soldiers. This is certainly a story that the Nuristanis were telling about themselves [...] from before the time of Marco Polo. It can be partially connected to Marco Polo's own interest in the Alexander romance, but also represents an attempt by these remote tribes to represent themselves as pre-Islamic (166).

Beginning with Kipling's nineteenth-century sources, I consider the role played by Kipling's story in promoting or at least sustaining interest in the legend together with evidence of the story's intervention in contemporary narratives' discussion of the issue. Jonny Bealby tends to treat 'The Man Who Would Be King' as an accurate and authoritative source-text to verify 'his own' observations. Bealby's writing is interspersed with quotations from Kipling's story and generally corroborates its assertions, claiming, for example: 'The people of Kalash [Nuristani village] believed that they were descendents of Alexander's army and that was enough for me [...] another thread of Kipling's story had been fulfilled' (220).

An article by Raverty in the *Journal of the Asiatic Society* (1859) recounts the following incident during the First Anglo-Afghan War:

> [Thirty to forty Kafirs] made their way into our lines with bag-pipes playing. An Afghan Peon, sitting outside Edward Conolly's tent, on seeing these savages rushed into his master's presence exclaiming; 'Here they are, Sir! They are all come! Here are your relations!' [...] I heard Conolly tell this as a good joke, he believing [...] that his Afghan attendant was not actuated by impudence in attributing a blood-connection between his master and the Kafirs (345).

Many writers, such as Bellew, claimed the legend was 'not without foundation', since 'ten thousand of [Alexander's] Greek soldiers had taken themselves wives of the country' (50). Although John Wood seems sceptical of the legend's truth, certain details of his narrative appear to support it. He comments, for example, on the 'open

forehead, blue eyes, and bushy arched eye-brows' of one 'Kafir' (186-
7). This description clearly draws on the Aryan myth as a means of
confirming its apparent truth.[50] Upon meeting his chief 'informant', a
traveller from 'Kafirstan', Wood provides further information as
though to support the idea of his possible kinship with the traveller:
'Cross-legged he would not sit, for in this respect Kaffirs differ from
all eastern nations, and like Europeans prefer a chair or anything
raised to a seat upon the ground' (1872: 186). Significantly, in
Kipling's story, Peachey offers the identical example of seating
preferences to Wood's:

> 'These men aren't niggers; they're English! Look at their eyes – look at
> their mouths. Look at the way they stand up. They sit in chairs in their own
> houses. They're the Lost Tribes, or something like it, and they've grown to
> be English' (269).

This passage seems to advance the theory of Nuristanis' possible
kinship with the English by appealing to the 'antecedent authority'
(Said 1979: 176) of early nineteenth-century explorers. Peachey later
declares: 'this book here [Raverty or Wood] says they're related to us
English' (254). Later in the story Dravot appeals to the legend in an
attempt to secure obedience from the 'Kafirs': 'I know that you won't
cheat me, because you're white people – sons of Alexander – and not
common, black Mohammedans''' (267). At this juncture, the story
departs from the legend since Dravot's faith turns out to be ill-
founded, suggesting, to a Victorian audience at least, that the
inhabitants of 'Kafirstan' are more akin to their Muslim counterparts
than to the English.[51]

In order to consider further the importance of Kipling's story to
contemporary narratives, it is necessary to make a brief foray into the
archaeological sub-genre of travel writing about Afghanistan. As a
classical scholar and archaeologist, Peter Levi's major interest is in
discovering 'traces of Greek elements', especially archaeological
remnants, 'in the life of central Asia' (28). At one point he declares
his intention to test the legend: 'It is an open question to what extent
the Greeks in Afghanistan or their successors until Abdur Rahman
ever did penetrate the more inaccessible valleys, and this was one of
the problems we set out to explore' (167). Although he suggests the

Alexander legend is supported by the linguistic findings of Sir George Grierson in 1900, Levi later dismisses the legend as a myth, possibly replacing it with another: 'Sometimes in Afghanistan we saw fair-haired and blue-eyed children, but in the only cases where we could question an adult about this colouring we found it could be traced to women who accompanied the British armies in the region of the Khyber Pass' (165 & 6). Levi usefully isolates three of the legend's component parts, which may be summarised as follows[52]: the belief that Nuristanis are related to Alexander's armies and, related to this, that Nuristanis are descended from the same 'tribe' as the Prophet Mohammed and, finally, the idea inherited from Wood's meeting with a Russian Jew, that the region contains one of the lost tribes of Israel (233). These component parts are significant in pinpointing Bealby's intertexts. At the beginning of his narrative he writes:

> ...it's the people who make the region so interesting and their roots have had anthropologists baffled for years. As Peachey and Danny [Dravot] were to discover on their journey, many are fair-skinned with blond hair and blue eyes...'*as pale as any Englishman*'. They sit on chairs or stools rather than on the floor as others in the region [...] And there [are people...], my fictional friends included, who claim that the Kafirs are in fact descendents of the armies of Alexander the Great, who marched through the area more than 2,000 years ago [...I] found myself thinking about the pagan past, the land Peachey and Danny had known, and wondering whether there could still be any pockets of the old polytheistic ways left. [...] Could a pagan tribe have survived [...] and still be hidden in the Hindu Kush' (21)?[53]

This passage provides a means of determining the intervention of Kipling's story in contemporary discussions of the legend. Bealby's narrative provides a rather jumbled version, retaining substantiating 'evidence' such as pale skin and Nuristanis' preference for chairs. Such details are present in Kipling's story as well as in Wood's travel account. The possibility of their arrival in Bealby's narrative via Kipling, rather than Wood, is strengthened by a number of factors, not least by Bealby's mission to travel in the footsteps of Kipling's fictional characters. More precisely, Bealby favours Peachey's understanding of 'Lost Tribes' (pagan tribes) (269) over Wood's lost tribes of Israel. Wood reports meeting a Russian Jew seeking the lost tribes of Israel in Nuristan, while Kipling's story departs from Wood's account in this respect by retaining the notion of lost tribes while dropping the Jewish context and instead conceiving of the tribes as pagan (269). Not only does Kipling's story (and its own intertexts) intervene in Bealby's narrative but it imbues the quest with considerable imaginative excitement, thereby fulfilling a key obligation of the adventure-travel sub-genre. At the slightest hint of the myth's truth the narrator writes: 'my heart jumped at the mention of Alexander, the acceleration of blood making my skin positively tingle' (182).

Rudyard Kipling and British news media coverage of Operation Enduring Freedom

Kipling's enduring influence on the history of British ideas about Afghanistan is partly explained by the immense popularity of his fictional renditions of the country during his lifetime, which guaranteed the popular dissemination of these writings' peculiarly mythologised conceptualisations of the country. The relative paucity of writings by prominent British literary figures since Kipling's death explains his privileged position as a commentator on Afghan affairs ever since.

Only a minority of British war correspondents were silent about Kipling during Operation Enduring Freedom. This is particularly true of the early stages of the military operations, when his writings were key to the process of (re)familiarising the British public with Afghanistan. News reports, especially newspaper articles, are littered with references to the canonical writer despite his problematic association with the long tradition of absentee authority. Extensive and widespread reference to Kipling is particularly problematic for news commentary with an explicitly informational remit. However, it is also worth noting that journalists have ascribed varying degrees of authority to Kipling's writing. Recalling her first visit to Afghanistan, Christina Lamb describes herself as a 'gawky English girl', a naïve young correspondent 'dizzy with Kipling' (2002: 2). This image of being off-balance seems to recommend that the British literary tradition be given a wide berth. An article for the *Sunday Times News Review* by Kipling's biographer Andrew Lycett adopts a similarly cautionary tone about the usefulness of Kipling's writing, stressing the need to adopt a nuanced understanding of Kipling's imaginative relationship with Afghanistan. In his article entitled 'How Kipling created the Afghan myth', Lycett describes Kipling as a 'lively though not totally reliable commentator [on the Great Game]' (30 September, 2001). Expressing reservations such as these about the legitimacy, ongoing or otherwise, of Kipling's authority provides readers with the extra critical tools to decipher those news reports that make less guarded reference to Kipling. Other articles identify Kipling's writings as influential in the formation of their initial impressions, impressions that were later called into question. An article by former SAS recruit Tom Carew in the *Sunday Times News Review* is a case in point. Although he quotes the standard lines from Kipling's 'The Young British Soldier' ('When you're wounded and left on Afghanistan's plains...'), he asserts that – contrary to expectations – he 'found the Afghans to be very pleasant' (September 23, 2001). However, despite Carew's implicit claim that his experience of Afghanistan modified expectations fuelled by the British literary imagination, a later deployment of the phrase 'chopped to pieces' suggests his narrative cannot quite break free of nineteenth-century conceptual frames. The close scrutiny of news media coverage in 2001 suggests that this state of affairs typifies news coverage, especially newspaper articles, which are news frame definers in the sense that they provide marginally more space to historicise and contextualise. While it is not necessarily advisable to take on trust claims that Kipling's authority is being questioned, the narratives of Carew and Lamb suggest that reference to Kipling, especially as an unreliable commentator, is to an extent mediated by journalists' differing senses of Kiplingesque mythology's ongoing relevance to contemporary Afghan scenes and settings.

As I have suggested, during the 2001 conflict, references to Kipling were legion. Indeed, they were almost standard in tabloids such as the *Daily Mail* and the *Mirror* as well as in the *Independent*, the *Scotsman*, the *Times* and the *Sunday Times*. Some newspaper articles confined themselves to commentaries about Kipling's fascination with Afghanistan, or to Tony Blair's rediscovery of *Kim* while at Chequers.[54] More generally, however, journalists turned to Kipling as a resource for describing Afghanistan to British audiences at the beginning of the conflict. In the *Mirror* Sandy Gall writes: 'When I first went to Afghanistan in 1982, I took a copy of Kipling. We walked for 12 days across the Hindu Kush, much of it through Pathan country and I re-read the Ballad of East and West [...] "There is rock to the left, rock to the right, and low lean thorn between..." – a good description of much of Afghanistan' (September 19, 2001). Far and away the most universally cited of Kipling's writings is the single stanza from 'the Young British Soldier'. Quoting Kipling during Operation Enduring Freedom had a particular impact on the way in which the conflict was reported. Despite the self-reflexive statements by journalists such as Lamb, and the inevitability of a coalition military victory, the much-cited stanza was (incredibly) posited as a prophetic prediction of imminent defeat for the anti-terror coalition. During the early stages of military operations, the appropriated stanza stood as an historically verifiable synonym for Afghan ferocity, spawning headlines such as 'The proud warriors yet to be defeated' (the *Daily Mail*, September 17, 2001). The article reads as follows: 'the precedents for [...the allied] invasion could hardly be less encouraging [...] Rudyard Kipling wrote chillingly of the dangers after British defeats in the last century [quotes the stanza from 'The Young British Soldier]'. Equally revealing was the articles' repeated deployment of the distinctly nineteenth-century phrase, 'cut to pieces' to describe the 1842 massacre. Further on, the same *Daily Mail* article elevates Kipling's fictional writing to the status of historical evidence, testifying to Afghans' propensity for excessive violence, which is then generalised as evidence of an ongoing, stable cultural trait: 'in this country of haughty warlords [...] fighting has always been a way of life' (22).

Television news reports do not habitually make direct reference to Kipling during Operation Enduring Freedom since, as I suggested earlier, they are particularly antithetical to historical contextualisation. However, news reports were evidently structured by nineteenth-century British preoccupations. Kipling's writing even gets occasional mention in post-9/11 television documentaries. A *Channel Four* documentary entitled 'The House of War' contains an interview with three journalists, one of whom suggests that Afghan General Dostum's authority is 'almost Kiplingesque': 'you'd see Dostum with his turban, a warlord, and then you'd see the CIA, so it's almost like 'The Man Who Would Be King' (4 July, 2002). Such statements tend to set political players such as Dostum adrift from the specific context of his rise to power and attach him to a generalised and abstracted rule of warlordism laced with 'Kiplingesque' espionage.[55] Other references to Kipling were more deeply buried. An article in the *Daily Mail* notes that, 'in one valley [of Afghanistan] the men might have blue eyes and blond hair, the genetic reminder that Alexander the Great marched through here 2,500 years ago [sic]' (19 September, 2001). The vague reference to Nuristan and the Alexander myth points strongly towards the unacknowledged yet favourite source: 'The Man Who Would Be King'.

Reliance on Kipling during the 2001 conflict inevitably carries the risk of displacing historically and politically disparate memories onto contemporary scenes and settings. It sets thematic agendas and is implicated in the proliferation of that which Cynthia Weber calls 'non-knowledge'; the 'incessant, conscious exchange of some narratives, images, and ideas so that others remain unconscious [...] exclusive focus on one story makes it possible to neglect other, potentially more important aspects of the same story' (in Kishan Thussu and Freedman: 190). Kipling and his associated tales of historical Afghan-British encounters may be said to provide some legitimate context for the recent attacks on Afghanistan. However, in an age where television news reports are edited down to the last second and newspaper articles to the last syllable, something has to give. It is interesting to consider which other stories were displaced into the shadows whenever Kipling was promoted as a commentator on Operation Enduring Freedom. Certainly, disproportionate emphasis on historically remote contexts hampered coverage of geo-political manoeuvres by the United States, Pakistan and other states with strategic interests in the region. These are elaborated upon in Part Three.

Mythologising Afghanistan

In examining travel narratives' competing tensions it seems desirable to avoid concentrating exclusively on representational continuity at the expense of instances of imaginative appropriation, or even subversion of dominant British renderings. The following brief examples illustrate the importance of understanding how, why and when narratives consolidate or dissemble from tropes and narrative conventions associated both with Afghanistan and the sub-genres of travel writing associated with writing about the region. Though Jonny Bealby tends to defer to judgements expressed in Kipling's writing, in an untypical moment his narrative subjects the genre's citationary tendency to a form of 'internal critique' (Holland and Huggan: 123): 'What *did* I expect to discover? The lost pagan land of my dreams? Myself? A descendant of Alexander the Great clutching a battered copy of *The Man Who Would Be King*' (193)? This passage foregrounds the close relationship between Kipling's story and the narrator's textually-inspired 'dreams', thereby suggesting the impossibility of unmediated 'personal vision' (Holland and Huggan: 10). In a similar vein, the narrator contests enlightenment notions of self-discovery as a likely outcome of travel: 'What *did* I expect to discover? [...] Myself?' Such a question is symptomatic of travel writers' preoccupation with the problem of cliché, which seems bound up with the desire to 'personalise' one's own narrative by distinguishing it from others. In this case, however, a preoccupation with cliché actually militates against the possibility of 'personal vision', which seems unattainable when placed against the dubious claims of Bealby's literary forebears ('lost pagan lands'; 'descendent of Alexander').

The sub-genre of adventure-travel is also submitted to a form of 'internal critique' in a passage cited earlier by Jason Elliot, where the narrator lists recurrent phrases in British depictions of Nuristanis as 'homicidal' or 'murderous-looking'. Not only does Elliot's narrative depart from established convention by exposing continuities in representation over an historical period of around fifty years, but his exposé implies that dominant patterns of representation actually preclude the possibility of 'personal vision'. Ironically, however, his passage ends in the following manner: 'Uncharitable descriptions – but the look of such faces made us all wonder. For the first time I felt my journey had really begun. At last, I felt with enormous satisfaction, I was off the beaten track.' (138) By departing from a representational convention, however, it resorts to a well-worn cliché about 'the beaten track', a phrase symptomatic of tourists' aspiration to the status of traveller which, as James Buzard has argued, is the 'product of nearly two hundred years' concerted stereotyping' (1993: 3). In this sense the passage falls in with the tendency of travel writing to depict Afghanistan as a non-touristic realm where experiences are anything but 'predictable and repetitive' (Buzard: 4). The narrator's reluctance to dismiss British representations of Nuristanis as entirely unfounded ('but the look of such faces made us wonder') strengthens the impression that Afghanistan is being placed at an anti-touristic remove from the scene of mass tourism.

Homicidal Nuristanis

A persistent claim by travellers relates to Nuristanis' supposed predilection for human slaughter. As contemporary travel writers often point out, there is abundant evidence to the contrary so far as Nuristani dealings with Europeans are concerned. Once again, even though the 1842 massacre took place elsewhere in Afghanistan, the homicidal Nuristani myth is not unconnected to it. European travel to Nuristan post-dated the First Anglo-Afghan War and, as Nuristan increasingly became a focus of intrigue, it was imbued with a synecdochic or *pars totalis* quality (Buzard 1993: 10), becoming the part that stands for the whole: Nuristan gradually became the distillation of all that has disturbed the British about Afghanistan. Kipling's 'The Man Who Would Be King', I would argue, both reflects and contributes to this process. Careful examination of the following extracts from his story reveals subtle yet significant slippage from the North-West Frontier Province to Nuristan:

> 'You'll be cut to pieces before you're fifty miles across the Border,' I said. 'You have to travel through Afghanistan to get to that country. It's one mass of mountains and peaks and glaciers, and no Englishman has been through it. The people are utter brutes, and even if you reached them you couldn't do anything [...] You *are* two fools [...] You'll be [...] cut up the minute you enter Afghanistan' (253-4).

Here, the narrator associates danger with Afghanistan in general and the North West Frontier Province in particular ('the minute you enter Afghanistan'; 'before you're fifty miles across the border') in language resembling nineteenth-century *Arabian Nights*-inspired commentaries on the massacre ('cut up'; 'cut to pieces').[56] Once again, images of dismemberment ('cut to pieces') hint at fears that go beyond personal safety, extending to what were once imminent threats to the British empire. The warning even contains traces of Marquis

Wellesley's prophetic warning against invading a geographically hostile country ('It's one mass of mountains and peaks and glaciers'). Significantly, however, in the space of a single sentence, British wariness of crossing the frontier is conflated with entering 'Kafirstan', thereby executing a conceptual and geographical leap from one region to the other by stating that 'no Englishman has been through it', a statement clearly untrue of the Frontier Province but true of Nuristan (at least in the year in which the story was set). This depiction of Nuristan as epitomising the violence and cruelty experienced during the 1842 retreat is entirely justified, in the story's terms, since Dravot comes to an unhappy end.

Contemporary assertions of Nuristanis as murderers without cause are legion. These are again in line with a wider British tendency to locate the cause of Afghanistan's ills in pathological cultural practices. I cite a number of examples, starting with Eric Newby's famous passage, which introduces the adjective 'homicidal', commonly utilized by subsequent travel narratives:

> ...I looked into his eyes; they were strange and mad. He had about him an air of scarcely controlled violence that I had noticed in some of the other [Nuristanis] in the hut. An air of being able to commit the most atrocious crimes and then sit down to a hearty meal without giving them a further thought. The man was a homicidal maniac. Perhaps they were all homicidal maniacs (196).

> ...From what I've heard they're a tricky bunch the Nuristanis, not quite as homicidal as they used to be, but tricky just the same (Jonny Bealby: 68).

> ...Because of Nuristanis' homicidal reputation, their cruel looks and penchant for armaments, I'd carried with me a deep sense of fear and trepidation throughout the trip (Jonny Bealby: 185).

> ...Eric Newby [writes that Nuristanis have...] 'an air of being able to commit the most atrocious crimes and then sit down to a hearty meal.' [An] [u]ncharitable descriptio[n] – but the sight of such faces made us all wonder (Jason Elliot: 138).

Despite this repeated refrain, it is important to consider any narrative interventions in the standard representational pattern. As I have mentioned, one such intervention can be found in Jason Elliot's narrative, which draws attention to the customary practice of reiterating the assertion by summarising the tendency of British travellers to embrace the homicidal myth and foregrounding it as a significant pattern of representation:

> The men watching us were a ferocious-looking bunch, ragged and turbaned and intense [...] for the most part the European eye is not used to such intensity and readily finds something intimidating in it; Eric Newby's adventures in the Panjshir valley and Nuristan are littered with references to 'villainous-looking', 'murderous-looking' and 'mad-looking' individuals, frequently 'smelly', 'verminous' and 'brute' (138).

Such a summary raises important questions about the 'intricate interplay of power, desire and place' (Duncan and Gregory: 1999: abstract) and suggests the value of attending to power's multiple dimensions as it interacts with a range of variables while working in complex relation with the unpredictability of place itself. Despite the prevalence of the homicidal claim, Elliot's passage suggests the potential for significant 'variations on the repetition' of 'certain rule-bound discourses' (Butler in Smith and Watson: xx).

Dervla Murphy's commentary on the homicidal theme reveals how the tension between expectation and experience operates in complex relation with factors such as gendered positionality. Murphy writes: 'This is the only country I was ever in where not one single man of any type has tried to 'get off' with me, so I feel no qualms about a night at the mercy of my five companions. They all look as though murder was their favourite hobby (and maybe it is – among themselves) yet they're as gentle as lambs with me' (100). Experience is implicitly theorised here as a simple counterweight to expectation, operating as a restraint against mere regurgitation of the homicide trope. However, the words contained in parentheses, '(and maybe it is – among themselves)', re-inscribe the myth even as the main clause of the sentence disavows it. Once again, Afghan violence lurks ominously close to the surface. By issuing only a partial disavowal, the narrator adopts an heroic stance, showing nonchalance in the face of latent Afghan violence. In this way experience interacts with other variables, particularly generic imperatives: adventure-travel must be exciting. However, elsewhere, Murphy's narrative provides more complex illustrations of the interface between gender and genre. In the following example, the narrator's experience of safe travel interacts with other variables such as gendered positionality to intervene in the homicidal myth. Once again, however, a generic imperative labours to defend the myth: 'It seems to be beyond dispute that Afghanistan has slightly more than its fair share of bandits, yet almost everyone who travels through is favourably impressed by the treatment they receive and it's high time the silly nonsense about the extreme dangers of this land were 'exposed' as exaggeration' (73). In this instance, the narrator's dissent from the homicidal claim seems partly predicated on rejecting long-held notions that a lone woman capable of travelling safely is an anomaly (Mills 1992: 23). Nevertheless, the myth's persistence is suggested by the assertion of a genuine threat ('Afghanistan has its fair share of bandits') raising the possibility that the sub-genre of adventure travel places high value on perpetuating rumours of danger.

There can be little question that the homicidal charge is routinely raised. However, as the previous examples show, this does not mean that it is never problematised. Although Bealby's narrative frequently corroborates Kipling's story, his experience of safe passage through the region leads to a questioning of the homicidal claim's foundation in reality:

> But now I wondered in how much jeopardy had our lives actually been? Had anyone [in Nuristan] actually intended us harm; to kill or to take us hostage? To Victorians, possibly, thanks in part to Kipling's tale, the land had been *a synonym for suicide*: a place so wild and savage that only a lunatic pair of renegades would ever dare to enter. But the fact remained that with barely a quarter of our journey left to go, only one Westerner had lost his life to violence in the province (186: italics mine).

This passage temporarily strips Kipling's 'tale' of its status as an authoritative source text: the Victorian notion of Nuristan's being a 'synonym for suicide' is, the narrative hints, exaggerated and perpetuated by Kipling's influential fictional rendering ('thanks in part to Kipling's tale'). However, even as the passage considers the complex interplay between text and experience, the dense network of textual referencing comes to light in the very phraseology in which the disavowal is expressed. Although it is difficult to prove that the phrase 'a synonym for suicide' is a reference, conscious or otherwise, to Robert Byron's narrative, which reports that 'a visit to Kunduz [west of Nuristan] is tantamount to suicide' (260), the theme of suicidal travel is remarkably prevalent in travel writing about Afghanistan. To name but two examples, Jason Elliot writes that: '[travel alone] would be suicide' (139), while Murphy announces: 'the whole trip wasn't far short of suicidal' (77). There are, of course, no reliable means of accurately tracing the exact path of phrases to particular passages. Nevertheless, the phrase's presence in Bealby's passage serves as a reminder that Nuristan is a site crammed with representations (Fowler 2004: 4). This justifies the study's sustained focus on those notional Afghanistans associated with the British history of ideas.

The Wild Westification of Afghanistan

Tropes of the lawless wilderness, and its metaphorical counterpart, utopia, were prevalent in the commentaries of Victorian travellers journeying to a wide range of destinations (Boehmer 1995: 44). Afghanistan is particularly amenable to notions of lawlessness since its uncolonisable reputation is the legacy of the First and Second Anglo-Afghan Wars. As I have suggested, Victorian travellers depicted Afghanistan as a grave threat to the safety of those British travellers who risked journeying through the country. Bearing in mind the importance of resisting easy parallels between the Afghanistan(s) of travel writing and the actualities of place, the question is perhaps not whether incidents of murder or robbery are statistically high in Afghanistan, so much as why 'lawlessness' is consistently presented as a pathologically embedded cultural practice rather than, say, an economic function. Part of the answer to this question lies in Victorian commentaries, where claims of Afghan 'lawlessness' have clear colonial origins, since Afghanistan's unpacifiable state was invariably attributed to 'the recklessness and unscrupulousness' of the Afghan race or the 'treachery of the Afghan character' (Keay 1851: 105 & 113). Keay's contention that '[t]he Afghans are a turbulent and lawless people – little inclined to succumb to authority' (487) is typical in its drawing of a correlation between lawlessness and Afghan 'character'. Kipling's *Kim* (1901) consistently presents Afghanistan as the antistudy of British India in its approach to law and order. This is apparent in the free indirect speech of Mahbub Ali, the horse-trader and British agent: 'he knew that south of the Border a perfectly ridiculous fuss is made about a corpse or so' (199). When Mahbub Ali presents Kim with a gun, which is accepted with a proper sense of sobriety, Kim comments that, should he kill, hanging would be the consequence. Again, Mahbub Ali's reply is telling: "'True: but one pace beyond the Border, men are wiser'" (244). In *Kim* at least, merely stepping across the border entails entering a space where Afghans habitually, and with a quiet conscience, violate all that British colonials apparently hold sacrosanct.[57]

Lawlessness is a prevalent theme in twentieth and early twenty-first-century narratives about Afghanistan. Jean Bowie Shor writes about her 1955 journey to north-eastern Afghanistan in the following terms: 'Our ascent toward the headwaters of the Oxus, and the divide beyond, would take us into a land of unnamed peaks, and untamed peoples, and beyond the protection of any sovereign or law' (172). Far from having been 'stripped of immediate pioneering thrill', Afghanistan is once again imaginatively transported to a bygone era of exploration. '[A] land of unnamed peaks',[58] the region acquires the associated dangers of 'untamed peoples'. Atypically, however, this passage is unusually specific regarding whose law the 'untamed peoples' are beyond since the cause is attributed, albeit implicitly, to localised power structures that coexist with the centralised political system. In this respect, Bowie-Shor's writing is an exception to the rule since recent narratives rarely specify whose or which law Afghans are 'beyond'; they are generally depicted as merely 'lawless'. The characteristic vagueness that accompanies the assertion of lawlessness supports the impression that this theme harks back to the nineteenth-century experience of Afghan intolerance of British invasion as well as to British interference with Afghanistan's foreign policy. Below are three more assertions of lawlessness, beginning with Jonny Bealby's commentary upon leaving Nuristan:

> ...at last the threat of murder had gone. The spectre of living in a lawless land, never knowing what might be waiting round the next corner, had weighed heavily on me (205).

...It was a wild and lawless place. At least the law was not our own (Elliot:138).

...The entire region [encompassing north-east Afghanistan] is still beyond the law (letter to Paine in Paine: xvii).

All three statements retain a colonial belief that crossing the border means that harm, even murder, is imminent. The extracts from Bealby and Paine display the usual lack of specificity regarding which laws Afghans fail to adhere to, although Elliot notes that it 'was not our own'. Elliot's qualification partially subverts the lawless claim by appealing to a form of cultural relativism, showing that contemporary British narratives do not always and inevitably regurgitate colonial complaints about Afghan disobedience. More generally, however, 'lawlessness' is viewed as a quintessentially Afghan phenomenon.

A useful starting point for understanding the roots of the enduring lawless trope is Eva Sallis' notion of 'dynamic dislocation'. I discuss the idea behind this term before discarding her problematic phraseology. Dynamic dislocation occurs when a given text (in Sallis' discussion it is *The 1001 Nights*) is removed from the original context(s) of writing. Sallis explains that dynamic dislocation has particular consequences for the way in which translations of the *Nights* were (and are) received in an historically and culturally decontextualised manner by European readers. The history of the *Nights*, Sallis argues, is best described as one of 'transformation' rather than mere translation (1999: 2). One consequence of the *Nights*' transformation was that, for nineteenth-century European readers, particular cultural premises that would have originally served as a backdrop for the tales' engagement with moral issues were foregrounded by European translators and readers as the tales' 'most compelling aspect'. The tales were thus 'reborn' into an 'alien environment' of antithetical relations between Christian and Muslim nations, and 'enslaved to the service' of European cultures (1, 11 & 7). Sallis suggests that the imaginative worlds of the *Nights* were 'cut loose from one history and insecurely attached to another' (58). In their use of the *Nights*, travel narratives about Afghanistan parallel this process of 'transformation'. Although India, Egypt and Iraq are the *Nights*' principal settings, travel writers frequently have recourse to the tales as a means of heightening a sense of the fantastic and exaggerating the place's remoteness to British experience. I provide three examples in order of publication. The first is from Dervla Murphy:

> One of the servants has just glided up with a new lantern to give me more light: it's all deliciously like the Arabian Nights (64).

> Ali Khan spoke of the cluster of huts clinging to the desolate mountain as though it were Baghdad under Haroun al Rashid, and our arrival worthy of the *Thousand and One Nights* (Jason Elliot: 178).

> [W]e were surrounded by characters forgotten by time, conjured from a page of Scheherazade (Jason Elliot: 93).

Of all travel narratives about Afghanistan, Elliot's is among the most self-reflexive and wary of its representational strategies, yet the tales' mere mention is sufficient to imbue everyday scenes with the *Nights'* associated sense of mystique and exoticism. Despite Afghanistan's geographical and historical remoteness from the *Nights,* archaic imaginative worlds associated with the tales are grafted on to Afghan locations. This process resembles Sallis' notion of dynamic dislocation. Nevertheless, closer scrutiny of the concept's component parts reveals the term's in-built limitations. Although Sallis usefully identifies a particular process of representative distortion, the terms 'dynamic' and 'transformation' carry positive connotations that sit uneasily with the notion of 'dislocation' and thus potentially detract from the very ethical problematic that Sallis highlights. I proceed with Sallis' insight but shed her phraseology.

When considering the lawless trope's evolution from the early nineteenth century to the present, it is important to stress that meaning about Afghanistan is also *interculturally* mediated. The processes which Sallis terms dynamic dislocation seem closely related to a process of cross-cultural comparison, especially retrospective comparison, whereby cultural phenomena are extracted from one context and likened to culturally, geographically and historically distinct settings. Sir Walter Scott's comparison of Afghans with Scottish Highlanders usefully illustrates this process. The Afghan-Highlander comparison is first made in Elphinstone's *Account of*

Caubal: 'the situation of the Afghaun [sic] country appears to me to bear a strong resemblance to that of Scotland in ancient times' (230). Here is Scott's commentary on Elphinstone's *Account* in the *Quarterly Review*:

> The genealogies of Afgauni [sic] tribes may be paralleled with those of the clans [...who] resembled these oriental mountaineers in their feuds [...] which serves strikingly to show how the same state of society and civilisation produces similar manners, laws and customs (quoted in Richards 1994: 126).

Standing behind Scott's reasoning is Adam Smith's notion of the progress of human history towards commercialism, which Smith sees as a mark of civilisation (Richards: 125). According to Scott, Afghans, or 'oriental mountaineers' shared 'the same state of society' as Highlanders and the comparison enables Afghans' relegation to a supposedly pre-civilised stage of social and cultural development. Richards argues that the justification for Scott's comparison 'is determined, with complete circularity of argument, by the very mode of categorisation' (126). Thus cross-cultural comparison is, as Sallis suggests, a dynamic process that has produced particular consequences: crucial details of Afghans' and Highlanders' disparate cultural, geographical and historical locations are subsumed into a category derived from Smith's progressive stages of civilisation.

While Afghanistan's portrayal as lawless has remained constant, the *lawless* trope has in fact been responsive to the rise and fall of political fortunes in the region. It has thus assumed a variety of forms that are culturally meaningful to readers back home. Increasingly prevalent since the United States' entry into the macro-political arena is the tendency to render Afghanistan as the Wild West of the East. In the British tradition, implicit connections are forged between Afghanistan's ungovernability during the Victorian era and 'lawless' frontiers in the history of the United States. Correspondingly, rural Afghanistan is symbolically overlaid with yet another context with well-established popular roots: regions bordering the North-West Frontier are transformed into the contested border between Mexico and the United States and populated with imagined bandits and desperadoes. There are countless examples of Afghanistan's Wild-

Westification and I quote but six, this time beginning with a narrative
by a writer from the United States whose use of the metaphor, as
earlier indicated, coincides with the rise of the United States as a
powerful presence in Central Asia:

> Tiluh Walduh was Hollywood's version of a Mexican desperado, tall and
> slender, with smouldering black eyes and a thin drooping handlebar
> mustache [sic] (Jean Bowie-Shor 1955: 229).

> 'You will find my land,' said Majid, 'something like your Wild West' (Jean
> Bowie-Shor: 132).

> Lowell Thomas wrote, 'you could find no men more worthy of the title
> "desperado" than the Pashtuns' (Jason Elliot 1999: 12).

> Their hard looks suggested something of the desperado (Jason Elliot: 257).

> Miners built Sar-e-sang village seven millennia ago, and walking through it,
> I wondered how much it had changed. It had the feeling of a cowboy town
> (Victoria Finlay 2002: 340).

> ...My grandfather had only one vice. He was addicted to pulp novels about
> the American Wild West [...] They reminded him of the unruly Pashtun
> tribes, whom no man has truly succeeded in conquering [...] he described
> the proud men of the Afghan Frontier in a style that owed as much to his
> treasured Wild West novels as to the *Arabian Nights Entertainments* (Saira
> Shah 2003: 117).

The imaginative transportation of Afghanistan to the Wild West[59]
uncovers the mechanics of Afghanistan's fictionalisation as well as
narratives' corroboration of well-established belief in Afghan
lawlessness. Victoria Finlay's town resembles a Hollywood film set
while   Jean   Bowie-Shor's   characters   resemble   'Mexican
desperado[es]'. Bowie-Shor's extract operates in a similar self-
authenticating manner to classical ethnographies; an Afghan
'informant' offers (and thus legitimises) the comparison with
ungovernable periods of United States history as a conceptual
framework for understanding Afghanistan. Saira Shah's narrative
makes an explicit connection between the Wild West and Pashtun

resistance during the First Anglo-Afghan War thereby amalgamating two disparate histories of rising and falling empires. This process of amalgamation is also at work in Lowell Thomas's imaginative fusion of Pashtuns with desperadoes (via Elliot). Complicating Shah's comparison, however, is the intrusion of a telling vocabulary item, 'unruly', which is strongly associated with Sir Alfred Lyall's much-quoted line, 'who would rule the unruly Afghan'.[60] In the context of Lyall's poem, the appellation 'unruly' conveys the perceived gravity of Afghans' insubordination at a critical moment in British India's history. Such textual moments suggest how nineteenth-century anxieties over the stability of colonial rule have become dislodged and transferred from their original contexts of writing while the fusion of disparate histories imaginatively embellishes the well-established sense of lawlessness. Although I have no wish to assert any unitary consciousness on the part of these writers, it is clear that earlier writings and representations provide a repository of phrases from which travel writers inevitably draw while, in the case of the Wild West comparison, gesturing towards the changing macro-political climate in which the narratives are embedded.

Despite the prevalence of the lawless trope, however, Jason Elliot's narrator once again counters this recourse to the inventory of ready phrases by describing some Afghan responses to the Wild West comparison: 'The laughter was unrestrained when [...] I mentioned that in Afghanistan I would meet only *wakshi* men – desperadoes and warriors' (329). Such derisive laughter seems to level an unspoken accusation of Elliot's unreliable narration which partially discredits depictions of Afghan desperadoes elsewhere in his, and others' narratives.

In conclusion to this section, the powerful significance of Afghan frontiers, combined with an enduring belief in Afghans' predilection for warfare, makes the Wild West comparison irresistible for many travel writers. While Elliot's writing suggests the potential for deviating from the customary charge of lawlessness, repeated reference to nineteenth-century Anglo-Afghan contexts (explicit or otherwise) creates a form of historical analogy that tends to promote a sense of lawlessness as historically documented and therefore culturally embedded.

Medievalising Afghanistan

As I discuss below, Afghanistan's depiction as contemporaneous with medieval Europe was a striking feature of news media coverage of the 2001 bombing campaign. Afghanistan's medievalisation has a long pedigree, however, that lies in direct continuity with twentieth-century travel writing about Afghanistan, most particularly the narratives of Robert Byron and Eric Newby. Of course, the practice of medievalisation belongs to older patterns of representation associated with narratives about South and Central Asia.[61] Melman notes that T.E. Lawrence 'medievalised Arabia and applied chivalric ideals to the Arab Revolt of 1916-18 which he helped organise'. She also observes how he 'resorts to a particular version of the pilgrimage paradigm: the Crusade' (in Hulme and Youngs: 115), although travel writers on Afghanistan tend to prefer the Chaucerian pilgrimage and people Afghan settings with monks and nuns.[62] Travel writers routinely relocate Afghanistan's contemporary scenes and settings to three distinctive historical eras: the invasion of Alexander the Great, the invasion of Genghis Khan[63] and, of particular relevance here, to Europe's medieval past (and sometimes to all three in the space of a paragraph).

Medieval characters turn up with some regularity in twentieth and early twenty-first century scenes of travel. I cite three examples, beginning with Robert Byron:

> We set off under the guidance of a peasant [...] whose hair was cut to the bob and fringe of a medieval page (217).

> In half an hour he brought back two passable horses with iron scoop saddles such as European knights used in the Middle Ages (Jean Bowie-Shor 1955: 188).

> The sensation of crossing the square was like that of entering a small Italian hill-town in perhaps the eleventh century, only that there was no mortar and no cut stones (Peter Levi:1984 [1972]: 183).

All three examples provide concrete criteria (a page-boy haircut, scoop saddles and architectural features) for likening Afghanistan to the Europe of the Middle Ages. Medieval artefacts, hairstyles and costume substantiate claims of, in Freya Stark's words, Afghanistan's 'medieval background' (1974: 58), acting as props to stage the country as medieval. In Robert Byron's narrative in particular, Afghanistan's medievalisation can be partly accounted for by the need for escape. Byron's journey was undertaken at a time when, in his own words, 'the Depression was in full swing [...] and Europe insupportably gloomy' (233). As Burdett and Duncan also point out, at the time of Byron's journey, Fascism was on the rise and escape from Europe seemed highly desirable (4). Aspirant knights (in the shape of a medieval page) suggest that, in the 1930s and Afghanistan's ensuing war-free decades, the country was a locus for escape. The chivalric emphasis of travel narratives such as Byron's and Newby's did not, however, prevail in reporting during Operation Enduring Freedom. This can be explained by the fact that Afghanistan was afflicted by military conflict and populated by the menacing figures of the Taleban.

Arthurian chivalry features prominently in Newby's narrative. This is illustrated by the following passage, where two Afghan men on horseback seem only at first to embody the lost Romanticism of a chivalrous age:

> They both carried long wands that looked like lances. The man riding pillion wore a red skull-cap; the other one the large floppy sort [...] the feeling of being transported into the Middle Ages was overwhelming. With some monks in the foreground fishing for carp it could have been an illustration in a pictorial history of England (198).

Once again there is a focus on tangible 'evidence' of medievalism; a 'skull-cap' and two 'long wands' support the subsequent assertion that 'the feeling of being transported into the Middle Ages was overwhelming.' The detail of 'wands' conveys an Arthurian sense of powerful wizardry and, in the manner of stage props commandeered for another purpose, the wands double up as 'lances' to enhance the medieval atmosphere. Moreover, the superimposition of monks 'in the foreground' Anglicises the scene in accordance with the conventions of the picturesque, taming Afghanistan's threatening aspects by likening it to a textbook illustration of pastoral bliss. A similar brand of nostalgia is to be found over forty years later in the following claim by Jason Elliot: 'There was an otherworldly character to Afghanistan, reflected in the pleasant anarchy of life, the medieval civility of its people's manners' (28). However, idyllic portrayals rarely last in narratives from the British tradition; the medieval coin has two sides. Once 'pictorial' images of rural, Arthurian England are introduced into an Afghan environment poverty impinges, traumatic colonial memories stir and claims of 'medieval civility' metamorphose into something altogether more sinister. Newby's description of the two horsemen continues thus:

> Close-to these men made a most disagreeable impression on all of us. The one with the skull-cap looked nothing more than an assassin. As well as his willow wand he carried a rifle slung across his shoulder. There was nothing medieval about the rifle, a 45 Martini-Henry that, although almost eighty years old, could still blow the daylights out of anything (198).

In this passage is found considerable textual upheaval since nostalgia for Arthurian Romance is at war with lawless tropes and the latent threat posed by Afghans (signalled by the rifle that 'could still blow the living daylights out of anything'). The rifle, about which 'there was nothing medieval', makes the 'wands' and 'lances' seem decidedly out of place. Moreover, since it dates back to the Second Anglo-Afghan War, it instantly raises the spectre of nineteenth-century Afghan-British conflicts. Pastoral and idealised medieval comparisons therefore tend to be problematised almost as soon as they are produced.

While escape is an important component of the medieval comparison, and one which was, as I have suggested, absent from the 2001 news coverage, narratives of travel tend to oscillate between the portrayal of Afghanistan as a pre-industrial rural idyll where Afghans practise the lost art of Arthurian chivalry and, conversely, branding Afghan cultural practices as medieval in the sense of being crude or cruel. Jason Elliot, for example, describes butchers' market stalls where a 'man hacked with iron axes at carcasses on wooden stumps [...] and laid out severed heads in long rows like the grisly trophies of medieval conflicts' (59). As I discuss presently, this representational counter-swing was most prominent in the recent media coverage. In travel writing, the chivalrous trope is invariably accompanied by its counterpart, which is 'medieval barbarity'. Contemporary travel narratives lurch between idealised and sinister medievalised depiction, depictions that either tame Afghanistan into a pre-industrial idyll or – conversely – build on its fearful reputation for the British. The crucial point is that likening Afghanistan to the Middle Ages was a feature of travel writing long before recent news coverage, which flipped the medieval coin onto its uglier face as Taliban methods of punishment were compared to medieval torture, or occasionally, to that of the 'Dark Ages'.

Travel writing thus set an important precedent for Afghanistan's medievalisation in the 2001 coverage. There are two further sources of these medieval tropes: the picturesque and the gothic. I deal with each in turn before dwelling on the connections between them. The abundance of castles and forts amounts to a form of Afghan picturesque that recent journalism about Afghanistan partially inherits. William Gilpin described the picturesque in the following terms: '[t]he picturesque eye is perhaps most inquisitive after the elegant relics of ancient architecture; the ruined tower, the gothic arch, the remains of castles, and abbeys' (in Ryan 1996: 76). Whenever such settings occur in colonial writing, they tend to support colonial ideologies. For example, Simon Ryan argues that the 'ideological function' of castles' frequent appearance in the journals of Australian explorers was to 'remind the reader of the uncivilised state of the country's inhabitants' (77). This interpretation seems pertinent for some, but by no means all, narratives about Afghanistan. It certainly appears to be the case with the castles in Jean Bowie-Shor's narrative: 'Everywhere history was mute before us, frozen in stone. Ruined castles perched in impossible places' (158).[64] The prevalence of castles and ruined fortresses builds up a picture of Afghanistan as a barren wasteland dotted, in the words of Robert Byron, with the 'worn grey shapes of a bygone architecture' (Byron: 245). Descriptions of castles and forts, which are always deserted, suggest the need for an 'implicit programme of action' on the part of more powerful nations (Said 1978: 208). To the extent that literal ruins imply cultural ruination, or the obsolete cultural codes of the country's inhabitants, such descriptions are not antithetical to the perceived need for some form of intervention to prevent further disintegration (Ryan: 79). This

latter state of affairs expresses the commonest ethical implication of
deploying this mode. In Jason Elliot's travel writing, however, the
Afghan picturesque does not go uncontested. In a distinctive passage,
he intervenes in the convention: 'On a high ridge I fancied I could
make out the crenellated wall of a pre-Islamic fort or the withered
ramparts of a monastery forgotten by time; both were tricks of the
light and mind' (163). As with other moments in this narrative, a form
of counter-narrative foregrounds the illusory and over-determined
nature of the traveller's gaze. The narrator's mistake is not merely a
'tric[k] of the light' but also of 'the mind.'

Travel narratives about medieval Afghanistan are partially gothic. The
'medieval Orient' has a long pedigree, merging, as Dale Townshend
argues, in the gothic form in William Beckford's 1786 novel *Vatek*.[65]
The gothic mode has been instrumental in mobilising the medieval
Orient, relocating the Islamic aspects of Afghan cultural practices to
Europe's medieval past. The gothic is notoriously 'cross-generic',
being a mixture of high and low cultural forms (Hogle 2002: 8).
Afghanistan's architectural and topographical features have powerful
gothic appeal, and travellers' depictions correspond with a number of
items on Jerrold Hogle's list of key gothic features and scenarios. In
the gothic, action generally takes place in 'an antiquated or seemingly
antiquated space'. This might be 'a castle', 'a foreign place', 'a vast
prison' or 'a primeval frontier'. Crucially, Hogle notes that 'within
this space [...] are hidden some secrets from the past (sometimes the
recent past) that haunt the characters psychologically, physically, or
otherwise at the main time of the story' (2). Travel narratives about
Afghanistan (and after them news reports) are haunted in comparable
ways, especially, as I have argued, by the 1842 retreat and the
associated sense of peril at crossing the North-West Frontier.

The partially gothic nature of travel writing and news coverage, which
tends to depict the 'ancient' Afghan landscape as littered with
medieval forts,[66] risks complicity with the gothic's well-documented
psychological functions. As Hogle points out, the gothic 'express[es]',
'resolve[s]' and disguises powerful western anxieties and desires,
'fears and longings [...] from the most internal and mental to the
widely social and cultural' (4). In travel writing, the gothic mode
seems conducive to repressing collective guilt and trauma over British

humiliations and violent interventions in Afghanistan's political affairs. As I argue below, persistent medievalisation in news media coverage tended to hinder the exploration of political anxieties in relation to Afghanistan. These anxieties clustered around the demonstrable precariousness of the historically amnesiac political rhetoric about Afghanistan's recent past and potential political culpability, especially regarding the role formerly played by coalition countries in the rise of the Taleban. As David Punter argues, throughout its history, the gothic has been a means of 'displac[ing] the hidden violence of present social structures, conjur[ing] them up again as past, and promptly fall[ing] under their spell' (in Hogle:16).

Medievalisation in news media coverage of Operation Enduring Freedom

A salient feature of news reports about Afghanistan at the time of Operation Enduring Freedom was the confusion of poverty-related 'medieval conditions' with 'medieval' or 'barbaric' culture. Again, this is a phenomenon shared with travel narratives, in which descriptions of material poverty frequently lead to a medieval atmosphere being evoked. It is a short step from discussions of medieval architecture or 'Afghan warlords' to a focus on Afghanistan's 'medieval culture' in need of external intervention. This is apparent in the *Daily Mirror* reporter Kevin Toolis's conflation of material Afghan poverty ('no roads, no medical clinics, no electricity') with 'travel[ling] back into medieval barbarity' (October 3, 2001). The following article by Ross Benson for the *Daily Mail* executes a similar manoeuvre when he suggests that 'the world has moved on since' his last visit to Afghanistan twenty years before. In the following extract, material poverty quickly becomes synonymous with cultural backwardness:

> The intervening decades have witnessed the rise of the computer, the invention of the Internet and the refinement of the satellite communications I am using to file this report.

> In Afghanistan, however, time has gone backwards. According to the Islamic calendar the year is 1379. It is a date the Taliban takes literally, and to journey through Afghanistan's mountain passes and along the ancient

> donkey tracks which serve as highways is to step into the Middle Ages
> (October 1, 2002).

As the multiple influences on this passage suggest, the discursive
origins of the medieval trope are various, not least the long tradition of
cultural hostility towards Islam and its perceived conservative and
illiberal outlook. Time's 'backwar[d]' travel is explained by Islam's
'anti-modern' nature through the narrative's emphasis on the apparent
significance of the Islamic calendar being set at 1379 as tangible
evidence of medievalism. By contrast, 'the world' (an exclusive but
naturalised category implicitly comprising those wealthy nations that
have enjoyed technological expansion) 'has moved on'. In this
context, 'mov[ing] on' expresses the universal desirability of
imposing technologically-driven modernity on societies across the
globe (Lugo: 2004). This ideological imperative is conveyed by the
passage's celebratory model of the information society ('the rise of the
computer, the invention of the internet'). The naturalised category of
'the world that has moved on' detracts from the uneven distribution of
technological benefits across the globe. Despite the fact that less than
ten percent of the global population has access to the internet,
Afghanistan, which clearly does not fall into the category of the
'world [that] has moved on', is abnormalised in misleading ways
(according to the Nielsen ratings statistics, ninety percent of the
world's population has yet to 'mov[e] on').[67] At the same time,
however, the passage reverberates with genuine personal shock at the
contrasting Afghan and British experiences of life in the twenty-first
century. Indeed, Benson's first-hand experience of being in
Afghanistan makes it difficult to deny the contemporaneity of Afghan
poverty.[68] In this sense, medievalising Afghanistan has an identifiable
consequence, function even, combating disquieting realisations of this
contemporaneity by casting off, in the Kristevan sense, troubling
connections between two apparently distinct and separate 'worlds'.
This is partly accomplished by banishing one of those worlds to a
different century. There are plentiful examples Afghans being
depicted as, in the words of journalist Peter Greste, isolated from 'the
world', 'tucked away in remote valleys, living and surviving in the
middle ages' ('An Afghan Odyssey' in 'From Our Own
Correspondent', 17 November, 2001). Once again, persistent
representations of Afghans as existing in unworldly monastic

seclusion are misleading in the sense that they detract from key material facts such as the phenomenon of Afghan migration. For example, Afghans make up more than half of the world's refugee population with 3.6 million refugees and 600,000 internally displaced peoples.[69] It is not merely travel writing, but international news media coverage, that is caught between what Holland and Huggan call 'competing drives' to tackle new and complex global realities or to revert to nostalgic 'site[s] of a simpler past' (24).

Persistent claims of medieval isolationism fly in the face of plentiful evidence to the contrary, suggesting that such claims speak volumes about the disturbingly interrelated economic and political fortunes of 'the world [that] has moved on' and the world that is left behind. Matt Frei's report for BBC1's 'Six O' Clock News' is another case in point:

> [Mid-shot of a turbaned Taleb peering over a wall, dressed in ragged clothes.]
> Frye: In his last remaining fiefdom, Taliban man is still stuck in a time warp.[70] Resolutely cut off from the outside world. We were such a novelty that some scaled trees [mid-shot of two Taliban climbing a tree. Close-up shot of a man peering at the camera through the branches] to get a better look. (20 November, 2001)

As I discuss later, depictions such as these divorce the Taliban from the very conditions that gave rise to their inception. The Taliban emerged partly as a result of the aftershocks from the Cold War. As William Voselsang points out, most Talebs came from the refugee camps (2002: 300). Nevertheless, Matt Frye's report pursues a metaphor of medieval feudalism before sliding back along the socio-evolutionary scale to (Neanderthal) 'Taliban man [...] scal[ing] trees' to catch a glimpse of the (elusive) sophisticated technology of (in Benson's words) the 'world that has moved on'.

Afghanistan's medievalisation often evokes laughter. In Andrew North's report for 'From Our Own Correspondent', the Governor of Herat, Ismael Khan, 'holds court in 'an almost medieval scene, except that for much of the time Ismael Khan had a mobile phone clamped to his ear' (16 September, 2004). Here, North's report disrupts its own scheme of representation by drawing attention to objects that are incongruous with medieval scenes and settings. Such manoeuvres anticipate laughter, yet this laughter is often double-edged. As with Robert Byron's description of Nuristanis with guns, artefacts often exercise their own form of incriminating agency, testifying to complex, multiple connections between two supposedly distinct spheres. This principle applies to news reports' depictions of 'ancient' or 'medieval' Afghan landscapes, where rusting tanks or bomb-craters offer visual testimony to Afghanistan's contemporaneity, exposing points of connection between economically and militarily disparate worlds.

Medieval tropes risk complicity with that which Jairo Lugo describes as a 'cybernetic paradigm' generated by free-market dependencies on information and communication technologies (ICTs). Lugo argues that this celebratory paradigm effectively 'recuperates' colonial narratives of progress. He suggests that, across the 'political spectrum', public and media discourses are 'impregnated' with neo-Hegelian conceptions of progress, constructing and promoting a model of technological and information-based modernity as desirable and inevitable for societies across the globe (2004).[71] As Benson's *Daily Mail* article illustrates, news coverage of Afghanistan frequently brings this 'cybernetic paradigm' forcefully into play. This paradigm is of course dramatically (and photogenically) rejected by the Taleban's literal destruction of ICTs. Incongruous though Ismael Khan's mobile phone might appear, then, its significance for news audiences relies on the assumption that modernity will inevitably replace 'medieval' cultural, social and political realities. Indeed, Taliban edicts on the consumption of ICTs, especially television,[72] are pathologised and abnormalised according to this same ideological dynamic. The following sentiment expressed by Yvonne Ridley is commonplace: '[the Taleban's] brutal and ruthless drive [...] seemed like madness to someone like me, who was brought up on television, telephones [...] music, dancing and singing' (2001: 140). The Taleban's consciousness of the power of mainstream news networks to define the political landscape is persistently under theorised in news reports and newspaper articles. I did not find any news commentaries that even considered the possibility that the communicative supremacy of global media networks was in any way relevant to the ban on televisions.[73]

Linked to globalisation's implicit narratives of progress are, as Lugo suggests, two ultimate goals and products: modernity in the shape of secular democracy and economic liberalisation. As scholars such as Tim Fitzgerald have pointed out, the ideal of secular democracy is discursively and conceptually flawed. Fitzgerald observes that the concept relies heavily on the essentialised English-language category of 'religion', which has, since the seventeenth century, been placed in opposition to 'secularity', encompassing the modern category of 'politics' and other supposedly 'secular' domains such as science and economics (2004).[74] As he points out, the 'historical separation and yet mutual construction of semantic fields is mirrored in the constitutional separation of church and state'. However, secular democracy, which tends to go hand in hand with free market economics, has many ironies. The propagation of free-market economics has Christian derivatives. As Gray points out, the International Monetary Fund peddles the post-Christian, Positivistic remnants of monotheism and retains a strong belief in salvation (2002 113;106) through economic means. Operations such as Enduring Freedom are the military extension of this brand of salvation. The category of 'religion', then, has an in-built, negative connotation, being 'formulat[ed] as essentially non-political' while 'politics' is constructed as 'essentially "secular" and "non-religious"' (Fitzgerald: 2004). In the context of Afghanistan, secular democracy's propagation in news reports conveys an unspoken ideal of 'good' or 'non-political' Islam. The problem with this is it sets up yet another narrative of good and evil, which tends to militate against making a contribution to news audiences' understanding of a given conflict's wider causes. Moreover, not only does this characterisation of 'religion' belie the historical experience of both Christianity and Islam, but also the promotion of the secular democratic ideal places ethno-linguistic constraints on audiences' conception of, for example, the viable range of political alternatives to military action. As Gray seems to suggest, medievalisation tends to reinforce celebratory narratives of modernity by obscuring the fact that '[t]here has always been more than one way of being modern' (81). Moreover, the persistent portrayal of Islam as fundamentally anti-modern leads to the designation of groups such as the Taliban or al-Qaeda as medieval. However, aside from radical Islam's geo-political drives, Gray also notes that it has 'secular derivatives'.[75] As he points out in his aptly titled *Al Qaeda and what it*

means to be modern, the 'intellectual roots' of al-Qaeda and the
Taliban are in the thinking of rational sceptics such as David Hume.
During the European Counter-Enlightenment, such thinkers rejected
reason itself (2003: 25). Al Qaeda's charter[76] draws on
'quintessentially modern' ideas, making the medieval comparison still
more obsolete; the 'medieval world may have been unified by faith,
but it did not scorn reason' as al Qaeda's charter does (26). Far from
being medieval, the form of Islam expressed by the Taliban edicts has
inherited German Romanticist protests against French claims to
embody universal civilisation. In the twenty-first century, this protest
has been directed against the missionary-like advancement of secular
democracy and free market economics (85).

A noticeable feature of British news reports about the Taliban was that
understanding the group's drives, origins and motives tended to come
second to their designation as the foremost enemy of secular
democracy. Contentions such as Benson's that in 'accord[ance]
[with...] the Islamic calendar', the year 2001 in 'the world' is actually
only 1379 in Afghanistan, feed easily into an established historical
tendency to report Islam as fundamentally anti-modern. To make such
a claim is to misidentify a specific feature of Saudi Wahaabism as
being representatively Islamic. However, Ahmed Rashid notes that, in
2001, those journalists with little knowledge of Islam were ill-
equipped to be discerning about the Taleban's highly unorthodox
interpretations of *Sharia* law. *Sharia* law in Afghanistan more
profoundly resembles Pashtun codes of Pashtunwali than Islamic law
as it is interpreted in other parts of the globe. For all their talk of
'Islamic' punishments, the Taliban were intensely ignorant of Islamic
history and often directed these punishments towards the persecution
of non-Pashtuns (2000:210). Failure to analyse the combination of
circumstances, local, regional and international, that gave rise to the
Taliban in the first place risks misidentifying the root causes of
Afghanistan's problems as primarily cultural, sectarian and religious,
leading commentators to proffer straightforward solutions (such as the
Taleban's removal) as a path to secular and economic liberalisation.

Conclusion

Part One has discussed the ongoing resonance of traumatic nineteenth-century Anglo-Afghan encounters for British travel writing about Afghanistan. For over a hundred years, travellers' narratives have been structured by worries over personal safety, assertions of Afghan lawlessness and depictions of murderous Nuristanis or petty village feuds. I have argued that travel writing about Afghanistan has a particular literary pedigree in which the writing of Kipling features prominently. Contemporary travel writers have inherited a number of assumptions and prejudices from Kipling and agendas of travel are set with an eye on his writing. Like many of the authors of his own sources, Kipling never visited Afghanistan and belongs to a long tradition of absentee authority. Because his work is so influential, this has particular ethical implications for travel writing that aspires to informational status. As Part Two explores, decades of warfare have meant that Afghanistan is associated with increasingly narrow purposes of travel. In recent years the most likely British traveller to Afghanistan is the war correspondent. It is therefore advisable to discuss British travel writing in relation to recent journalistic reporting. As already illustrated, Kipling's writings were regularly consulted by British journalists at the beginning of the 2001 conflict. I will also argue, however, that travel narratives by journalists are subject to a unique set of narrative pressures, most particularly the need to transmit authority. Part Two considers how this need tends to foster reliance on representational strategies associated with the parallel genre of ethnography.

Part One has illustrated how attention to the specificities of place and its associated histories of cross-cultural encounter necessarily supplements and modifies generalised theories of travel writing. The politics, and even the aesthetics, of location impinge on contemporary travel narratives in very particular ways, sometimes leading to significant deviations from wider generic tendencies or conventions of representation. For example, Afghanistan's Wild-Westification means that travel narratives rarely comply with a well-documented tendency to feminise the Orient. On the contrary, Afghanistan is frequently masculinised. To many travel writers it is 'a big boy's country' (Bealby: 69). To subsume Afghanistan into a 'zone of repetition' such

as 'the Oriental' (Holland and Huggan: 67 & 68) would risk
overlooking the nuances of its site-specific trends. I have also argued
that Afghanistan's undiminished reputation as an 'off-the-beaten-
track' location combined with a paucity of travel writing about the
country have tended to dull the urge, noted by critics in relation to
much contemporary travel writing about more frequently visited
regions, to parody or satirise the pronouncements of earlier travellers.
Partly as a means of intensifying the 'thrill' of its outlandish
reputation, recent travel narratives about Afghanistan are more than
generally disposed to manifest nineteenth-century preoccupations and
to corroborate, rather than contest, the conclusions of antecedent
writings.

Part One has also examined the way in which travel writing and, more
recently, news media coverage routinely superimpose historically and
geographically alien contexts (such as medieval Europe and the Wild
West) onto Afghan scenes and settings in ways that tend to foster an
analytical reliance on the notion of 'cultural interiority', or
'ethnopsychology'[77], as an all-purpose explanation for Afghan poverty
or conflict. I continue to investigate this tendency in Parts Two and
Three. There are, of course, clear disadvantages associated with
confining the discussion of such phenomena as medievalisation or
Wild-Westification to a single country. There is a danger of playing
down the significance of these tendencies in travel writing about other
locations. Nevertheless, Part One has been able to map Afghanistan's
medievalisation from the late 1930s to the present. Paying exclusive
attention to Anglo-Afghan contexts has allowed me to consider in
some depth how and why, in British imaginations, certain 'mud' came
to 'stick'.

I have argued that it is not only travel writing, but also journalism, that
is torn between complex global realities and a nostalgic reversion to
earlier pasts. As I have suggested, 'medieval Afghanistan' remains a
compelling construction for the British. This is partly due to
contemporary Britain's social and political self-construction as the
'world that has moved on'. Medievalisation tends to reinforce
celebratory narratives of modernity and is implicated in the
advancement and imposition of secular democracy. In the 2001
coverage, the continual slippage from scenes of Afghan poverty to

Afghan medievalism tended to sideline any discussion of the conflict's wider causes and contexts. Moreover, persistent depictions of Afghanistan as existing in a geo-political vacuum tended to detract from material realities, such as mass migration, that might have assisted news audiences to understand the degree of social and economic upheaval perceptible to journalists the moment they crossed the Afghan border. Part Three picks up on incriminating points of connection between economically and militarily disparate worlds, points of connection from which medievalising commentaries tend to avert their gaze.

Despite the unusually high degree of consensus among travel narratives about Afghanistan, the discussion in Part One has not been restricted to an exclusive focus on representational continuities at the expense of instances of imaginative appropriation or the subversion of dominant renderings. Instead I have attempted to balance the 'relative weight of textual determinants' (Hulme and Youngs: 8) against the desirability of assessing the potential for significant 'variations on the repetition' of 'certain rule-bound discourses' (Butler in Smith and Watson: xx). Part Two moves the argument forward to consider the tendency of travel narrative to corroborate nineteenth-century ideas in terms of 'push' and 'pull' factors. Certain factors push narratives towards sustaining the assertions of nineteenth-century commentators while others draw them away from simple reiteratation of well-worn notions. Genre is central to this process. The demands of different generic conventions exert pressure in distinct and complex ways. The example of Wild-Westification suggests that particular generic conventions can initiate revisions of established traditions of representation. As Part Two goes on to examine, therefore, factors such as intentionality can be balanced against a range of other factors that facilitate divergence from representative norms. Authorial agency is by no means discounted, however. While travel writing's predilection for citing earlier sources sets thematic agendas and defines discursive parameters, Jason Elliot's generally self-reflexive travel writing shows that strategic citation can introduce a metafictional dimension whereby representational patterns are foregrounded and thereby subverted. Parts Two and Three therefore attempt to consider the interaction of diverse factors such as authorial agency, gendered positionality, changing political circumstances (especially pertaining to warfare), shifting imperatives, incompatible or competing tropes (as was seen with the Afghan picturesque and homicidal Nuristanis) and, finally, significant upheavals in sub-genre, most particularly the rise of journalistic and pseudo-ethnographic travel writing.

Part Two:
Where ethnographers fear to tread: the counter-influence of classical ethnography on travel writing and journalism about Afghanistan.

Following the attack on the World Trade Centre in 2001, travel narratives were perhaps inevitably enlisted in the scramble for knowledge about Afghanistan. Afghanistan became the sudden focus of international attention and there was a rush of publications as travel books, ethnographies, historical accounts and political analyses were (re)printed, or reissued.

Part Two concentrates on the books of two journalists who have turned to travel writing to record their personal and professional experiences in Afghanistan. Christopher Kremmer's *The Carpet Wars* and Christina Lamb's *The Sewing Circles of Herat* were both published for the first time in 2002 by Harper Collins. Kremmer, an Australian national, spent ten years writing about Asia for print and broadcast media. He won an award for his first travelogue, *Stalking the Elephant Kings*. Lamb, a British national, was named Foreign Correspondent of the Year for her reporting from Afghanistan and Pakistan for the *Daily Telegraph*. Kremmer's and Lamb's professional identities as journalists are particularly relevant to my discussion since, I will argue, the counter-influence of classical ethnography on contemporary travel writing about Afghanistan is partly related to travel writing's deficit of, and resultant quest for, narrative authority. Although neither Kremmer's nor Lamb's narratives purport to be ethnographic,[78] I will argue that, when journalists turn to travel writing, certain professional imperatives exert pressure on the narrative to accrue a greater degree of authority than is generally possible with travel writing. After all, as Steve Clark points out, travel writing has been a 'middlebrow form throughout its history' (1999: 1).[79] As Part Three explores, professional imperatives are by no means the sole explanation for the phenomenon I have termed pseudo-ethnographic travel writing. Nevertheless, Part Two's focus on narrative authority in travel writing by journalists is fully justified by the fact that, as Peter Hulme and Tim Youngs have argued, '[m]uch contemporary travel writing has been written by journalists who have a deep investment in maintaining their credibility' (2003: 10).

Since travel writing predates ethnography, much research has centred on the influence of travel writing on ethnography (rather than the other way around). Ongoing debates over the crisis in anthropology mean that scholarly investigations of ethnography's indebtedness to travel writing tend to be valued for their contribution to the crisis debate. Less attention has been paid to the question of counter-influence: the presence of ethnography in contemporary travel narratives. Attending to ethnographers' and travellers' accounts of Afghan games reveals that recent travel writing about Afghanistan relies heavily upon the long-established (and much maligned) textual practices of those varieties of ethnography closely associated with the pre-crisis period. For want of a better term, I refer to pre-crisis modes of ethnography as *classical ethnographies*.[80]

Placing my close readings of Kremmer's and Lamb's narratives in the context of recent anthropological debates over dilemmas of cross-cultural representation, I consider the ethical and ideological implications of travel writing's dependency upon ethnography's previous incarnations. Contemporary ethnographers have made sustained and rigorous efforts to disentangle ethnography from its colonial roots. However, I ask whether travel writing about Afghanistan is doomed to repeat classical ethnography's mistakes. To what extent do (and can) Kremmer's and Lambs' narratives eschew ethnography's colonial component? Alternatively, is contemporary travel writing about Afghanistan inflected with ethnographers' sense of discursive crisis? While Kremmer and Lambs' narratives appear to disassociate themselves from Orientalist discourses about Afghanistan (Said's *Orientalism* is in Kremmer's bibliography) I consider the possibility that ethnographically-loaded travel narratives may be hostile to any anti-imperial purpose.[81] Of course, ethnography is not the sole, or even main, influence on Kremmer's and Lamb's narratives. Kremmer's and Lamb's travel writing relies on a wide range of texts about Afghanistan (from which both books inherit a number of prejudices). However, it is their professional identity as journalists that is the major focus of attention for Part Two, which examines the ethnographically-loaded nature of travel writing by two war correspondents.

Part Two raises a number of questions. Do the professional imperatives and narrative conventions of journalism and war reporting compound the problem of ethnographic borrowing, or do they provide a route map for negotiating ethnography's abandoned mine fields of cross-cultural representation?

Inevitably, I will argue, Kremmer's and Lambs' narratives are complicit (in very specific ways) with some of classical ethnographies' most problematic modes of representation. However, Part Two takes into account recent interventions in the crisis debate by feminist anthropologists who regret the determinism associated with the postmodern turn in ethnography and who, like many feminists in the parallel field of literary criticism, resist precluding the possibility of agency. Ruth Behar's questions about feminist anthropology mirror those asked of women's travel writing by Mills and others: '[h]ave ethnographic authority and the burden of authorship figured differently in the works of women anthropologists? [...] What is the cultural logic by which authorship is coded as "feminine" or "masculine," and what are the consequences of those markings' (1995: 15)? What happens to what James Duncan describes as the 'usual masculinist fantasy of the Orient as a liminal zone of unrestrained sexuality' (in Duncan and Gregory 1999: 143) when a woman writes about it? Finally, what is the relationship, if any, between the writer's gender, the negotiation of conventional plots or patterns of representation, and the facilitation of informants' agency? Reading these interventions back into Kremmer's and Lambs' texts, I consider the possibility that, at certain critical junctures, their travel narratives occasionally manage to eschew excessive narrative and interpretative authority.

Ethnography as travel writing

Although the rise of formal ethnography is generally considered an early twentieth-century phenomenon, Joan Pau Rubies suggests that the 'ethnographic impulse' has been present in travel writing since the early modern period, when travel writers often consulted manuals to assist with organising their writing and observations. Mary Louise Pratt notes the distinctively proto-ethnographic quality of some sixteenth-century travel writing, such as Hans Slade of Hesse's captivity narrative, which contains chapters with such titles as: 'what their dwellings are like', 'how they make fire' and 'what they believe in' (in Clifford and Marcus 1986: 34). During the Enlightenment, travel writing's persistent return to themes such as political order, kinship, warfare and justice signalled the emergence of a set of analytical categories that prefigured twentieth-century ethnography (Pau Rubies in Hulme and Youngs 2003: 243-252). Ethnography's emergence in the 1930s has been described by Pau Rubies as a 'split between the 'professional' ethnography of the anthropologist and the literary late-romantic travel writer, given to *subjective musings* rather than to […] systematic observation' (258 & 259).

Because travel writing and ethnography have been, and remain, mutually dependent genres, the question is not so much how travel writing and ethnography differ as how this difference has tended to be perceived by ethnographers. In her influential essay 'Fieldwork in Common Places' (in Clifford and Marcus: 37), Pratt has noted the tendency of classical ethnographies to distinguish themselves from antecedent genres such as travel writing. She observes that, by the late nineteen-eighties, it was the 'well-established habit' of ethnographers to 'defin[e] ethnographic writing over and against older, less specialized genres, such as travel books, personal memoirs, journalism, and accounts by missionaries, settlers, colonial officials', and so on (27). Since its birth in the early twentieth-century, ethnography has tended to redraw, define and police its generic boundaries[82], developing formalized systems of observation so as to create and maintain a distance from travel writers' more self-evidently subjective ruminations (Pau Rubies in Hulme and Youngs: 257 & 258). However, as Pratt has pointed out, the blindness of classical ethnographies to the fact that travel writing, rather than science, is its principal antecedent, has meant that, until recently, anthropologists have tended to overlook the possible ethical consequences of ethnography's generic entanglement with travel writing (in Clifford and Marcus: 27 & 34).

It would be reckless to suggest that the differences between travel writing and ethnography are a figment of anthropologists' collective imagination. There are, of course, many genuine points of departure. David Scott identifies one major difference as being a matter of differing commitment to viewpoint and perception:

> It is the business of ethnography to study in a given culture both the *how* and the *what* of semiosis, not only the way signs interact but also the way they may be understood from a native perspective to act on and transform the real. Travel writing, on the other hand, while often operating within a project broadly analogous to that of ethnography, focuses more on how the other or a different episteme is experienced by the individual consciousness (2002: 210).

Another major difference pertains to narrative conventions. Even while ethnography shares many of travel writing's conventions, the latter tends to subordinate description to narrative while classical ethnographies tend to embrace description and suppress narrative, especially personal narrative (Pratt in Clifford and Marcus: 41). Until recently, personal narrative tended either to be relegated to the margins of the formal ethnography or to be published elsewhere in a separate account. Pratt attributes classical ethnography's separation of personal narrative and impersonal description to its traditional alignment with the authoritative discourses of science (41). Perhaps the most crucial point of departure relates to the ethics of representation; while exoticising strangeness is virtually a contractual obligation for travel writers, ethnography's agenda has generally been culturally relativist, locating 'difference' within an allegorical framework of 'sameness'.[83]

The 'crisis' in socio-cultural ethnography[84]

The crisis in socio-cultural anthropology is key to my discussion of counter-influence since ethical debates associated with the crisis highlight the problems associated with classical ethnographies, problems, as I will argue, that are inherited by Kremmer's and Lamb's narratives. Furthermore, focus on the recurring themes of the crisis makes it possible to establish whether or not their travel writing is inflected with a parallel sense of discursive crisis.

The crisis in ethnography has been variously denied, challenged and refuted.[85] Debates centre on how the crisis has been narrativised, how it was initiated, when or why it took place, whether or not it took place at all, and, finally, how to respond to the insights that it has provided.[86] According to postmodern versions of recent anthropological history, by the late nineteen-eighties, ethnographic writing began to be subjected to intense critical scrutiny and questions of such enormity were raised as to precipitate a discursive, methodological and ethical crisis. Whether or not this version of events is acceded to, there is broad agreement among anthropologists that key concepts (such as the culture concept) and textual practices (such as synecdoche) have, and ought to have been, thoroughly challenged and variously adapted, avoided, or supplanted by more self-reflexive models.

In his 1983 essay 'On Ethnographic Authority', James Clifford made tentative statements pertaining to what he referred to as 'the current crisis - or better, dispersion - of ethnographic authority':

> The activity of cross-cultural representation is now more than usually in question. The present predicament is linked to the breakup and redistribution of colonial power in the decades after 1950 and the echoes of that process in the radical cultural theories of the 1960's and 1970's (118 & 119).

In the same essay, he focused on anthropology's '*crise de conscience* with respect to its liberal status within the imperial order' (119). Clifford's introduction to the seminal collection of essays in *Writing Culture* (1986)[87] made an unequivocal declaration of anthropological crisis.[88] Clifford's more recent writing continues to centre on the issue of excessive ethnographic authority, insisting that there is 'no politically innocent methodology for intercultural interpretation' (2000: 19). The link between anthropology, colonialism and imperialism or, as David Richards puts it, the 'misrecogni[tion of] colonized people as primitives' (1994: 237), has been a recurring theme of the crisis debate. Talal Asad's essay in *Writing Culture* stresses the ongoing relevance of ethnography's colonial heritage to the crisis by underscoring the significance of the disparity between what ethnographers *claim* to do in the field and what their countries' governments *actually* do (in Clifford and Marcus: 144).

Ever since the publication of *Writing Culture*, feminist ethnographers have launched a compelling and sustained attack on its exclusions and silences, most particularly Clifford's denial of the relevance of feminist empirical work and theory to the crisis. Feminists argue that Clifford's infamous denial is symptomatic of the gender politics of theory transformation within the academic community.[89] Published nearly ten years after *Writing Culture*, Ruth Behar and Deborah Gordon's *Women Writing Culture* expresses feminists' ongoing struggle to make inroads into this process of retrospective disciplinary rehistoricisation. While Marcus' conclusion to *Writing Culture* suggested that ethnographers produce 'mixed genre texts' where 'ethnographic detail shares textual space with other varieties of writing' (188 & 189), Behar argues that many so-called innovations suggested in *Writing Culture* were a feature of feminist ethnography 'throughout the twentieth century'. She suggests that, though 'women had crossed the border between anthropology and literature', they usually did it '"illegally" as aliens who produced works that tended to be viewed in the profession as "confessional" and "popular"' (4). Ethnography about Afghanistan has generated its own example of this phenomenon. Veronica Doubleday's 1988 study *Three Women of Herat*, emerged from a tradition of proto-professional ethnographic writing linked to the "untrained" wives of anthropologists (see appendix two for a description of her ethnography).[90] Despite the fact that Doubleday appears in the acknowledgments sections of anthropological colleagues working on Afghanistan, I have been unable to find a single review of her study.

The overriding concern of feminists regarding the postmodern turn in ethnography concerns political paralysis. Margery Wolf points out that feminist critics have an uneasy relationship with postmodernism because, while postmodernism concerns itself with the 'demolition of grand narratives (narratives which have silenced women and minorities)', deconstructionist approaches risk deauthorising feminist counter-narratives. It is not here possible to do justice to the contribution of feminist contributions to anthropological theory and practice. Since the nineteen-seventies (and arguably long before this), feminist theory has interrogated anthropological premises and units of analysis (questioning the primacy of gender and the category 'woman'), challenged essentialist practices, raised questions about anthropology's underlying assumption of sameness and gone against the grain of anthropology's moral project of minimizing difference (especially in relation to the question of universal solidarity among women).[91] However, I return to the relevance of the most salient feminist discussions towards the end of Part Two

Ethnography about Afghanistan

This section provides a brief overview of the work of six anthropologists specializing in Afghanistan: Louis Dupree ([1973] 2002), Nazif Shahrani ([1979]2002), Whitney Azoy ([1982] 2003), Veronica Doubleday (1988), Margaret Mills (1991) and Nancy Tapper (1991).[92] As the bibliographies of Kremmer and Lamb attest, when contemporary travel writers enter Afghanistan, 'the field' is already filled with ethnographic writing. Of the six ethnographers, two (Azoy and Dupree) can be traced as direct intertexts: both appear in Kremmer's bibliography, while Dupree is present in Lamb's. Importantly, while the travel narratives of Kremmer and Lamb inherit the ethnographic stances of Dupree and Azoy (identifiable as a direct influence on Kremmer's discussion of *buzkashi* or, to use the Kirghiz name, *olagh tartish*,[93] and Lamb's discussion of Afghan games) they are also subject to the more nebulous and pervasive traits and discourses of classical ethnographies in general. Kremmer and Lamb inherit interpretative frameworks, ethnographic principles and analytical processes that are traceable, but not necessarily exclusive, to specific ethnographies about Afghanistan.

It is difficult to exaggerate the impact of more than twenty years' civil war on ethnography about Afghanistan. As Shahrani puts it, 'Afghanistan was lost to anthropology after April 1978' following the establishment of a Communist government in Kabul.[94] Tapper stated in her 1983 review of Azoy's ethnography that '[t]he current tragic situation in Afghanistan has closed that country to Western ethnographers for the foreseeable future [...] a fact which enhances the documentary importance of field studies undertaken in the country in the last decade'. As a result of the country's inaccessibility during this period, many studies suffered severe delays in publication.[95] The work of Tapper and Mills was published relatively recently (1991) despite the fact that their fieldwork was conducted before 1975, although both studies were partially revised by their authors with post-crisis insights in mind. In an attempt to diminish her own study's narrative authority, Mills' narrator presents the ethnography as 'my story [...] about some stories, my own dialogue with some conversations' (2). Notably, those ethnographies that are absent from the bibliographies of Kremmer and Lamb are more profoundly inflected with a sense of discursive crisis than Azoy and Dupree's studies.

Louis Dupree, whom Azoy describes as the 'grandfather' of ethnography about Afghanistan, published his study *Afghanistan* in 1978. This study, reissued in 2002, is unmistakably classical in its application of outmoded concepts and suppression of informants' voices. Azoy's *Buzkashi. Game and Power in Afghanistan* was first published in 1983 and republished in 2003. Azoy's study was applauded by reviewers in the early nineteen-eighties, as, in the words of William L. Richter, a 'stimulating [...] study of buzkashi, the Afghan national game, and of the value of the game in understanding the turbulence and subtlety of Afghan politics' (1984: 270 – 272).[96] Republication and reissue have specific ramifications for the authoritative status of ethnography about Afghanistan. As with Azoy's *Buzkashi, Game and Power in Afghanistan*, Shahrani's *The Kirghiz and Wakhi of Afghanistan* was republished with a new preface and epilogue following the September 11th attacks. Each contains a new preface addressing the possible causes of the rise of the Taliban in Afghanistan. In the quest for knowledge about Afghanistan after 2001, republished studies are imbued with a specific form of authority, signalling a tendency to look to outmoded studies of Afghanistan for anthropological insights (cultural rather than political) into the root-causes of conflict fought on Afghan soil. The back cover of the second edition of Azoy's ethnography extends its afterlife in the public domain by stating: 'sadly but truly, buzkashi continues to prove itself to be an apt metaphor for ongoing Afghan political control and chaos'. Of course, awarding this degree of interpretative authority to the ethnographies of Azoy and Shahrani is in many senses antithetical to contemporary notions of ethnographic responsibility and principles of de-authorization. Indeed, Shahrani has since criticised his own study for 'adher[ing] to all the long-held conventions of scientific ethnographic presentation [...:] ethnographic truth, objectivity and impartiality' (www.indiana.edu/anthro/faculty/nazif/html).

Azoy's *buzkashi* account nods to the work of Clifford Geertz to whose synecdochic analysis of Balinese cockfights and Moroccan *suqs* his study is indebted. A brief comparison suffices to point up the resemblance between their styles and modes of representation which reflect the literary turn in classical ethnographies:

> To the foreign eye, a mid-Eastern bazaar, Sefrou like any other, is a tumbling chaos: hundreds of men, this one in rags, that one in silken robes, the next in some outlandish mountain costume, jammed into alleyways, squatting in cubicles, milling in plazas, shouting in each others' faces, whispering in each others' ears, smothering each other in cascades of gestures (in Richards 1994: 112).

> Powerful men on powerful horses mass with one another in a mayhem of frantic movement: pushing and shoving and changing position and trying to grasp the carcass, headless and hoofless, from the ground. The men are now yelling past one another at the top of their lungs and now urging their horses onwards with an incongruously soft hiss (Azoy [1982] 2003: 1 & 2).

The resemblance is striking; gone in these passages is the subordination of self-evidently subjective narrative to description. Each passage depicts a scene (or, more accurately, amalgamates numerous scenes) of 'tumbling chaos' and crams them with active verbs that depict 'frantic movement'. Geertz and Azoys' 'shouting', 'shoving', 'milling' subjects also emit whispers, or 'soft hiss[es]' audible only to the omnipresent anthropologist who amplifies these for the reader. Most relevant to my discussion, however, is the ethnographic strategy of imposing interpretative clarity and analytical sense upon a scene that the text has itself rendered chaotic (Richards: 221). This is accomplished through the use of synecdochic metaphor, a strategy associated with classical ethnographies that, I will argue, accounts for the most pressing aspect of the counter-influence of these ethnographies on Kremmer's and Lamb's narratives.

The counter-influence of classical ethnographies on the travel writing of journalists Christopher Kremmer and Christina Lamb

'Why can't we just study them for a while like good 'ol anthropologists?' (NGO worker in Kremmer: 119).

Paul Rabinow once noted a 'curious time lag as concepts move across disciplinary boundaries' (in Clifford and Marcus: 242). I suggest that the time lag principle applies equally to concepts and practices associated with classical ethnographies as they migrate back and forth across generic boundaries. In borrowing from classical ethnographies, Kremmer and Lamb redeploy concepts and authoritative modes of discourse that are, in Renato Rosaldo's words, 'already old-fashioned in [their...] homeland' (in Clifford and Marcus: 77). Utilizing the insights of contemporary debates in anthropology, this section examines the nature of those borrowings, the conditions that necessitate or compel them and, finally, their ethical and ideological implications.

I begin by considering two key and interrelated factors that necessitate or compel Kremmer's and Lamb's ethnographic borrowing. The first pertains to the relative statuses of travel writing and ethnography, the latter of which has been constructed as more rigorous and credible. The second relates to Pratt's observation that travel writing has 'never been fully professionalised or disciplined' (in H.L. Gates jnr. 1986: 156). Throughout the eighteenth century, European travellers were enlisted by scientists and scholars to provide information from their travels (Pau Rubies in Hulme and Youngs: 257). While this means that there is an historic proto-ethnographic association between travel writing and information-gathering, the rise of ethnography clearly supplanted the role of the travel writer as an information-producing subject (Pratt in Gates: 252). Kremmer's and Lamb's professional identities as journalists promotes two textual practices that are, once again, interrelated. Firstly, in order to accrue authoritative status, their narratives must somehow rid themselves of travel writing's excess baggage (exoticism; eroticism; hyperbole) which tarnishes its reputation as an authoritative discourse. Secondly, both narratives borrow heavily from classical ethnographies' legitimating rhetoric. Although the presence of one text in another is conventionally held to be radically deauthorising (since it belies any coherent or unified intention) (Allan: 6), I suggest that, in terms of narrative authority, the reverse is true when it comes to Kremmer's and Lamb's travel writing. This is because, for the non-specialist reading public, classical ethnographies provide, or appear to provide, a certain depth of insight and analytical rigour.

The notion of professionalisation is critical here. How is a generally low-status genre to transmit this sense of credibility? In a passage where Kremmer's narrator reflects upon his traveller predecessors, there is an attempt to raise their collective professional profile: '[l]ike prophets, travel writers are inspired by the journals of their predecessors, and leave their own revelations for those who come later' (62). Travel writing is here lent spiritual weight, not least because a prophet is the ultimate symbol of truth-seeking and revelatory utterance. A more self-evidently neo-professional impulse is detectable in Kremmer's preface, however, which reads as follows:

> This book took shape over a decade of work in Afghanistan, Pakistan, Kashmir, Iran, Iraq and the Central Asian republics, at a time when events in much of the region were of little concern to most people elsewhere. Since the attacks on New York and Washington, many have realized that a crisis, even in a remote corner of the world like Afghanistan, can precipitate disaster at home. Understanding the causes and effects of injustice in Muslim societies has become critical to the restoration of our own security. The carpet business might seem a curious place to seek such an understanding, but [...] [i]n any case, I present Muslim society here as I found it; it is a personal portrait of a different world in which many of my friends and interlocutors made or sold rugs (xi).

Although, of course, Kremmer's travel book does not purport to be an ethnographic study and although 'work' seems a more than fair representation of his experience as a journalist, key vocabulary items suggest that his travel narrative is being upgraded in the sense that its author is framed as a qualified practitioner with an experience of intensive dwelling among Muslims. As I explore below, his encounters with Muslim 'interlocutors', are ethnographically resonant. Furthermore, his stated goal, to promote an '[u]nderstanding [of] the causes and effects of injustice in Muslim societies' may be read as a declaration of professional responsibility imbued with a moral imperative remarkably consistent with ethnographic ideals of promoting cross-cultural understanding through culturally relativist means. Worth noting is the connotation of the collective 'our', which implies a non-Muslim readership. The primacy of western, over Afghan, imperatives is also striking. These factors combine to build a picture of the professional journalist-ethnographer, who uses pseudonyms to protect identity and makes implicit claims to truth-telling: '[t]he encounters that provided the raw material for this book generally appear here in chronological order, albeit at times heavily compressed' (xi).[97] The renunciation of artistic licence reinforces a sense of the text's ever-present will to truth.

The upwardly mobile orientation of Kremmer's and Lamb's writing is made further apparent by their evocation of an anthropological rite of passage: fieldwork. Clifford argues that the consolidation of ethnographers' professional power between 1900 and 1960 was partly accomplished by establishing a strong disciplinary consensus over the importance of fieldwork, which became the norm among trained university specialists around 1930.[98] Once the scientific validity of intensive fieldwork had been established, as little as a single sentence could convey a metaphor for experience and expertise (Clifford 1991: 121 & 124). Kremmer's and Lamb's subtitles rely upon the authorizing metaphor of fieldwork. Kremmer's subtitle is: 'Ten Years in Afghanistan, Pakistan and Iraq', and Lamb's reads: 'My Afghan Years'. While it is a principle of anthropological fieldwork that it entails '[p]rolonged exposure' to informants' lifeways that ensure that the anthropologist 'will', as anthropologists John Monaghan and Peter Just maintain, 'accidentally encounter most social phenomena of significance' (2000: 19), this period rarely exceeds eighteen months (1983: 121). Even though Lamb's subtitle is vague as to the number of years spent, the plural 'years' is common to both subtitles. Kremmer's ten years are particularly weighty, exceeding (by far) standard anthropological claims to expertise. To summarise, then, both travel books wield powerful ethnographically resonant peritexts[99] that direct the reader to expect an authoritative account. Authorial agency is not the only factor in play. Having said this, while Lamb's narrative shares many of Kremmer's strategies for gaining narrative authority, its professional status is not so overtly marked. The *my* of her subtitle ('My Afghan Years'), suggests a more personal account and a

paperback edition of the book (published one month later in December
2002) replaces the original subtitle with 'A Memoir of Afghanistan',
which cannot be said to evoke the trope of fieldwork. In addition,
Amazon's website classifies her book as *Biography*, a classification
that is consistent with a tendency, identified by Mills (1992: 32), to
read women's travel writing as biographical. This suggests that, when
it comes to women writers, the interventions of publishers do not
always enhance the account's authority. The significance of this
potential point of divergence is explored towards the end of Part Two.

Traditionally, ethnographic authority is partially predicated on
ethnographers' withdrawal from the field to write the account. This is
not of course unique to ethnography. Maria Frawley observes this
imperative at work in the proto-ethnographic travel writing of Harriet
Martineau, who insists that proper retrospection requires a return to
western soil (1996: 47). Frawley suggests the imperative to return
home is a legacy of the Romantic quest narrative, something Richards
identifies as an important literary inspiration for the ethnographic
return from the field. Typically, the quest narrative entails a knight's
embarkation on a quest for truth. The knight undertakes challenging
tasks (fieldwork) before returning to the 'mundane world' (the
university institution) 'endowed with special gifts, powers or insight'.
The ethnographer's 'goal and prize' is ethnographic knowledge (52 &
53). The opening scene of Lamb's travel narrative suggests that the
imperative to withdraw from the field has some bearing on her
narrative's description of the act of 'writing culture': 'I begin to write
in the pale light of dawn […] On my desk is a handful of letters from a
woman about my own age in Kabul' (1). The office location signals
her retreat from Afghanistan to a space of reflection. It is dawn, which
not only represents the beginning of her narrative, but a time of day
associated with solitude, prayer and a profound degree of
introspection. On her desk, like a stack of field notes, is 'a handful of
letters' from her main Kabul contact, Marri. I am not suggesting that
this is consciously done. However, by triggering a series of
anthropologically charged associations, this opening scene establishes
an implicit narrative of professionalism. Once again, it is more than
understandable that a journalist might strive to produce an such a
narrative. Nevertheless, at work here is a manoeuvre that ensures the

adopted genre of travel writing does not impede the narrative's ability to transmit authority.

The paratextual dimensions of Kremmer's and Lamb's texts are critical to a discussion of their neo-professional impulse, since their books are embedded in global marketing structures and sales imperatives that exceed any authorial intention. Both books contain bibliographies, footnotes, indexes, and (in Kremmer's case) glossaries. These are all features that one would expect from a formal ethnography (or indeed a scholarly work) in the sense that readers are instructed to take the text seriously (Watson 1987: 39). Both books are hard to classify because they contain extended passages detailing historical and political events, although personal narrative predominates. The books are classified in bookshops not merely as *Travel* but as *History* or *Asian History*. However, despite being published on the same subject by the same publisher in the same year by two writers of the same profession, Kremmer's book is now classified on Amazon as *History*, while Lamb's is accorded a less certain knowledge-status including, as I mentioned, *Biography* as well as *History* and *Travel and Holiday*. Kremmer's book is awarded an unqualified knowledge status while Lamb's is presented as straddling the personal and the scholarly. This said, even when, as I shall discuss later, Kremmer's and Lamb's narratives undercut their own textual acts of dominance, their paratexts invariably accrue, rather than eschew authority.[100] A brief example of the use of photographs and captions in Lamb's travel book serves to illustrate this point. When she enters Mullah Omar's abandoned house, she writes that one of the guards 'kept asking for his photographs to be taken in the most unlikely places, such as standing in the cot bed of one of Mullah Omar's children' (255). The following page contains a corroboratory black and white photograph with the caption: 'A guard perches on a child's cot inside the house owned by Mullah Omar, Kandahar 2001'. Not only does the caption echo (and confirm) her description of the event, but it is further endorsed by a date so as to suggest the accuracy of her eyewitness account. The result is significant: the travel book is presented as a text that carefully and accurately documents, rather than merely narrates, her experiences among Afghans. Overall, the effect is to raise the narrative's truth-status.

Buzkashi as synecdochic metaphor

'[T]here are three dimensions to the social significance of *buzkashi* in Afghanistan: (1) as a commemoration of cultural heritage, (2) as a metaphor for unbridled competition, and (3) as an arena for political process' (Whitney Azoy, *Buzkashi, Game and Power in Afghanistan*, 1983: 10).

'The goat-grabbing game of life was tougher than anything happening on the field' (Kremmer, *The Carpet Wars*, 2002: 57).

Bearing in mind their professional identity as journalists, I turn to the use of synecdoche in Kremmer's and Lamb's narratives as a means of addressing the problem of narrative authority. Although synecdoche predates the rise of ethnography, the notion of counter-influence is more appropriate than that of 'influence', since counter-influence best captures the power dimensions of the generic interplay between travel writing and ethnography. The question of counter-influence makes it both necessary and desirable to examine ethnography as comprising a series of narrative conventions, many of which were inherited from travel writing.

Synecdoche, which gained ethnographic currency around the 1930's, is literally 'a figure of speech in which the part is made to stand for the whole'.[101] In ethnography, synecdoche is linked to the literary turn in ethnography, most specifically with Clifford Geertz, and is variously defined as: 'the [...] evocation of a social whole through representation of its parts' (Webster in Richards: 221) and, more explicitly, as '[the] seek[ing] out of cultural 'texts' that the people of the society [under study] themselves find compelling [...] not only to understand them as they see them, but to see the ways the themes of these 'texts' illustrate other aspects of the society' (Monaghan and Just: 45). As a critic of synecdoche, Richards provides a less charitable definition: 'a familiar trope for representing otherness by describing a single cultural aspect which appears immensely significant as a key to the whole culture [sic] but which is nonetheless a riddle or seemingly inexplicable event to the reader' (221).

As with many of ethnography's conventions, synecdoche can be traced back to the nineteenth century and beyond.[102] James Buzard has identified synecdochic metaphor (or, in this context, *pars totalis*) as a prevalent feature of anti-touristic discourse. *Pars totalis* is, typically, a 'valued moment' that somehow expresses the whole; particularly the essence of a visited place. Thus, throughout the nineteenth century, tourists represented place through 'a series of mnemonic stereotypes' about Paris, Rome, Italy, or the Rhine. *Pars totalis* is a means of organizing a vast number of competing observations and experiences of a place, which Buzard likens to the hearing of a 'resounding C major' that 'elides what challenges its definitions' (1992: 12). In this sense, it can be compared to literary assertions of textual unity and the possibility of interpretative closure. Indeed, Monaghan and Just lay a similar charge at synecdoche's door. Synecdoche, they argue, is rather 'too simplistic and reductionist, because of its tendency to view cultures in terms of one or two key themes' (44). In his historicisation of synecdoche's use by ethnographers, Clifford identifies synecdoche as one of a series of 'methodological innovations circumventing the obstacles to rapid knowledge of other cultures'. Although a sense of the impossibility of reaching anything like a full understanding of other cultures had plagued ethnographers' intellectual forebears, synecdoche allowed ethnographers from the 1930s onwards to grasp at the 'cultural whole' (too difficult to master in a short period of fieldwork) through attending closely to 'one or more of its parts' (1983: 125). While Kremmer and Lamb are not ethnographers, these more pessimistic assessments of synecdoche raise important ethical concerns in relation to the extension of its anthropological 'shelf life' in their writing. As I explore below, this is because their narratives fall in with a tendency (noted by Afghan ethnographer Shahrani) to explain Afghanistan's problems almost exclusively in terms of its 'culture'.

Despite the widespread condemnation of synecdoche among contemporary ethnographers, Azoy's buzkashi metaphor has retained its currency as an authoritative discourse rather than being discredited as 'bad' ethnography. The metaphor gained considerable popular currency[103] in the United States after being adopted by journalists at two particular historical junctures. In the first instance, it was used as a means of explaining political manoeuvres in the struggle against Soviet invasion. As I discuss in due course, it was used more recently to expound upon the significance of September 11th and its relationship to contemporary Afghan politics. Azoy has sanctioned

this journalistic foraging in a series of articles about *buzkashi* in the
Bangor Times and the *Wabash Magazine*.[104] Journalistic requisitions
combine with Azoy's post-September 11th articles to extend Azoy's
buzkashi metaphor long past its ethnographic sell-by date so that, in
effect, it straddles two decades of anthropological debate. This
figurative and disciplinary extension can be seen at work in an article
by Azoy published shortly after the twin tower attacks where he
writes: '[h]undreds and thousands of Afghans are riding away to
would-be refugee status at the closest border [...and will] continue to
ride away as long [as] the impression of Taliban debility can be
managed and enhanced. The better the impression management, the
quicker the riding away' (*Wabash Magazine* 2001: 2 & 3). This
'riding away' is symptomatic of what Azoy describes as 'an age-old
Afghan dynamic', presumably encoded in the game of *buzkashi*.

Kremmer's and Lamb's writing is subject to a powerful synecdochic
undertow that can be traced to the ethnographies of Azoy (Kremmer
on *buzkashi*) and Dupree (Lamb on children's games). Azoy's
opening scene provides a useful starting point for highlighting his use
of synecdoche:

> Under a cold winter sky the landscape of northern Afghanistan stretches
> towards a bleak horizon. Here on one rim of the Central Asian steppes, the
> hard ground runs - gray, yellow, and brown - in an empty latitudinal band
> below the Hindu Kush. It is less country-side than wasteland [...] Beyond a
> last outlying mud hut, the featureless steppes begin again, desolate and only
> somewhat less dusty on account of a recent cold rain. And not far from the
> village, on marginal ground, hundreds of horsemen gather over the
> mutilated carcass of a calf.
>
> The dead calf is hard for an outsider to see. Unless the earth is still really
> moist, great clouds of dust hide much of the central action (1).

Countless details in this passage suggest that this is a symbolic as
much as a literal setting. The landscape is scored with peripheral lines:
the 'rim of the Central Asian steppes', the 'empty latitudinal band',
and the 'marginal ground' on which the horsemen are gathered,
denoting a cultural location at the edge of civilised existence. A
Conradian outpost (the 'last outlying mud hut') situates the scene and
its inhabitants at the farthest reaches of progress.

The passage illustrates three ethical consequences of deploying synecdoche. The first is the assertion of a timeless 'Afghan dynamic'. This opening passage utilises what Vincent Crapanzano terms *'temporal deixis'*: a series of buzkashi games (in Geertz's ethnography it was a string of cockfights) are conflated into a 'single, constructed performance' (in Clifford and Marcus: 75) so as to suggest the games' profound metaphorical resonance. Despite each game of *buzkashi* being anchored in specific contexts, the amalgamation of a series of games effectively denies each game its social, cultural and political co-ordinates. There are several clues to suggest that *temporal deixis* is in operation in Azoy's passage.[105] The winter season and 'a recent cold rain' suggest a single occasion and yet the narrative quickly slips into reporting general rules: the 'calf is hard to see [...] [u]nless the earth is still really moist'. This points up a second ethical consequence of synecdoche; the slippage from the literal to the symbolic that confers on the anthropologist the authority to generalize about a cultural rule, or rules. This is made possible by what Richards calls the clinching of the culturally typical or representative, with all the insight that implies (221). As the setting slips from the literal to the symbolic, *buzkashi* is transported into a symbolic realm and, in the symbolic realm, *buzkashi* encapsulates 'an age-old Afghan dynamic'. In Azoy's terms, this 'age-old dynamic' may be effectively summarized as political unruliness, the importance of reputation and an Afghan predisposition towards political chaos, rather than political order. This illustrates a third ethical consequence of synecdoche. Synecdoche enacts a form of interpretative tidying by identifying an internal cultural dynamic and shutting out the complex international dimension of wars fought on Afghan soil. In this way, games and wars alike are removed from their context. *Buzkashi* (in its metaphorical sense) is utilized to explain, in terms of an internal cultural dynamic rather than economic or geo-political terms why, 'after two dozen years of conflict, Afghanistan remains beleaguered by [...] self-seeking warlords' (22).

Ethical concerns about the use of synecdoche centre on the form of textual dominance that it makes possible. The work of Geertz perhaps best exemplifies the adroit use of synecdochic metaphor and, as I have mentioned, Azoy's study is indebted to Geertz's classic analyses of

Balinese cockfights and Moroccan *suqs*. Richards makes a damning appraisal of Geertz's rendering of a Moroccan *suq* as culturally representative and decipherable by the expert eye of the ethnographer. Richards identifies three eyes present in the crowded scene of Geertz's *suq*. There is the 'foreign eye' (that of the reader, disorientated by the *suq's* chaos) and the 'indigenous eye' (that of the local, 'blinded by the miasma of its social reality and its inability to read the text of which it is subject'). Last, but certainly not least, there is the 'third eye' of the anthropologist, with the ability to 'clinch the typical, the representative, the "synecdochic" and the insight to decipher the *suq's* true meaning. The indigenous eye, immersed in its own familiar realities, is unseeing. So caught up are the Moroccan subjects of the 'text' in 'the game of their lives that they cannot communicate or understand the rules they are playing'. By contrast, the untrained 'foreign eye' of the reader has the potential to understand the 'riddle' of the *suq* (with the help of the anthropologist). The 'indigenous eye' is thus rendered 'foreign' to its own cultural practices while the 'foreign eye' and the 'third eye' become 'true natives of the text' in a way that ensures their dominance (221-223).

Azoy's narrative creates four categories purporting to capture *buzkashi's* 'real significance': the literal game itself (the 'first-order game'), the 'competition for control over the first-order game' (the 'second-order game'), 'competition for control over the entire celebratory enterprise which the *buzkashi* represents' (the 'third-order game') and 'the competition for control over the entire real-world political process in which *buzkashi* participants (and everyone else in the society) are encapsulated' (the 'fourth-order game') (17). However, having creating these categories, the narrator encounters a seemingly insurmountable hurdle: his informants disagree with his interpretation. Azoy confesses that these informants 'dismiss' *buzkashi* as 'only *shouq*', which he translates as 'leisure' (8). Furthermore, the informants' notion that *buzkashi* is 'mere *shouq*' is dismissed by Azoy as an 'often voiced, in fact, normative, notion' (8). How, when his theory is almost universally rejected by his informants, might its credibility be recovered? '[T]he majority' of *buzkashi* participants', he argues, are 'in effect, half-conscious of *buzkashi* as an arena in which events have real-life implications of authority and power' (16). *Buzkashi's* ostensibly political symbolism is likened to 'subliminal advertisements [...which are] all the more effective because those who absorb them are not consciously aware of it' (4). *Chapandaz*, or special *buzkashi* riders, are believed by participants and spectators to be the game's real players. However, Azoy dismisses this as a 'superficial' assessment (16). The 'indigenous eye' is drawn to the movements of the *chapandaz*, who occupy the literal spatial (but symbolically false) centre of the *buzkashi* field. Meanwhile, Azoy's all-seeing 'third eye' resists the hypnotic pull of the scrum that occupies this false centre and instead locates power's true, symbolic centre at 'the sidelines': '[t]he political leaders – khans, governors [...and] heads of state' (16). *Buzkashi's* significance and power's true location *is* discernible to the 'foreign eye', but only through the expert guidance of the 'third eye' of the anthropologist.[106] The interpretative vision of the 'third eye' here surpasses that of Afghans, and Azoy stands at the top of the hierarchy of understanding (Crapanzano in Clifford and Marcus: 74).

One further means of combating the informants' rejection of his cultural interpretation of *buzkashi* is to attribute the latent recognition of the game's synechdochic potential to a single informant, named Sardar Mohammed Hafiz Nawabi, whose suggestive utterance is stated here: '"If you want to know what we are really like, go to a *buzkashi* game"' (x). The narrative is disarmingly frank about the necessity of including such a statement as a means of self-authentication: 'Nawabi['s] [...] 1976 introduction to the *buzkashi* world remains my touchstone of credibility' (xvi). This statement reveals more than it knows, namely, his text's subjection to wider ethnographic imperatives to gain 'credibility' by authenticating cultural interpretations via one's informants.

Kremmer also provides an authenticating informant, named Rasoul, who materialises shortly before a *buzkashi* game and makes a statement that suggests how Kremmer's narrative trails in Azoy's wake: 'This game [*buzkashi*] can tell you a lot about the character of the northern Afghan' (45). Adopting a more formal register than Azoy's informant, Rasoul's statement resounds with anthropological confidence. Rasoul deploys a more ethnographically informed vocabulary than Azoy's informant ('the character of the northern Afghan' rather than 'what we're really like') by making the refined distinction of 'northern Afghan' rather than merely 'Afghan', a distinction Azoy generally fails to make (see appendix one).

Azoy's second chapter, entitled 'Reputation and the Unruly Afghan' contains an epigraph from Victorian poet Sir Alfred Lyall's 'The Amir's Soliloquy', which ends: 'who would rule the unruly Afghan' (21).[107] Naming the chapter after a colonial poem means that Azoy's study is anything but counter-intuitive, since it replicates rather than investigates, nineteenth-century discursive frameworks. Rather than interrogating the colonial anxiety expressed by Lyall's poem, Azoy simply 'rediscovers' a colonial commonplace: he describes *buzkashi* as a 'metaphor for the particular sort of unbridled competition – chaotic, uninhibited, uncontrollable – that lurks below the apparently cooperative surface' (14). Following the soliloquy's logic, Azoy both resurrects and reincarnates age-old British fears, augmented by the first and second Afghan wars, that colonial authority is never fully assured. This sense of 'lurk[ing]' threat generates metaphors of ungovernability: Afghans are 'uncontrollable', 'unbridled', 'chaotic' and their cooperation is only 'apparently cooperative', a mere performance of submission. It therefore seems no coincidence that Kremmer's *buzkashi* account begins with the following incident:

> In March 1980 fifty Russian soldiers were invited to the outskirts of Mazar-e-Sharif to watch a game of buzkashi [...] But as the Russians watched the game, the Afghans were watching the Russians and when their guests were entirely engrossed, fell upon them, beating and trampling them to death [...] On the field where the killings had taken place years before, Rasoul and I took our seats under an aluminium sky, nervously eyeing the crowd for any sign of a repeat performance (55).

While this anxiety may well be the legacy of specific colonial memories of massacre during the First Anglo-Afghan War, it seems likely that this particular expression of anxiety has been filtered through Azoy's text, which, in turn resurrects colonial characterizations of Afghan society as 'unruly', violent and 'chaotic', rather than ordered, rational or strategic.

Kremmer's *buzkashi* account mirrors Azoy's slippage from literal description to synecdochic metaphor. This is also evident in Kremmer's claim that '[t]he goat-grabbing game of life was tougher than anything happening on the field' (57). This slippage is also evident in the following observation:

> There were, supposedly, two [*buzkashi*] teams, but without uniforms it was difficult to tell them apart and rumours swept the bleachers [around us] of sneak defections mid-game, much as the various Muslim militias kept switching sides in the civil war (57).

The difficulty of telling teams apart is imbued with symbolic significance as the narrative makes a conceptual leap from the 'first-order game' (a detail about lack of uniforms) to the 'fourth-order game' of Afghan politics and the charge of changing sides during the civil war. Once again, this explanation relies heavily on the concept of an internal cultural dynamic rather than on the international dimensions of wars fought on Afghan soil, most particularly the policy of Pakistan and the United States to 'kee[p] Afghanistan weak and divided' by switching their support between opposing military and political factions (Rubin and Benjamin 2000: 2).

The deployment of a carpet metaphor throughout Kremmer's travel account suggests that his narrative is subject to a synecdochic drift not wholly attributable to Azoy's study but rather to the more pervasive and nebulous counter-influence of classical ethnographies. The book's title (*The Carpet Wars*) indicates that carpets might have something to tell us about the causes of war in this region. Kremmer's carpet metaphor is not always synecdochic. In his text, carpets serve as a symbol of Afghanistan's ancient trade and glorious past. Carpets are presented as a kind of antidote to encroaching modernization, a means of 'retailing [...] conversation outside time' (40). The inside jacket cover describes Kremmer's carpets as a 'symbol of Islamic society's genius and resilience'. However, at several junctures the metaphor becomes synecdochic, offering itself as an interpretative totality emphasizing the whole at the expense of multiple, conflicting realities.

The synecdochic drift of Kremmer's narrative is apparent from the outset, during the opening scene of *The Carpet Wars* where he visits a carpet merchant in Kabul. The carpet shop is depicted as a site of learning, an impression reinforced by his sense of reverence upon going into it: '[s]eeing [....the shop owner's] stockinged feet, I slipped

off my shoes and entered' (2). The scene inside the carpet shop is
loaded with anthropological significance:

> Rolled up rugs lined the walls, insular and secret. But, knowing them well,
> Tariq was more interested in unravelling me. What was my name? My
> country? Was I married? Did I have children? Satisfied with my answers, he
> rose from the floor and unfurled a rug, releasing a flurry of dust particles
> that danced in a narrow shaft of light streaming through a crack in the
> ceiling.
>
> 'Baluchi!' he declared, with a smile that said 'yes, it's true',
> adding, in case I didn't know, 'Made by nomad tribes. Desert people.'
>
> The claret red and celestial blue wool hung lankly from Tariq's
> hands, presenting a galaxy of eight-pointed stars bordered by brilliant dots
> in ivory and yellow. Like a matador tempting a bull to charge, he turned the
> rug slightly left and right, highlighting its lustre (3).

Implicit in this scene is the notion that the carpets, and their
merchants, are key to understanding something about 'Afghan
culture'. '[R]olled up', 'insular and secret', the carpets are not unlike
scrolls awaiting scholarly interpretation. As culture's guardian, Tariq
'guide[s]' the narrator through 'his nation of rugs' (4). The shop is
both a place of apprenticeship and a space of revelation: as each rug,
or cultural secret, is 'unfurled', it releases 'a flurry of dust particles
that danced in a narrow shaft of light streaming through a crack in the
ceiling'. A kind of mystical insight, available to those of uncommon
sensitivity is implied by the 'narrow shaft of light', which sets up an
association with a religious sanctuary, or place of truth, illuminating
tiny 'dust particles' ordinarily invisible to the eye. Once exposed to
Kremmer's gaze, the rugs reveal themselves to contain a universe of
meaning ('a galaxy of eight-pointed stars'). This gaze is essentially
benevolent, an impression heightened by the evocation of a pastoral
scene. Tariq becomes 'the shepherd of this matted flock [who] tutored
me in the clarity and fidelity of dyes' (4). The encounter's
anthropological potential is intimated by Tariq's attempts at
'unravelling' the narrator by asking questions to map his cultural
location. Having perceived his trainee to be worthy of learning, Tariq,
the merchant, teaches him to read rugs as an informant might teach an
anthropologist to read his culture, deftly 'highlighting' the
peculiarities of each rug, or each cultural practice. A passage soon
afterwards renders the scene's anthropological overtones still more

discernible: 'But as the day wore on, the conversation broadened like a river [...] coursing through the life and times of the rug merchant of Kabul' (4). This sentence deepens the impression that the encounter is not really a lesson in buying carpets but rather an in-depth interview between a journalist-ethnographer and his informant.

A common marker of anthropological professional experience is the telling of anecdotes to recollect previous states of ignorance at an earlier stage of research in the field. Clifford calls this phenomenon the '[*b*]*ildungsgeschichte* of [...] ethnography' (1983:132). Kremmer's narrator himself adopts this strategy as a means of demonstrating his growing expertise in reading carpets. Recollecting his first carpet-buying error, he recalls being seduced by sales-pitch, composed of '[s]uperlatives [that] enriched the merchants' patter' (10). Examining this earlier interpretative deficiency in the light of experience, his mistake is evaluated as follows: 'The printed receipt made no false claims: the merchants had merely exploited my fantasies' (10). This self-reflective moment conveys a sense of movement beyond this early place of ignorance to more discerning and dispassionate observation: 'Ten years since my first carpet purchase, I was no longer the callow victim of the predators who lurk in rug shops' (45). Examined in isolation, this *bildungeschichte* moment might appear relatively insignificant. However, I suggest that Kremmer's narrative accumulates authority through a combination of ethnographically resonant strategies such as the subtitle's evocation of ten years' fieldwork experience and the use of footnotes. When shown into an interview with General Dostum alongside a 'small group of foreign reporters', he distinguishes himself from other journalists in the following manner: '[w]ith chairs in short supply, I sat on the edge of his carpet, an old sign of deference, or fear' (59). This is more the action of a culturally knowledgeable anthropologist than a journalist.

Synecdoche is closely related to another discarded tool of anthropological analysis: the culture concept. While there is disagreement over the way in which classical ethnographies have variously conceived of culture in the past[108], there is broad agreement among contemporary anthropologists that deploying the concept precipitates a theoretical nose-dive into homogenisation. James Buzard notes that an influential notion of culture is enshrined in

Raymond Williams' classic anthropological definition of culture as: 'a whole way of life'. Buzard detects the nostalgia that underlies this apparently value-free definition, that is, the quest for a perceived lost wholeness, or social coherence (10). The notion of *culture* has also been condemned by Stephen Tyler as a 'non-entity' reproduced via scientific discourse as though it were 'fully observable' (Tyler in Clifford and Marcus: 130). More recently, Arjun Appadurai has criticized the culture concept for encouraging 'highly localized, boundary-orientated, holistic, primeordialist [sic] images of cultural form and substance' (in Brightman 1995: 521). Synecdoche's reliance on the culture concept can be observed in his discussion of some new handmade *Mori Bukhara* rugs, of which he disapproves:

> Alas, a typical *Mori Bukhara* rug [...] is a rug of no consequence. No matter how detailed the design, how fine the knotting, how lustrous the wool, they are usually quite ugly, with dreary colours and robotic execution. The vital element of cultural continuity is missing, swept away by politics, urbanisation and modern methods of production (155).

At one level the *Mori Bukhara* might be read as a cautionary tale of the perceived decline of traditional cultures due to modernisation and, dubiously, to contact with the so-called outside world ('politics, urbanisation and modern methods of production' are viewed as contaminants). On another level the *Mori Bukhara* is being compared unfavourably to its imagined opposite: a carpet of genuine consequence. According to the logic of this passage, a rug of consequence provides demonstrable evidence of 'cultural continuity'. To whom is such continuity so 'vital'? A rug collector, certainly. Yet the note of nostalgia ('[a]las') that creeps into the narrative is highly suggestive of this passage's relationship to outmoded conceptualisations of culture as an homogenous entity with well-defined parameters. On one level the passage laments a perceived decline in 'traditional culture' that results in Afghanistan's descent into an ignoble present, indicated by the inferior rug's 'robotic execution'. But here again, it seems worth asking in what sense the rug's execution might be 'robotic'. Because the rug is 'hand made', this seems more than a bourgeois lament at the onset of mechanisation and 'modern methods of production'. Which nameless, 'vital' entity, or value, is being 'swept away' through contact with the 'outside world'? I suggest that, just as the rug of genuine consequence is the opposite of the *Mori Bukhara*, so syncretic, or hybrid cultures become the supposed opposite of traditional cultures, conceived of here as an integrated whole. It is at this juncture that the carpet becomes *the carpet* and invested with notions of 'cultural continuity'. In Kremmer's narrative, cultural continuity is prized more highly than cultural discontinuity, or heterogeneity. What is being regretted is the perceived passing of an homogeneous culture, a notion described by Robert Brightman as 'anthropological totalization' (517) entailing conceptions of culture deemed unworkable by contemporary anthropologists. Contemporary ethnographers have since radically altered their approach to culture. Anthropologists such as Anna Lowenhaupt Tsing describe their ethnography as a pile of stories that contradict and interrogate one another to ensure that supposed underlying principles and socially unifying structures are never privileged over heterogeneity and discord (1993: 33). Kremmer's synecdochic reliance on the culture concept provides one further illustration of how contemporary anthropological debates have had very little impact on Kremmer's discussion of *Mori Bukhara* rugs.[109]

Children's games as an explanatory metaphor

'Like other individual aspects of a total cultural environment, play and recreational activities reflect the values, the ethos of the society' (Louis Dupree *Afghanistan*: 209).

'Even activities that seemed peaceful, like boiling eggs, in Afghanistan involved some form of warfare' (Christina Lamb *The Sewing Circles of Herat. My Afghan Years*: 287).

When Jonny Bealby plays a cricket game in Gilgit, one of the Indian players calls it 'the Great Game' (*For A Pagan Song*: 91), illustrating how readily games with a small 'g' become metaphorically linked to political wranglings over Central Asia. Sports such as cricket have long inspired politicised analyses of the relationship between coloniser and colonised. When Lamb's narrator deploys synecdoche in her extended discussion of Afghan games, it is difficult at first glance to determine which tradition, anthropological or colonial, stands most squarely behind her analysis. It soon becomes apparent, however, that Dupree's *Afghanistan* speaks powerfully through Lamb's narrative in two related ways. First, it supplies an interpretative framework, which Lamb's narrative builds upon, and, second, it directs her conclusions. This leads her narrative to make particular claims about Afghan attitudes to war.

Dupree's ethnographer-narrator describes *Afghanistan* as 'an attempt by an anthropologist to ferret out the patterns, *functional and dysfunctional*, in the total synchronic – ecological – cultural sense' (xxi, italics mine). There are at least two reasons why Dupree's discourse might trouble contemporary ethnographers. The phrase 'total [...] cultural sense' betrays the statement's reliance on the culture concept. This is more apparent still in his later statement: 'Like other aspects of a total cultural environment, play and recreational activities reflect the values, the ethos of the society' (209). Afghan games, it is implied, are key to understanding attitudes that are quintessentially Afghan. Dupree's notion of 'functional and dysfunctional' patterns conceptualizes culture in terms of psychological health. In this sense, it measures Afghan cultural practices against an implicit European norm. This principle governs the framing questions with which Dupree's discussion of Afghan games are prefaced: '[a]re they games of skill or brute strength, mental exertion or violent contact, physical or mental coordination? [...] Is cheating accepted or at least the attempt respected? Does chance or luck control, or is strategy the key' (210)? These binary opposites have built-in conclusions so as to create a hierarchy of skills: 'mental co-ordination' and 'strategy' are pitched against 'brute strength', 'physical [...] co-ordination', 'cheating' and 'luck'.

Dupree inherits from his colonial predecessors the notion that Afghan society is, in Dupree's words, 'fundamentally warlike', and he argues that the 'ideal [Afghan] personality type is the warrior-poet' (210). Embellishing this theory, he characterizes Afghan attitudes to war in the following manner: '[w]ar in Afghan society relates to the family, tribal, kin-blood honor [sic], and is not an amorphous, ill-defined loosely implemented ideology [...] but is an immediate face-to-face confrontation with a real, nearby enemy, a confrontation involving *zar, zan, zamin* (gold, women, land)' (211). According to this assessment, Afghan wars, blood ties and local grievances prevail over wider political concerns. Parochial disputes outweigh the long-term or strategic objectives, while the competition for resources ('gold, women, land') takes precedence over abstract principles ('ideology'). As with his series of framing questions about Afghan games, an implicit set of binary opposites is created: parochial battles for resources (Afghan wars) are contrasted with ideologically motivated conflict (wars fought in the western hemisphere).

Like Dupree, Lamb depicts kite-flying as essentially an Afghan activity, which it is not (I return to this significance of this in due course). Here is Dupree's description of kite-flying: 'a favourite urban sport [...that] provides boys with a[n] opportunity for individual competition' (212). Provided we forget Dupree's set of evaluative questions about Afghan games and sports, his depiction of kite-flying seems predominantly descriptive. It is Lamb's narrator who adopts, adapts and applies Dupree's questions and uses their evaluative logic to make explicit, rather than implicit judgements about Afghan cultural practices. I quote from Lamb at length:

> In Afghanistan, warfare was part of life even when the country was not at war, particularly among the Pashtun [...] The Afghan scholar Louis Dupree wrote of visiting a village in the southern eastern province of Paktia in 1962 and witnessing attempts by one tribe to steal some trees of another, sparking off a long-dormant feud. Within a week ten of the hundred men in the village had been killed.
>
> 'Fighting is our problem', said one of the other men. 'We fight with everything. Afghans are world champions in fighting.'
>
> It was hard to disagree [...] All their legends revolved around fighting and so did their hobbies. It wasn't just the obvious ones such as bird-fighting, cockfighting and wrestling or *buzkashi*, the Afghan version of polo and pre-cursor to the western game, with a live goat (or sometimes the heads of Russian soldiers) used as a ball. Even activities that seemed peaceful, like boiling eggs, in Afghanistan involved some form of warfare.
>
> Kite-flying was another unexpectedly martial sport [...] I had wondered why the kites had no tails and why so many ended up trapped in trees and powerlines. Then it was explained to me that the point of kites was not to watch them soar and dive in the sky but to use them to fight other children's kites. Warrior kites. This was done by coating the string with a mixture of

powdered glass and rice-flour, and then flying the kite towards an
opponent's to try to slash his string (187).

This passage confirms Dupree's *Afghanistan* as an important intertext,
first by its explicit mention and, second, through the testing (and
confirmation) of its study that Afghan games reveal something
pathological about Afghan attitudes to war. The opening statement
claims that that 'warfare was a part of life even when the country was
not at war', thereby advancing a study that resonates with Dupree's
sense of cultural dysfunction. The notion gains further credibility by
being ventriloquised through the authenticating voice of an Afghan
informant ('Fighting is our problem'). Afghans' inability to be
peaceful is presented as a fixed trait, or cultural disposition, and the
'unexpectedly martial' nature of kite-flying is offered as clinching
evidence of this dysfunction. The normative, or culturally functional,
response to kites is to watch them 'soar and dive'. By way of
confirming this idea, lasting peace is connected to this normative
response. On the previous page, the narrator states that, since
England's last civil war three hundred and fifty years ago, 'people in
England have pretty much lived together peacefully' (187). By
contrast, kite-flying in Afghanistan is loaded with sinister,
synecdochic significance: 'the point [...] was [...] to use them to fight
other children's kites. Warrior kites.' Following Dupree's logic,
Lamb's narrator concludes that decades of warfare in Afghanistan can
be explained by Afghan pathology. Indeed, her focus on children only
enhances the sense that violence exists in the very germ of 'Afghan
culture'.[110]

A brief foray into history of the so-called warrior kites' history
exposes its dubiousness as a metaphor for Afghans' 'fundamentally
warlike' nature. The form of kite-fighting described by Dupree and
Lamb is also played throughout the Punjab, Rajasthan and Gujarat and
has its origins in Hindu mythology.[111] Kremmer (who recognises that
this form of kite-flying is not exclusive to Afghanistan) uses kite-
flying to suggest a Pakistani predilection for warfare: 'in Pakistan
even children's kites carry a hidden menace, their strings coated with
finely ground glass capable of cutting other kids' strings in dogfights
[...] in a children's version of an air defence exercise' (143-144).
Here, generalised notions of Islamic militancy[112] are grafted onto

Pakistan, illustrating how synecdochic analyses tend to militate against the proper historicisation of cultural practices.

The apparent soundness of Afghan games as a metaphor for Afghans' 'warlike' nature is challenged by Lamb's discussion of egg-fighting. Egg-fighting is subject to the same synecdochic treatment as other Afghan games: 'Even activities that seemed peaceful, like boiling eggs, in Afghanistan involved some form of warfare' (187). However, an earlier sentence undermines the warlike Afghan study by identifying a possible parallel with a game played by British children who belong, according to Lamb's analysis, to a peace-loving society: 'From what I could make out the egg game was a messier variant of playing conkers' (185). The culturally relativist comparison of egg-fighting with conkers instigates a textual wrestling match between opposing anthropological agendas. Anthropology's allegorical project of sameness requires parallels to be drawn between British and Afghan children so that similarities are discovered, while synecdoche works to isolate that which is quintessentially, pathologically Afghan, that which is different.[113] This illustrates how authorial intent is one of a number of factors to be taken into consideration when analysing the impact of anthropological debates on travel writing. Lamb's narrative here subverts synecdochic logic, not because of any post-crisis conscience on the part of the author, but rather because the text itself manifests a theoretical and ideological conflict within the discipline of anthropology.

Lamb's commentary on kite-flying illustrates why synecdoche, which lends a spurious coherence to multiple and competing socio-political realities (Gilmore in Lindisfarne 1991: 83) has largely been abandoned by contemporary ethnographers. Her conclusions are consistent with what Shahrani identifies as the tendency of ethnographies about Afghanistan to play down the importance of wider political factors. Ethnographies about Afghanistan, Shahrani argues, have 'managed to ignore' the 'painful and pervasive sociopolitical issues' of the various wars in which Afghanistan has become embroiled: '(colonial, anti-colonial, nationalist, revolutionary, and interventionist' (www.indiana.edu/anthro/faculty/nazif.html). The briefest history of Afghanistan's struggle against Soviet invasion suffices to illustrate this point. This struggle had complex international dimensions so that major political players acted according to their conflicting national self-interests. During this particular struggle, the Hazaras were backed by Iran, Ahmad Shah Masud was supported by France, and the Uzbek General Dostum had assistance from Russia (Ali:214). These dimensions present an obvious challenge to the insular analyses of cultural causation. Despite this, Kremmer's and Lamb's texts repeatedly seek to locate the cause of Afghan wars within the discursive anomaly of 'Afghan culture'. In his Author's Note, Kremmer makes the following claim: 'Generally the despots and militias responsible for this [recent Afghan hardship] have been homegrown' (xi). Placed against his commitment to contributing an '[u]nderstanding [of] the causes and effects of injustice in Muslim societies' (xi), his reliance upon the culture concept describes a pathology that is not only Afghan but (once again, in an ever-widening circle of generalisation) Muslim.

The use of synecdoche has further ramifications. In *The Road to Oxiana*, Robert Byron comments that '[Afghan] women as usual are invisible' (240). Azoy makes a similar observation about a family compound: 'Behind this wall remain the family women, with whom unrelated males are forbidden all contact. Nor are enquiries made, even the most perfunctory; for the visitor, this secluded domain may as well not exist' (33). This phrase captures a general tendency to exclude Afghan women from cultural analyses or to subsume them into the normalised category of *he*. Azoy's study follows this trend by observing that '[m]illions of men live in this area [of Northern Afghanistan]', thereby emptying the region of Afghan women (47). In Azoy's study, women neither play nor watch *buzkashi* games. If *buzkashi* is the key to understanding politics, then, we might easily conclude that Afghan women are devoid of political agency because they are generally absent from *buzkashi* matches. This might not have been such a serious problem if Azoy's study professed to be about Turkmen or Uzbek masculinities. However, only once does the study come close to acknowledging the theoretical implications of deploying the *buzkashi* metaphor to generalize about Afghan politics: 'In no other form of sanctioned activity', he states, 'are the cultural values of masculinity – courage, strength, dominance, host generosity – so vividly embodied' (11). *Buzkashi* might legitimately be defined as an arena where masculinities are performed and defined. However, though Azoy here touches upon women's exclusion from his study, the ethical consequences of its gender-blindness are never considered.

Gendered positionality is also of central importance to travel writing about Afghanistan. Kremmer's carpet metaphor relies on a gendered dynamic. Despite the apparent benevolence of Kremmer's gaze, the carpets are imbued with femininity. He '[r]eclin[es] like a sultan' while the rugs are paraded before him, 'tossing and turning' as though performing a dance for his delectation. When he finally makes his selection, the rug is described in the same, unmistakably gendered terms: 'a dusky beauty had caught my eye, a small prayer rug' (6). Afghan culture parades itself, or rather herself, before him. In this sense, Kremmer's narrative reproduces, rather than subverts, what James Duncan describes as the 'usual masculinist fantasy of the Orient as a liminal zone of unrestrained sexuality' (in Duncan and Gregory 1998: 143). Indeed, the understanding of an 'entire [Afghan] culture', which the carpet metaphor gestures towards revealing, is based upon the narrator's conversations with carpet merchants, who are all men. When the narrator claims that 'the [Afghan] diaspora had turned every second Afghan [in Peshawar] into a rug merchant' (159), he refers to every second man, not every second woman. On one occasion, the narrative hints at its exclusions and silences by mentioning that the weavers of Turkmen carpets are women, who produce 'the spectacular weavings their culture is most remembered for' (50). Nevertheless, Kremmer's attempt at interpreting and translating an 'entire culture' is severely hampered by his lack of access to Turkmen women. This forces him to resort either to the dubious practice of reading women via the cultural objects they produce, or to deduce women's heavily mediated thoughts from the explanatory narratives of male carpet merchants such as Tariq or Habib. In an isolated self-reflective moment, the narrator denounces women's exploitation in the carpet industry, even noting his own complicity with it: 'All the men did was sell or steal them [women's carpets]. Or, in my case, buy them' (51). This last statement addresses the tension between his book's discussion of carpets as cultural artefacts and his status as a collector who is complicit in the act of transforming those same carpets into merchandise. Even so, the exclusionary practices of Azoy and Kremmer are deeply embedded, falling in with the historical tendency of ethnographers to privilege men's versions of history and interpretations of cultural meaning (Lowenhaupt Tsing: 33). I return to this theme in due course.

Implied insight: synecdoche and journalism's pseudo-ethnographic content

A cartoon on the website of the Revolutionary Association of the Women of Afghanistan (RAWA) shows two armless, turbaned men galloping their horses round one another in perpetual circles, each with the bloody foreleg of a goat carcass between their teeth. Both men frown with determination and yet hold white flags of surrender under the stumps where their arms once were. As they circle one another their horses' hooves crush the bones of Afghan civilians. In the background their potential saviour, Uncle Sam, leans on a stick watching from sidelines as though contemplating the likely victor.[114] The referent, of course, is *buzkashi*, or goat-grabbing, and the cartoon has its precursor in Azoy's use of the game as a metaphor for a perceived Afghan predisposition towards anarchy and factionalism. Despite anthropologists' recognition of synecdoche's tendency to lend spurious coherence to multiple cultural and socio-political realities (Gilmore in Lindisfarne: 83), the *buzkashi* metaphor was widely taken up by British journalists during Operation Enduring Freedom. Among British journalists, the metaphor has retained its currency as providing authoritative insight into the root causes of conflicts fought on Afghan soil.

As I have suggested, journalism is a transgeneric form[115] that relies, to a significant extent, on the discourses and methodologies of classical ethnographies. Ethnography's influence on British journalism is as nebulous as it is pervasive. Pseudo-ethnographic discussions of *buzkashi* in news reports do not necessarily proceed from direct perusal of the pages of influential studies such as Azoy's by individual journalists. As with Kipling's writing, the passage of ideas through time is notoriously difficult to map. However, as discussed later in Part Two, Azoy's study was repeatedly cited as a source by many US journalists who made free use of the *buzkashi* metaphor during the Soviet occupation. In 2001, British news media coverage tended to become pseudo-ethnographic[116] at the first mention of *buzkashi*; discussion of the game quickly slid into the symbolic realm.

An article by Mark Franchetti in *The Sunday Times* suggests that ethnographers such as Azoy borrowed the metaphor from earlier military sources. Franchetti's description of the game as played with a goat's carcass (rather than a headless calf, which is how the game was played by the time Azoy wrote about it) confirms that Azoy's study had a military precedent:

> Military observers draw a startling parallel between the struggles for control of Afghanistan and a national sport called *buzkashi*, in which horsemen with whips fight over the carcass of a headless goat: it is a dirty debilitating game and the prize has seen better days (14th October, 2001).

As I have argued, ethnographic synecdoche has its forebear in nineteenth-century travel writing, where a 'valued moment' or insightful observation was used to suggest the essence of a place visited (Buzard 2001: 12). Franchetti's symbolic presentation of the game as revealing something about Afghan 'struggles' for political control matches definitions of synecdoche as the 'evocation of a social whole through representation of its parts' (Webster in Richards 1994: 221). Military sources' use of *pars totalis* with respect to *buzkashi* thus became formally ethnographic in Azoy's *Buzkashi. Game and Power in Afghanistan*. In this sense, while unspecified 'military observers' precede anthropologists, Franchetti's description of the game cannot be said to be *un*ethnographic any more than the First Anglo-Afghan War can be imagined in isolation from Kipling's later writings about it.

Journalism rarely purports to be ethnographic even when correspondents openly admire anthropologists' work.[117] In an interview with the author of this study, Lamb speaks of the Duprees with great respect: 'Louis and Nancy Dupree were real authorities on Afghanistan [...] I would be flattered to be compared to that kind of work [...because] their work on Afghanistan is very authoritative' (appendix six). Such a statement underlines the appeal of ethnography for those whose writing aspires to informational status. As I will explore, however, it is not merely ethnography's authoritative element but the pressures on journalists to provide insight, or the appearance of insight, that increase the temptation to resort to certain shortcuts to understanding. Another factor conducive to pseudo-ethnographic journalism is the increasing numbers of non-specialist journalists who are 'parachuted' in and out of conflicts at impossibly short notice. As anthropologist Ulf Hannerz points out, parachutists have extremely rushed itineraries and minimal time for any advance preparation. A lack of relevant language skills means that parachutists cannot easily be 'sensitive to perspectives and reverberations' in voices in the streets as more experienced correspondents, and especially ethnographers, might. Hannerz argues that this often forces them to rely on 'received wisdom: established interpretative frames and preconceptions brought in from elsewhere' (2004: 134). Even so, inter-referentiality is a more complicated business than Hannerz's statement allows. As Part One explained, 'responsible' programmes of 'informed reading' invariably increase, rather than decrease, the degree of inter-referentiality.

The pressure exerted on news reports by ethnographic writing, and the conditions that foster its influence are complex and various. An obvious first line of enquiry pertains to the content of journalism courses in the United Kingdom. Ethnographic principles and techniques are not necessarily taught explicitly, though they are often covered implicitly, with regard to interview techniques, cross-cultural communication, hazardous assignments and so on.[118] More obvious examples of ethnography's influence on journalism can be found in long-standing mainstream programmes, such as BBC *Radio 4*'s 'From Our Own Correspondent', which is founded on the ideal of sustained and intensive cross-cultural contact. The programme is described on the BBC website as encouraging reflection on 'the stories behind the headlines', envisaging its contributors as 'sit[ting] down [to...] compose his or her thoughts' after 'a busy day in the field'.[119] The programme ostensibly takes advantage of correspondents who have accumulated greater than usual experience of intensive dwelling among the local population. Much value is placed on the use of unofficial sources for reports, 'ordinary Afghans', whose voices are then mediated through that of the correspondent who narrates her or his report.

Ethnographers themselves have become interested in the obvious overlap between ethnography and journalism and offer some helpful insights. In *Foreign News. Exploring the World of Foreign Correspondents*, Hannerz notes that journalism is 'a craft in some ways parallel to ethnography', especially in the sense that foreign correspondents resemble ethnographic writers. He considers journalists and ethnographers to have the following similarities: 'Like anthropologists, news media foreign correspondents report from one part of the world to another. We share the condition of being in a transnational contact zone, engaged there in reporting, representing, translating, interpreting – generally managing meaning across distances, although (in part, at least) with different interests, under different constraints' (2004: 3 & 6). These similarities[120] help to explain why much of the metaphorical reductionism in articles and news reports by journalists has synecdochic overtones.

There are, of course, crucial differences between journalism and ethnography. As Mark Pedelty points out, 'for these "participant observers" [foreign correspondents], violence is not a matter of "values" in the moral sense [...] but instead "value" in the economic' (1995: 2). It is these conditions that create a pressing need to provide, or to appear to provide, 'depth' of coverage. Resorting to synecdoche enables tentative conclusions to be reached about conflicts fought in Afghanistan. As a unit of analysis, 'Afghan culture' is advantageous to journalists in a hurry since it appears to facilitate a degree of retreat from the controversial realm of international politics. In such an environment, understanding, or the illusion of understanding, becomes a commodity in itself in ways highly likely to optimise audience satisfaction. As DelZotto points out, the news becomes a simplified product for public consumption (2002: 143). Other crucial differences leave anthropologists with the upper hand. While they tend to self-censor according to academic fashions, or at least are answerable to the institutions and bodies that fund their research as journalists are beholden to their editors, they enjoy clear advantages in their quest for insight and understanding. Inadequate though it may be, an 18-month period of intensive fieldwork dwarfs the average stay of a foreign correspondent, which is unlikely to extend beyond 18 days. Moreover, since participant observation remains a key tenet of fieldwork, anthropologists (and correspondents producing reports for programmes such as 'From Our Own Correspondent') obtain much of their information first-hand while a foreign correspondent's sources are generally third or fourth-hand. Participant observation is the implicit model of news coverage, which relies for its authority on projecting a sense of the correspondent as an on-the-ground eyewitness even though, as Hannerz and Pedelty have discussed, this is generally very far from the case. The *buzkashi* metaphor is thus advantageous in the sense that it neatly 'diagnoses' the problem of Afghan attitudes to politics, implying insight without necessarily requiring a complicated socio-political context or even extensive interviews with non-official actors in the conflict.

Buzkashi is the theme of Richard Miron's radio report for 'From Our Own Correspondent', entitled 'Fierce battles over dead goats' (*Radio 4*, Monday 7th January, 2002):

> [*Buzkashi*] is like polo in that two teams on horseback face each other.
>
> But there, more or less, the similarities end.
>
> Instead of a ball, the riders compete over a goat's carcass, and while polo tends to be a pursuit of the well-heeled, played on carefully tended turf, *buzkashi* is a game of the people, played raucously – in this instance on dusty open ground next to Kabul's stadium.
>
> [...] It is, it seems, a game with a rich history, being based upon tales of great battles fought by ancient Afghans on horseback. [...] But to [my friend] Saroj, this was more than just a game [...] maybe also *buzkashi* serves to describe aspects of Afghan society as a whole, with its mixture of ethnic groups and political factions.
>
> But in recent years the country has failed to work as a team, communicate and succeed.
>
> Now, of course, many Afghans hope they have the chance to reach a positive conclusion.
>
> [...] As to the final result of the *buzkashi* game, unfortunately I could not work it out as the action became increasingly shrouded in a mass of yellow dust, making the goings-on even more impenetrable.

There can be little doubt that Miron's report is pseudo-ethnographic in the sense that it culls synecdochic strategies of representation from anthropological modes of representation. The narrative also yields to an ethnographic imperative to gain 'credibility' by authenticating cultural interpretations via one's informants, in this case through Miron's friend Saroj. However, the report is ethically problematic in the sense that it deploys synecdoche while remaining free from the obligation to subject its mode of analysis to anthropological scrutiny. Miron's treatment of *buzkashi* is not thoroughly elaborated, nor is it particularly precise. The facts of the game itself are under-researched: while the piece implies that *buzkashi* is a 'raucou[s]' distortion of polo, it is more accurately the forebear of its wealthier relative. A second misleading claim is that *buzkashi* is 'a game of the people'; this is belied by a caption beneath a *buzkashi* pony on the same page, which reads: '[h]orses are trained for years before they can take part', hinting at the game's connection to personal wealth and sponsorship.[121] So, too, is the game removed from its shifting social contexts, since it is restricted – in its most traditional form - to special occasions such as weddings or carnivals. The commentary itself inherits three broad tendencies of synecdoche's application. The expression 'Afghan society as a whole' is invested with the nostalgic yearnings associated with the culture concept. A second characteristic is apparent in a manoeuvre, executed in Azoy's own analysis, whereby the category of 'men' is conflated with that of 'women' to form 'the people'. While women are not always excluded from spectatorship of the game, they certainly do not participate.[122] Exclusionary practices have historically been deeply embedded in synecdochic analyses of *buzkashi* and, since women cannot be counted among the game's players, 'work[ing] as a team', their agency as social and political actors is indirectly discounted. The third inherited feature relates to Richards' rather uncharitable definition of synecdoche as isolating a single 'cultural aspect which appears immensely significant as a key to the whole culture but which is nonetheless a riddle or seemingly inexplicable event to the reader' (1994: 221). As Miron's description of *buzkashi* slips from the literal game to the symbolic realm, it clearly purports to provide insight into 'Afghan society as a whole', characterising it, as does Azoy, as one of 'ancient' factionalism and strife. Nevertheless, some 'yellow dust' billows over the scene, rendering the workings of *buzkashi* - and by extension Afghan society - finally 'impenetrable'. While this strategy may be said have the effect of undermining the metaphor's usefulness for explaining the root cause of Afghan conflict, there is no mistaking its inexorable analytical drift towards cultural, rather than political explanation. This is an ethical consequence shared with ethnographic synecdochic analyses. By enacting a form of interpretative tidying, it identifies an internal cultural dynamic, shutting out the complex international dimension of wars fought on Afghan soil. Finally, the metaphor is extended beyond the game's possible insights into reform of its rules: deeply embedded in this commentary is a positive outcome from Operation Enduring Freedom in the shape of liberal democracy and accompanying economic reform, possibly implied by the potential transition from 'raucou[s]' barbarity (or political unruliness) on 'dusty open ground' to 'carefully-tended turf'. When used to this effect, metaphorical reductionism is actually misleading, since the implied model of strong, centralised and hierarchical governance is very far from describing Afghanistan's historical forms of governance, nor is it compatible with leadership models associated with the Sunni Hanafi sect, to which ninety-percent of Afghans belong. As Rashid points out, governance in Afghanistan has generally taken the form of a skeletal government with as little state interference in local and regional affairs as possible (2000: 83). In this sense I would suggest that the metaphor offers little or no insight to its British news audiences.

As I have suggested, the pseudo-ethnographic content of Miron's piece is readily explained by the programme's anthropological leanings. However his reference to *buzkashi* is very far from being an isolated case. The game proved an irresistible unit of analysis in television news during Operation Enduring Freedom. Perhaps the most prominent example is John Simpson's report for BBC1's 'Six O' Clock News' where, elevated on a platform with a *buzkashi* team playing below and behind him, he offers the following summary of Afghan politics: 'So a deeply political game is going on here, which made it highly suitable that a *buzkashi* match, the ferocious Afghan version of polo, should have been staged today, played not with a ball but a headless calf. Politics here is fierce and the Northern Alliance is determined to propel itself into power' (6 November 2001). Once again, the source of Afghan conflict is located in Afghan ferocity:

'played not with a ball' (by implication, the culturally normative mode of play) 'but a headless calf'. Squeezed into the end of a short report, the *buzkashi* metaphor produces an illusion of depth whereby anthropological totalisation (Brightman 1995: 517) becomes journalistic totalisation.[123]

When it comes to reporting *buzkashi*, therefore, anthropologically-inspired news media coverage tends to replicate ethnography's problematic interpretative practices. In his ethnography, Azoy quotes a governmental leaflet about *buzkashi*, which describes the game as 'exclusively Afghan [...] reflect[ing] the boldness and fierce competitive spirit of the Afghan people' (109). However, a complaint by a Turkmen reader of Azoy's manuscript challenges the idea that *buzkashi* is 'exclusively Afghan'. The Turkmen's objection is relegated to a footnote, which urges Azoy to 'report the Kabul government suppressions of Turkoman and Uzbek *buzkashis* in the countryside' (108). When journalists identify the game as simply 'Afghan', therefore, their analysis becomes unwittingly bound up with Pashtun quests for dominance and the suppression, or in this case, the strategic appropriation, of non-Pashtun identities and cultural practices. However, Azoy describes the Turkmen's objections as 'marginal notes' and his footnote represents the study's sole mention of such suppressions. As Shahrani points out, however, *buz kashi* is the Persian, rather than the Turkic or Uzbek name. He therefore terms *buzkashi* as the 'traditional kirghiz game of *olagh tartish*' (106). Azoy thus fails to address directly the charge that persistent use of the name *buzkashi* risks complicity with such acts (acts in which this study, which uses *buzkashi* throughout, is likewise implicated). Azoy's ethnography could not be described as counter-intuitive, therefore, since it endorses rather than investigates this nationalist construction by drawing parallels between the game and 'Afghan culture'. By playing down the significance of the game's contested meanings, the ethnography thus goes with the grain of these acts of historical amnesia in order to facilitate its synecdochic analysis. While it is not the remit of news media coverage to be counter-intuitive, it nevertheless follows in Azoy's wake.

Since 2001 conflict, *buzkashi* metaphors for political anarchy have seen many parallels, one of which can be found in Jenny Cuff's 2004 pre-election report 'Challenging prize for Afghan poll winner', where a game of musical chairs on Afghan television is similarly invested with synecdochic meaning:

> The next item was a game of musical chairs. Five young men battled it out until there were only two left, circling the last plastic seat. One grabbed the back of it and would not let go. As the music stopped, his taller rival – brown suit flapping – landed on his lap, then slid to the floor. Musical chairs is what the leaders of Afghanistan are playing right now as they prepare for the first national election. But there are forces at work here that do not want anybody to grab the central seat of power [...] Over the coming months they will find out who the contestants are in the presidential election – and whether there is a genuine chance for change or just a re-arranging of the furniture ('From Our Own Correspondent', Saturday 26 June).

Analytically tidy though such a report may be, its substitution of macro politics for micro politics is particularly problematic since, in its keen pursuit of the furniture metaphor, not a single political actor receives a mention. Absent, too, is the context of long-established Afghan practices of devolved, rather than centralised power. Taking the place of such context is a disparaging view of Afghan politics as random and chaotic. Neither is there any mention of sustained Afghan resistance to governments sponsored or supported by international political powers, from Shah Sujah through Soviet rule through to the present. Again, it seems unlikely that the musical chairs metaphor is capable of delivering a great deal of insight.

Crucially, the journalistic predilection for metaphorical reductionism is unsurprising in the face of tight deadlines driven by commercial imperatives and evolving technologies. Lamb describes the negative impact of the pressure to produce reports quickly:

> As correspondents in the past we had a lot of time to think about what we were writing. I could reflect at my leisure on what I wanted to say. Now you only have a short time and then you have to file. That's why I really like to write books because there is no way you can convey properly in news articles the reality of the place and it's very easy to give a very misleading view (appendix six).

Recent technological innovations have further removed the possibility of time for reflection. As Lamb suggests, the rapid filing of reports was generally impossible during the Soviet occupation when war correspondents travelled through high mountain ranges with groups of mujaheddin. These trips, as Giradet recalls, were most likely to result in 'a series of lengthy articles plus two or three television reports' produced upon return to Peshawar or the United Kingdom (Giradet in Giradet and Watter 1998: 51). Nowadays such pressures perhaps make analytical shortcuts inevitable. Lamb explains the special appeal of *buzkashi* for journalists:

> I don't like using images like that. I think it's a real problem for a reporter when you see only fragments of what's happening and I think this problem should be made clear. Particularly in a country like that, so huge and so diverse. But then journalists are working within such restricted space, trying to convey something in a small amount of words and those [kinds of metaphors] are an easy way out (appendix six).

Journalism is commonly caricatured as a process of simplification followed by exaggeration. When explaining political and cultural complexities seems too tall an order, well-worn ethnographic metaphors clearly assist in the process of simplification and exaggeration. For journalists in a rush, therefore, following the tracks of ethnographers such as Azoy, makes a great deal of sense.

Buzkashi's appeal cannot be accounted for by time pressures alone, however. Synecdoche's link to the literary turn in ethnography closely parallels the indispensability of metaphorical reductionism to 'great piece[s] of journalism' (Stewart: 30). Few journalists can resist a good metaphor. Indeed, it would be difficult to communicate to news audiences without metaphorical language. Whether it be newspapers or television news reports, news media coverage of Operation Enduring Freedom contains abundant evidence of the quest for metaphors that appear to deliver insight whether this be delivered through metaphors of political chaos (as in *buzkashi* or musical chairs) or through the faces, aspects or case-studies of single characters, made, in the words of journalist Stephen Franklin, to 'serve as a metaphor for Afghanistan's dismay and tortured disintegration' (*Columbia Journalism Review* 2002: 7). It is important to consider precisely what is sacrificed on the altar of good writing. What is the ethical price of a good piece of journalism? The clearest consequence is an analytical shortfall and corresponding tendency to shirk socio-political complexities. Moreover, pseudo-ethnographic journalism, which is signalled by the widespread journalistic preference for 'Afghan culture' rather than 'Afghan society', both under-theorises and pathologises the former by implying a causal relation between socio-religious attitudes and Afghanistan's frequent experience of conflict.[124]

My critique of news reports' pseudo-ethnographic content extends beyond the charge of metaphorical reductionism, however. It pertains to journalism's often untapped potential to redress classical ethnography's overemphasis on cultural interiority, a tendency already observed by Shahrani. It seems justifiable to expect that journalism operates under certain imperatives to, at the very least, set the everyday habits of Afghans in their social, economic and political contexts. Journalism's pseudo-ethnographic content is therefore worrying in the light of its rejection of the opportunity, especially considering the BBC's public service remit to inform the British public, to redress this historical imbalance through sustained attention to the contexts of the 2001 conflict.

I turn briefly to one area of reporting that did receive some exceptional coverage: Afghanistan's opium trade. This shift of focus allows me to consider the relevance, and potential contribution, of anthropological insights into dilemmas of cross-cultural representation. This is not to suggest that careful attention to the precise economic conditions that give rise to poppy-growing was universally the case: generalised statements that 'poppy grows like weeds' are common, as are unsubstantiated accusations, such as Cuff's contention that 'warlord' Gul Agar's wealth 'is said to come from the drugs trade' ('File on Four', *Radio 4*, 29 June 2004). Nevertheless, Andrew North's report 'Following the Afghan drugs trail' does focus on socio-economic contexts and narrates the verbal exchange, albeit heavily edited and mediated through his commentary, between an Afghan poppy farmer and Antonio Maria Costa, head of the UN office on drugs and crime. The report appears on the 'From Our Own Correspondent' website under a photograph of a farmer

picking poppies above the caption: 'Farmers say they are confused by
government policy.' I quote it at some length:

> It looks like any other, except there was no poppy-growing here last year.
> Nor was there much else in the rest of Kunduz province. But all that's
> changing. Even in traditionally low-producing areas, farmers are sowing the
> crop, anxious not to be left out.
>
> The 78-year-old farmer is found in the huts nearby.
> "Yes, it's the first time I've grown it," he admits reluctantly.
>
> "But why this year?" demands his Italian visitor.
>
> "Well everyone else is doing it, so why shouldn't I?"
>
> Laughter from the crowd of officials and soldiers looking on.
>
> "But don't you know this is against Islam?" says Mr. Costa, holding up a
> poppy bulb.
>
> The farmer looks up plaintively. "There's freedom now, it's a democracy
> isn't it?"
>
> The crowd roars.
>
> [...] Others [in the region] may be profiting from drugs by levying taxes on
> drugs cargoes passing through their areas. And the underpaid police are
> easily corrupted and too under-resourced to fight back (4 June 2004).

The report gestures towards a form of complexity communicated
through the deceptively simple dialogue, suggesting a range of reasons
for poppy-growing, including confusion over government policy, lack
of policing due to 'under-resourc[ing]', corruption due to low police
wages, and widespread disobedience as an indication of poppy-
growing's economic function. Furthermore, the farmer's strategic
appropriation of the discourse of democracy parodies the notion of
choice and undermines Antonio Maria Costa's assumption of strict,
universal Afghan adherence to Islam, offering a challenge that extends
beyond the bounds of their reported conversation. In this last respect,
North's report seems in tune with some 'post-crisis' ethnography,

seeming here to follow a directive of Anna Lowenhaupt Tsing's to offer readers (in this case news audiences) a pile of stories that contradict and interrogate one another to ensure that supposed underlying principles and socially unifying structures are never privileged over heterogeneity and discord (1995: 33). Playing to the strengths of ethnographically-inspired journalism, then, North's report conveys competing understandings of democracy and choice, Afghan piety and notions of Islamic duty.

Travel writing, ethnography and Afghan agency in Christopher Kremmer and Christina Lamb

Taking anthropological debates over informants' agency (or lack of agency) as its cue, this section concentrates upon two related questions. The first concerns the degree to which Kremmer's and Lamb's texts variously deny, withhold, concede, or promote agency among the Afghan subjects of their discourse, especially Afghan women. The second considers the relevance of authorial interventions to denying or granting Afghan agency. To return to Behar's question: '[h]ave ethnographic authority and the burden of authorship figured differently in the works of women anthropologists? [...] What is the cultural logic by which authorship is coded as "feminine" or "masculine," and what are the consequences of those markings' (15)?

Before examining these questions in detail, it seems important to produce a sufficiently nuanced definition of agency. This is because, as Laura Ahearn observes, the way in which we theorise agency has particular implications for our conceptions of personhood, intention, action, causality and, I might add, authorship (2001:112).

Although my primary interest lies in the way each text denies, withholds, concedes, or actively promotes informants' agency, it is first necessary to consider the related issue of authorial intent, or authorial agency. Need agency be deliberate or intentional? Because meaning about Afghanistan is intertextually situated (Appadurai in Ahearn: 112), the entanglement of Kremmer's and Lamb's travel writing with the discourses of classical ethnography suggests that, irrespective of intent, it is impossible either to control meaning or achieve full awareness of the range of discourses and textual conventions from which each narrative, or rather series of narratives, derives. It would be misleading to privilege authorial intent (gender-related, anti-imperial, or whatever) above other salient factors such as genre, which (as I have shown) certainly promotes, if it does not determine, particular narrative frames and representational tendencies.

Of course, generic conventions and the influence of antecedent writings are not the sole factors that militate against authorial purpose. Historical location, socio-political and gendered positionality all combine to mediate understandings of Afghanistan in very particular ways. Need authorial agency therefore be deliberate or intentional? I suggest that the subversion of representative orthodoxies in Kremmer and Lamb cannot automatically be attributed to political intent anymore than nineteenth-century reiterations of colonial commonplaces was necessarily deliberate.[125] Moments of apparent subversion may have other causes such as the confluence of, or conflict between, genres or ideological positions. By prising authorial agency free of notions of individual agency, it becomes possible to avoid making value-judgements about travel writing as though it proceeds directly from the individual conscience in an unmediated fashion. Agency need not be individual. To conceptualize it as such risks re-establishing dubious connections between free will and atomic individualism associated with philosophical action theory, which, as Ahearn points out, tends to locate agency 'inside the mental process of particular individuals'. Ideally, she argues, human actions should not be divorced from the structures and discourses that shape them. She suggests that language, culture and agency are instead relocated from within individuals themselves to 'the interstices between people' (112-117).

A further question raised by Ahearn about agency is whether agency need be human (112). With regard to this question, it is helpful to examine points of friction between the synecdochic elements of Kremmer's narrative and the actual carpets under discussion. The carpets' symbolic meaning remains reasonably stable throughout the text. However, the narrative's synecdochic elements meet some resistance in the form of the carpets themselves. The following description of refugees' carpets is clearly at odds with the text's dehistoricised, depoliticized synecdochic correlation between carpets and Afghanistan's past. Wandering through some ruins, the narrator spots some graffiti on the wall:

> [S]omebody had scrawled 'jihad' in the Pashto language beneath a clever likeness of Najibullah hanging from the gallows. In the refugee camps in Pakistan they wove similar images into their carpets (23).

The correlation between carpets and Afghanistan's distant past is disputed by the descriptions or photographs of the carpets themselves. Photographs of carpets with guns and political slogans woven into them (140) and even a 'knotted replica of the American five-dollar note' (292) belie any straightforward association between carpets, antiquity and, by extension, cultural stasis. Thus an inanimate object (an Afghan carpet) counters the narrative's predilection for understanding Afghanistan's present in terms of its past and challenges the apparent neatness of the carpet metaphor.

Further examples of the possible agency of inanimate objects can be found in Kremmer's descriptions of Afghanistan's landscapes. Here is one example:

> [A] gas pipeline led the way across a timeless landscape of sickle-wielding farmers and camel drivers wrapped in shawls to avoid the sting of a sandstorm. Across the road [...] bored soldiers manning tanks and gun turrets looked on (64).

Again, key descriptive details subvert the powerful, organizing trope of the 'timeless landscape'. While the 'sandstorm' and 'sickle-wielding farmers' support his metaphor, evidence of recent economic, political and military intervention (the 'gas pipeline' and soldiers in their tanks) busily dismantle it. Even without the soldiers' help, an inanimate gas pipeline exercises a degree of agency, hampering the narrative tendency to marshal textual details in the service of synecdochic metaphor. Since agency can be exercised (with the reader's assistance) by inanimate objects, authorial agency, especially subversive agency, cannot automatically be attributed to authorial intent.

One further problem with theories of agency is that the significance of anterior writing is sometimes overlooked. As ethnographers have come to recognize, there are no unmediated spaces; 'the field' is always already filled with writing;[126] travel, missionary, colonial, journalistic and ethnographic.[127] While on the one hand the presence of texts in one another is de-authorizing, it also has important implications for the accumulation, or refutation, of what Said calls 'antecedent authority' (1979: 179). Kremmer's and Lamb's bibliographies offer a useful guide to the narratives' precise textual influences. Azoy, Burnes, Byron, Chatwin, Dupree and Elphinstone are strong and influential co-presences. Lamb foregrounds some of these presences from the beginning: 'What I knew of the Afghans was a romanticized vision distilled from Kipling's *Kim* and various nineteenth-century British accounts' (37). Not only does this acknowledge the impact of fictional representations of Afghans upon her travel writing (or, at least, considering her retrospective tone, its initial impact) but the metaphor of distillation usefully captures the often nebulous influence of earlier accounts of Afghanistan. The narrator's ambivalence about Kipling means that he cannot be established as a clear authority, since her depiction of his work is partially de-authorizing. His writing is characterised as providing 'visions', personal impressions and imaginary representations. The accounts are 'romanticised', rather than realist and, at this stage in the travel narrative, about to be tested and, I dare say, corrected, by Lamb's narrative, which replicates, negotiates, refutes, concurs with and deviates from these existing representations. If Kremmer's and Lamb's books are echo chambers, they are variously hewn.

Ultimately, the influence of anterior writings is important to my discussion, because Kremmer's and Lamb's narratives are an unruly compound of discourses and genres. Neither book is internally unified, nor yields determinate meanings, hence the advisability of attending to their ambivalence, contradictions and anxieties as well as to instances of ideological agreement and representative similarities among travel books about Afghanistan.

I return to the question of the degree to which Kremmer's and Lamb's texts variously deny, withhold, concede, or promote agency among the Afghan subjects of their discourse. Contemporary ethnographers tend to avoid assuming that, even in classical ethnographies, the ethnographic subject is always effectively muted. Aihwa Ong argues that it is a 'betrayal' to refuse to recognize informants as 'active cultural producers in their own right, whose voices insist on being heard and [who] can make a difference in the way we think about their lives' (in Behar and Gordon: 354). It seems important, then, not to doubly empower those texts that seek to deny agency by our presupposing its impossibility.

The ability of 'informants' to resist narrators' acts of palimpsest may be illustrated by a moment in Lamb's narrative where she remembers a Zambian man she met some years earlier:

> [A] man in a government office where I was trying to buy a map had questioned what I was doing there. He did not seem to understand the concept of foreign correspondent, instead asking me, 'Are you an explorer?' I told the official that I tried to go and find unreported places and people to write about. For a moment he looked confused, then he nodded vigorously, 'Ah, I see, you are an old-fashioned voyager' (144).

Despite the narrator's protestations of ideological innocence, the Zambian determinedly re-situates her in a colonial context, tracing and re-tracing lines of continuity between a colonial past (explorers and voyagers) and an imperialist present (embodied in her role as a correspondent). As though in recognition of the unacknowledged parallel between the reporter's task of writing about 'unreported places and people' and the classical ethnographer's remit to do the same, he refuses to accept the label 'foreign correspondent' as constituting a genuine line of demarcation between past ('old-fashioned voyager') and present British dealings with Afghanistan. It may be that this rather active mode of reading attributes more subversive agency to the Zambian than actually exists. However, this brings me to another important principle of informants' agency: the birth of the ethnographic reader. Following intertextual theorists, Clifford notes that the reader's interpretation of any single ethnography lies 'beyond the control of any single authority'. Hence the reader of ethnography, or indeed of travel writing about Afghanistan, may 'read against the grain of the text's dominant voice', by seeking out intimations of resistance and 'reinterpreting the descriptions, texts and quotations gathered together by the writer.' Thus it becomes possible to develop a subversive collaboration between reader and informant, whose statements are half-concealed (1986: 141).

Lamb's narrative provides further evidence to support Clifford's conceptions of the birth of the postmodern, postcolonial reader. In a letter to the narrator, an Afghan teacher, Marri, directs her 'not just [to write about] the men of beards and guns' (77), thereby issuing a directive not to deny women and peacemakers a voice. This exhortation accomplishes two things. First, it draws attention to the fact that reporting on the war on Afghanistan focuses disproportionately on the official actors of war,[128] among whom 'men of beards and guns' feature prominently. In this way it raises the possibility of pursuing another story, or stories. Second, it provides a litmus test of Lamb's own 'balance' of coverage. This means that when, elsewhere, the narrator characterizes Afghanistan as 'this country of warring tribesmen' (128), Marri's exhortation lingers like an accusation. Returning to the relevance of authorial agency to Afghan agency, then, Lamb's inclusion of Marri's words provides a limited opportunity for an Afghan woman to act as a commentator upon Afghan affairs.

Gender, genre and authorial agency

As my close readings demonstrate, Kremmer's and Lamb's narratives are complicit (in very specific ways) with some of ethnography's most problematic modes of representation. However, this section takes into account recent interventions in the crisis debate by feminist anthropologists who regret the determinism associated with the postmodern turn in ethnography and who, like many feminists in the parallel field of literary criticism, resist dismissing the possibility of agency.

In her study *Gender and Agency*, Lois McNay celebrates the decline of univocal models of patriarchy. This decline can be accounted for by the addition of variables such as class, economics, politics, even personal autonomy, into the analysis. To these variables I add genre, narrative convention, and the interplay between them (2000: 156). By taking a broad range of factors, or variables, into account, it becomes possible to avoid adopting deterministic and binaristic approaches to travel writing. As Wendy Mercer points out, close readings of nineteenth-century travel writings often 'confoun[d] the binarism of the man = coloniser/ woman = colonised hypostudy' (in Clark 1999: 163). With contemporary travel writing, too, it is simplistic to argue that a woman's writing is double-voiced, while a man's is somehow more self-assuredly univocal. However, avoiding deterministic readings can prove difficult for feminist theorists since, as McNay observes, feminism has inherited a deterministic component from Lacan and Foucault. The notion that women's identity has been formed 'through an originary act of constraint' has hitherto proved a useful way of explaining 'the deeply entrenched aspects of gendered behaviour while eschewing reference to a presocial sexual difference' (2-3). Extending this to conceptualizations of the author, this determinism risks denying the author self-consciousness, or creative and intelligent powers of negotiation. McNay suggests replacing deterministic models with a more 'generative' model that allows 'renewed understandings of ideas of autonomy and reflexivity, understood as the critical awareness that arises from a self-conscious relation with the other' (5). I wish to adapt this idea to my conceptualization of authorship by allowing that a degree of authorial awareness or self-consciousness may indeed be present, albeit in highly mediated and compromised forms. This more nuanced conception of authorship gestures beyond what McNay refers to as the reductive and 'dichotomous logic of domination and resistance' (155).

If, as McNay suggests, dominant norms are socially and historically variable, then they are constituitive, rather than wholly, determining (34). By the same token, since generic norms are not fixed, but rather variable, then it follows that the narrative conventions of ethnography are also constituitive, yet not fully determining of Kremmer's and Lamb's narratives. As with Bordieu's tennis player whose strokes are practised mechanically and in accordance with certain principles of good play, the player's actual strokes during the game are spontaneous and unpredictable (39). This captures the inherent creativity that should not be dismissed, but rather incorporated into any discussion of authorial agency.

What is the relationship of gender to authorial agency? While acknowledging gender to be an 'imaginative construct', Lowenhaupt

Tsing draws attention to its significance as a 'point of divergent positionings' (9). Which, if any, 'divergent positionings' have consequences for Kremmer's and Lamb's withholding, conceding or promoting agency among the subjects of their discourse? If the anthropological ideal is to promote agency among female, as well as male, informants, Kremmer falls short of this ideal for one simple reason. Despite his stated aim to facilitate an '[u]nderstanding [of] the causes and effects of injustice in Muslim societies' (xi), he is largely denied access to Afghan women. The problem of access is common to Kremmer's male predecessors, who often rely on second-hand accounts of the lives of Afghan women. One ethical implication of this is that male travellers are deprived of the armoury of experience with which to combat stereotypical representations.[129] More generally, however, Afghan women are notably absent from the account, which seriously undermines the validity of male-authored texts' generalizations about 'Afghan culture'.[130] With the exception of his 'interlocutor' Zhala, Kremmer's narrative consistently lacks face-to-face encounters with women.

Lamb's narrative, too, overwhelmingly privileges male informants. However, a reviewer of Lamb's claims that 'the women of Afghanistan remain largely invisible' in her travel book (Beecham 2003) is rather unfair. In statistical terms, there is a clear difference between Kremmer and Lamb. Kremmer's narrator briefly includes the words of two Afghan women while Lamb's narrative quotes thirteen, sometimes extensively. Access provides the most obvious explanation for such a disparity, but it cannot be ruled out that Lamb's sense of solidarity with, and political commitment to foregrounding the experience of, Afghan women may also have been a factor.

Beyond this, does the 'cultural logic' by which travelling is coded as male have an impact on Kremmer's and Lamb's texts? Which 'divergent positionings' does such coding bring about, and what are its consequences? Certainly, Lamb's narrative communicates unease about her relationship to travel from the outset. Her inside cover reads: 'This book is dedicated to Lourenco who thinks Mummy lives on a plane and the fond memory of Abdul Haq who told me "You're a girl. You can't go to war in Afghanistan"'. The latter claim, that only men can travel 'to war', is belied by the book's very existence, which testifies to the false assumptions on which such a claim is founded (including Abdul's infantilisation of the narrator). Later on, when contemplating her possible return to Afghanistan following September 11, the narrator spots 'the holiday faces of my husband and son [which] smiled out trustingly from a [...] yellow frame' (6-7). For a woman, especially a mother and wife, travel cannot be guilt free, especially when her relationship with Lourenco is characterized by absence. As a woman in transit, she deviates from the state of familial normality implied by the 'holiday faces'. Their confidence that she will prioritise them (they 'smil[e] out trustingly') is shown to be misplaced. Furthermore, travel entails a form of infidelity (Afghanistan is her 'lover') entailing the transgression of her feminine duty as wife and mother. There is no corresponding passage in Kremmer's narrative. His wife is mentioned once, but not in relation to dilemmas of travel.

To return to an earlier question, what happens to what Duncan describes as the 'usual masculinist fantasy of the Orient as a liminal zone of unrestrained sexuality' (in Duncan and Gregory: 143) when a woman writes about it? Does Lamb's narrator renounce the Flaubertian 'paradigm' of the East as a servant, or lover (Melman: 6)? Her introduction actively reworks it in a masculinised form. In this sense she diverges from the paradigm without flouting it. Returning to London from Central Asia she relates her experience in sexual terms: 'Afghanistan felt like a guilty secret, my Afghan affair' (4). The erotic undertones of this statement are later made explicit: Afghanistan becomes a 'love affair' (4), that seduces her from the stability of family life to spend time with the 'dashing young guerrillas' with whom she travels as a war correspondent (5). However, this does not mean that the importance of positionality to the reproduction of such paradigms should be prematurely dismissed.

Utilizing feminist insights about ethnography and female informants' agency, I ask to what extent Kremmer's and Lamb's narrators set out with an 'assumption of male agency' and, if they do, does this belief mute the voices of female 'informants'? Tapper points out that '[f]eminists and anthropologists have very properly raised doubts about the universality of female subordination' (20). In the case of Durrani women, she argues, 'male prestige is heavily dependent on women', who have the 'capacity to undermine male ambitions and damage' their social standing (22). Tapper's study offers a point of departure from other ethnographies by adopting an understanding of 'masculinity [as...] fluid and situational' (Cornwall and Lindisfarne 1994: 3), focusing upon subordinate men and superordinate, as well as subordinate, women. This signals a wider feminist project to counter the myth of universal male dominance. After all, as Lindisfarne (previously named Tapper) points out, not all men are successful patriarchs, neither is their power 'imminent in all social situations' (in Cornwall and Lindisfarne: 86 & 4). A comparison of Kremmer's and Lamb's treatment of their female informants sheds further light on this issue. To what extent is each woman accorded, or denied agency? Zhala Najrabi is introduced to Kremmer's narrator as one of Balkh University's women students. Here is his first impression of her:

> Zhala Najrabi was a model of precociousness, if not a model student. She was twenty-one, had a petite figure, and green eyes that flashed boldly whenever she said something outrageous, which was quite often. When I asked if she was married, intended to marry or ever wanted to marry, she flicked her auburn ponytail coquettishly.
> 'I am happy to be free,' she said. 'Anyway, I have my exams to finish.'
> Hearing this, her friends who had gathered around [...] exploded into laughter. Zhala's long, painted fingernails were the only thing she studied assiduously. She was passing – barely – and was smart and pretty enough to get away with it, amusing and scandalizing the entire campus with her blue jeans and independent attitudes [...] [S]he bustled off, leaving me engulfed in a heady veil of perfume, [and] I cried out for an interview, which she granted (52).

The sincerity of Zhala's declaration of independence from men is belied by her over-refined appearance, 'coquettish[h]' flick of her hair and 'heady veil of perfume', trailing Orientalist fantasies in its wake. His narrative maps the journey of his eyes along Zhala's 'petite figure', from her flashing 'green eyes' to 'her blue jeans'. Agency is withheld at this juncture: Zhala is denied the textual space, to represent herself. Her replies to his question are compressed into a single sentence, which serves as her sole defence against the narrator's heavy mediations and interventions. Zhala is provided with one sentence to defend herself against the narrator's questioning of her claim to be educated by legitimate means (against the implication that prettiness, more than studiousness, enables her to pass her exams). Of course, the narrator's heavy-handedness does not prevent the reader collaborating with Zhala, either by choosing to believe the sincerity of her statements, or else by gathering evidence from elsewhere in the chapter to contradict the notion that 'Zhala's long, painted fingernails were the only thing she studied assiduously'. Later, in his only interview with a woman, the narrator's eyes linger on her 'eye-catching red dress with a gold embroidered breastplate' while Zhala lists 'her competencies: diploma in personal computing, comfortable in WordPerfect, Lotus and Excel, fluent in English and Dari. In her spare time she worked as a nurse at a Tajik refugee camp run by Medicins Sans Frontières' (54). Choosing to suspect Kremmer's narrative interventions perhaps testifies to the redemptive power of what Margaret Mills describes as new, critical 'reading styles' (17), which ensure that the narrator is not awarded interpretative supremacy. This implies that there is an ethical responsibility, or at least opportunity, for the reader to intervene critically in Kremmer's commentary.

Lamb's narrator introduces Zena Karamzade as having been a 'second-year medical student at Herat University when the Taliban came and abolished female education' (162). Zena, and another Afghan woman named Leyla, detail their defiance of Taliban rule by co-operating in the establishment of a so-called sewing circle, a secret literary circle and an illegal school. In contrast to Zhala, Zena's narrative runs more or less uninterrupted for four pages. In this respect, Lamb's travel book resembles the ethnography of Mills, whose study is written up with post-crisis theoretical insights in mind. While Lamb no doubt exercises editorial control over the exchange with Zena (she does not go so far as Mills, who provides the full transcript of a storytelling session complete with listeners' interjections both as a direct transcription and in its translated form), Lamb's narrative loosely adheres to the following principle, set out by Mills in the introduction to her ethnography: 'My intention in this volume is to provide that "sufficient length"' in order to 'giv[e] the storytellers' words "autonomous textual space"' (17). Zena is here awarded a degree of textual autonomy. In a further gesture of empowerment, Lamb's narrator even attends to that which Tapper terms '[s]ilential relations' (20), or 'non-verbal utterance', in an attempt to remove the disadvantage conventionally experienced by 'subordinate informants'. This means that, when the narrator briefly intervenes in Zena's narrative, she enhances the dignity of her story: 'As Zena spoke her eyes burnt with injustice and her breath made clouds of steam in the cold air' (163). Although Lamb's narrator falls short of the ideals of polyphony by retaining editorial control (and which travel writer is likely to go this far?) her supportive intervention is at odds with those of Kremmer in the case of Zhala.

Does Lamb's gendered positionality (as opposed to any gendered interiority) predispose her narrative to promote agency among those Afghan women she writes about? Detailing her experiences as a young war reporter in 1988, Lamb makes explicit reference to her gender as a point of interpretative divergence:

> Most reporters covered the war from Peshawar where there was a five-star hotel and the seven mujaheddin parties fighting the Russians had their headquarters, making it easy to arrange trips 'inside', as we called getting into Afghanistan. There was an American Club where one could drink Budweisers, eat Oreo Cookie ice-cream and listen to middle-aged male correspondents in US army jackets with bloodstains and charred bullet holes on the back hold court with stories of conflict and 'skirt' from Vietnam to El Salvador. Their eyes had seen so much that they saw nothing, they knew the name and sound of every weapon ever invented, their faces were on the leathery side of rugged and even at breakfast there was Jim Beam on their breath [...] most had children in various places but never carried their photographs, and all of them went to the Philippines for R and R [Rest and Relaxation].

> It was different for me. I was a young girl in a place where women were regarded as property along with gold and land – the three zs of the Pashtuns, *zan, zar* and *zamin* – and kept hidden away behind curtained doorways (36).

The end of this passage is clearly borrowed from Dupree ('*zar, zan, zamin* (gold, women, land)' (211). The co-presence of Dupree's text immediately complicates any notion of authorial autonomy, since Lamb inherits from Dupree an assumption of male agency and a corresponding sense of female victimhood (encapsulated by the phrase 'kept hidden away'). However, working against this inherited grain is a clear assertion of difference on the basis of her gendered position. Although she identifies herself as part of a reporters' collective ('we'), she is misaligned with the male reporters' lifestyles and modes of behaviour. Her narrative is double-voiced in the sense that it is laced with a consciousness of women's exploitation (prostitution in the Philippines, 'stories of 'skirt'', and abandoned children). She is both in place ('we'), and out of place ('they') at the same time. Poised at the edge of their discourse, the narrator, being neither a male reporter, nor an Afghan woman, appears positioned, as Ahearn suggests, in the interstices between the two groups. Although she sides with the women at the receiving end of her colleagues' exploits and, by extension, Afghan women at the receiving end of men's oppression, her sense of sympathy nevertheless remains shackled to an assumption of male agency and female victimhood. In this sense, this passage fails to distance itself from models of universal female oppression.

By stating 'it was different for me', Lamb's narrator hints at the idea that women travellers, or at least, war correspondents, may be gifted with a different (by implication 'better') moral vision. Whether the narrator conceives of this moral vision as deriving from a sense of gendered interiority is difficult to determine. Caught in the middle of the battle of Jalalabad, Lamb's narrator implies that a woman is predisposed to deviate from certain masculine narratorial norms: '[t]he real story of war wasn't about the firing and the fighting, some *Boy's Own* adventure of goodies and baddies' (73). However, her renunciation of one mode of storytelling does not work to de-authorize her own account, quite the contrary. The issue of deauthorisation is difficult, however, since Lamb's text is marketed and categorised in ways that might make further deauthorisation seem like risking self-effacement.[131] Nevertheless, it remains important to address the question of whether this degree of self-reflexivity is sustained throughout the text. As I have shown with Lamb's narrative, her synechdochic analysis of Afghan games, and the orthodox conclusions to which it leads her also corroborates Sidonie Smith's contention that 'transgressions of the assignment of race do not inevitably lead to radical interventions in imperial assignments of racial characteristics' (220). Moreover, her claims to a different vision are complicated by the fact that, at moments, Kremmer's narrative comes close to Tapper's view of masculinity as 'fluid and situational' (in Cornwall and Lindisfarne: 3). At one point he deflates the heroism that Lamb caricatures in her passage about the American Club. When caught in some crossfire, the narrator asks 'Who are we? What are we achieving here?' and the reply comes back from a fellow reporter, 'I think we're trying to prove our manhood' (32). This exchange interrogates the determinism of the *Boys' Own* adventure story stereotype. By foregrounding masculinity both as a performance ('trying to prove'), and as a pathological response to danger (a futile act of risk-taking), Kremmer's passage suggests that the discourse of male reporters continues to be structured[132] by heroic models of masculinity. Kremmer's negotiation of this position, however, suggests that these models can be interrogated and, to a degree, remoulded. To return to Lamb's caricature of male reporters, it is clear that, in Kremmer's narrative at least, male reporters adopt a far more nuanced and self-critical relationship to masculinities than Lamb's narrator allows. On another occasion, Kremmer's narrator contrasts himself with a male reporter, Robert, who is described as wearing a 'chic [military] outfit' (19) and full of 'military jargon' to 'talk up the danger' from some outgoing fire (22). By contrast, his narrator detaches himself 'from the rest of the party' and walks 'alone' through the ruins to read the graffiti. By distancing himself from the group of male reporters, he provides a spatial metaphor for his own departure from that which Lamb's narrator characterises as masculinist discourse derived from *Boy's Own* adventure stories. In other words, men's travel writing and journalism are possibly more self-reflexive than she allows.

As I argued in the Introduction, 'centres and margins shift against various horizons of power' (Smith: 110). So, too, does Tapper's notion of fluid and situational masculinities apply to femininities. There are some power issues about which Lamb's narrative maintains a silence. In the following passage, she discusses the Mosque of the Holy Relic where a *kherqa*, the Sacred Cloak of Prophet Mohammed is kept:

> [T]here is a constant line of men leaving their sandals at the door and shuffling through to marvel at the surprisingly long marble tomb and touch the glass case containing Ahmad Shah's brass helmet. Before leaving they bend to kiss a length of pink velvet said to be from his robe. It bears the unmistakable scent of jasmine (38).

Reporting the scent of jasmine raises an intriguing question. How, if the mausoleum is only open to men, can the narrator know that it smells of jasmine? There are a number of likely explanations, all of which possibly implicate Lamb in an act of dominance. It is possible that she has been granted entry on account of her western status. In this case, she remains silent about a status frequently predicated on skin colour, that of honorary manhood. Another possibility is that Afghan women *are* allowed to enter the mausoleum and have been effaced by the narrative. In this case, the narrator is complicit in a long history of women's textual erasure. A third explanation is that she does not enter the mausoleum but relies on eye-witness accounts. In this case, she adopts the omniscience of the ethnographer whose 'third eye' penetrates the mosque wall to enter forbidden spaces from which the 'foreign eye' is barred (the word 'unmistakable' conveys a strong experiential element).

Behar deploys the term 'double crisis' to denote the crisis in ethnography and the crisis in feminism, each of which emerged from the 1980's 'like parallel lines destined never to meet' (in Behar and Gordon: 3). However, the faint possibility of these lines meeting is suggested when a letter from Marri to Lamb offers a critique of universal sisterhood: 'I dream of a life like that. It's funny we live under the same small sky yet it seems we live 500 years apart' (30). Marri concentrates upon that which divides, rather than unites them. The letter's inclusion represents a departure from classical ethnographies by providing 'autonomous textual space' for Marri's letters. This allocation of textual space to Marri provides an instance where a post-crisis anthropological principle is put into practice by a travel narrative. Elsewhere in the narrative Marri's persistent denials of sisterhood appear to penetrate the narrator's consciousness: 'As I watched these Hazara mothers unable to feed their babies, I thought of my own well-fed son back home, dressed in a different outfit every day [...] parties with cake and balloons, holidays in the sun' (24). This study's conclusion returns to the possibility that, in the words of W. H. Auden, travel writing at least presents the opportunity to offer a form of cultural critique, 'mak[ing] one reflect on one's past and one's culture from the outside' (in Youngs 2004: 74).

Conclusion: textual negotiations and anthropological solutions

Kremmer's and Lamb's writing about Afghanistan suggests that a limited degree of authorial agency is in operation, although this agency is sometimes difficult to distinguish from other factors. While both texts tend to comply with representational norms and narrative conventions, there is ample evidence of resistance to, or negotiation of, these same norms and conventions. Evidence of textual negotiation is most readily located in passages of anti-narrative. Anti-narrative may be defined as writing that breaks away from what Said calls the 'discursive finality' of the conventional plot (1978: 182), that which tampers with narrative convention or familiar patterns of representation. The following example from Lamb's text has political, even anti-imperial, resonance:

> On the steps of the hotel a polite young man in a pinstriped suit [...] addressed me in perfect English. 'Excuse me, are you a Britisher? [...] You are the first [real] Britisher I have met. Do you mind if I ask you a question?'
>> 'Not at all. Go ahead.'
>> 'Can you please tell me how many positive adjectives there are in the English language?'
> Since the Taliban had ridden into town [...] it would have been impossible for this man to speak openly to a Western woman. Now he finally had the opportunity and his first question was on a point of grammar. To my shame I didn't have a clue.
> We both stood there silent for a while, dissatisfied by the encounter. In my bag I had a bundle of pens to give to children and I wondered whether to offer him one, but it didn't seem quite appropriate.
>> 'Oh well, I was extremely honoured to meet you,' he said eventually and walked away (146-7).

This scene registers and replays scenes of colonial first encounters in ways that suggest more active and creative re-workings than deterministic approaches to authorial agency might allow. The scene is not devoid of tension ('finally he had the opportunity'), yet this tension is quickly deflated. Though positioned as a source of knowledge, the narrator falls far short of the Afghan's expectations ('I didn't have a clue') thereby eschewing any sense of superiority. Furthermore, while the narrator seems culturally predisposed to infantilise him (she considers giving him a pen intended for children), she wonders whether giving gifts is any longer 'appropriate'. The exchange of goods for cultural information is, of course, all too familiar to the anthropological encounter. In this respect the scene is particularly 'dissatisfy[ing]', since the potential informant 'walk[s] away'. Being woefully inadequate to the task, the gift can no longer guarantee the disclosure of cultural information.

Although agency is not synonymous with resistance, my discussion centres on evidence of textual negotiations that have the counter-intuitive potential to interrogate or intervene in patterns of representation inherited from colonial writing about Afghanistan. Since textual negotiation is possible, it is also desirable, and travel writing's close relationship to ethnography suggests that anthropology's recent theoretical insights may be of some relevance for travel writing. (This prospect is discussed at greater length in the study's conclusion). By adhering to the principle of providing 'autonomous textual space' to her storytelling informants, for example, ethnographer Mills is able to minimise, though not eliminate, her account's interpretative authority. Although I have argued that the counter-influence of ethnography on Kremmer's and Lamb's accounts is predominantly classical, by adopting a more nuanced understanding of agency I have shown that certain negotiations (while not always deliberate and possibly limited) are perfectly possible. This is evident in the allocation of space in Lamb's narrative, for example. Sandwiched between each of her chapters is one of Marri's letters, or an edited extract from her diary. The result is to weaken Lamb's authority as a commentator because, while the diaries and letters are edited, Marri's words frequently contradict or problematise conclusions reached elsewhere in the narrative. Despite the reluctance of Lamb's narrator to engage in any direct criticism of the 2001 bombing of Afghanistan, Marri's letters and diary entries offer their own criticism of the principles behind it: 'I hope they [Tony Blair and George Bush] do not come and bomb and then forget us again' (77). Elsewhere, Marri interrogates the manner in which the interim government was chosen ('They have chosen us a government in Bonn' (179)). She also voices concern about the new cabinet: 'Father says it is a cabinet of Old Enemies' who 'will all shoot each other' (209).

A second principle increasingly encouraged by anthropologists since the 1980s is that of partially de-authorizing ethnographic accounts by curbing the interpretative power of the all-seeing narrator. In an unrepresentative moment, Lamb's narrator adheres to this principle: 'The more times I went into Afghanistan to cover the war the more I realized that there were many realities, and the best I could hope for was a few fragments, never the big picture' (65). This statement effectively de-authorizes her narrative in the sense that it precludes the possibility of reaching any global understanding ('the big picture') and by acknowledging the account to be necessarily and inevitably partial, composed of 'a few fragments' that cannot be synthesized, synecdochically or otherwise, into an understanding of Afghanistan as an imaginary cultural whole (also see appendix six).

One further recommendation made in the spirit of postmodernism by Graham Watson in his famous 1987 article is the need 'to learn to live with' a lack of interpretative closure, or 'unending ambiguity'. He suggests that effective self-reflexive ethnography might cause the reader to 'ask himself [sic] whether or not the observations took place' (36). Feminist ethnographers might justifiably argue that they transgressed officially sanctioned generic boundaries by smudging the line between truth and fiction long before Watson's suggestion. Of the group of ethnographies about Afghanistan, Mills' study of Herati storytelling adheres most closely to this principle by describing itself as 'a story about some stories' (2). One technique utilized in experimental ethnographies has been to, as Lowenhaupt Tsing puts it, stretch the genre of ethnography beyond its professionally sanctioned perimeters (8). Travel writing has always relied on parallel genres, but Lowenhaupt Tsing's suggestion of strategic 'genre-stretching' makes a useful proposal for further textual disarmament. On an isolated occasion, Kremmer's text engages in this form of 'genre-stretching'. After 'run[ning] aground in the middle of the desert' (345), the narrator loses his temper when the Afghan driver attempts to mend the engine with some glue:

> From the beginning I had hated everything about this driver: his sparse, clumpy beard, his rodent features, his dull leer, and his nose on the wheel.

> My hand was lifting, drawn up by the power of a psychotic urge to batter
> him, when suddenly a loud voice rent the sky above the stranded car.
>> 'Leave him to me!' cried the voice of the Almighty. 'For he is a
> driver, and they are a stiff-necked people.'
>> So I heeded the word of the Lord and let the driver be (346).

It is difficult to exaggerate how exceptional, and therefore how
striking, is this passage, which departs dramatically from the realms of
scientific, even ethnographic, possibility. By so doing, the narrative
risks jettisoning any sense of professional respectability borrowed
from parallel genres, such as ethnography. Temporarily abandoning
his role as a relatively impartial observer providing insight into
'Muslim societies', Kremmer becomes self-evidently unreliable, first
verging on the edge of psychosis, then purporting to receive a divine
revelation. The overt fictionality of this passage invites far-reaching
questions about the narrator's commitment, or indeed ability, to tell
truth.

In his essay 'Travel Writing and Ethnography', Pau Rubies suggests
that by the late twentieth-century travel writers 'seemed to find
themselves in a deep crisis', since '[a]s the encyclopaedia of natural
and human history was being completed and [...] formal empire
shrank, the period following the Second World War generated a new
condition that seriously affected the role of ethnography within travel
writing'. Consequently, the travel writer was deprived of a 'pure,
uncontaminated' tribal subject (in Hulme and Youngs: 259). As Part
Two demonstrates, there is little evidence that the discourses of
ethnography are redundant so far as travel narratives by journalists are
concerned. Journalists have a special attraction to ethnography. In
fact, travel writers who are *not* professional journalists have tended to
write in non-metaphorical ways about kite-flying (Elliot: 449;
Somerville-Large: 48; Levi: 200; Payne: 170), cock-fighting (Byron;
Levi) and even *buzkashi* (Somerville-Large: 117). While
contemporary ethnographers have begun to progress beyond a period
of extended debate over cross-cultural representation, writers such as
Kremmer and Lamb are turning to outmoded ethnographies as a
means of accruing greater, not lesser, authority to their travel
narratives. As increasing numbers of correspondents reporting
Afghanistan turn to travel writing, the need to professionalise the

genre tends to militate against principles of de-authorization. Contemporary travel writing about Afghanistan therefore seems dangerously likely to repeat at least some of the mistakes associated with classical ethnographies. So long as travel writers remain relatively unaffected by ethnography's long-running sense of discursive crisis, their narratives are inevitably complicit (in very specific ways) with some of ethnography's most problematic modes of representation.

Kremmer's and Lamb's texts suggest that there is some relationship between gender and the facilitation of agency for Afghan women, although this relationship is not clear-cut. While both Kremmer and Lamb overwhelmingly privilege male informants, Lamb's access to Afghan women means that many of these encounters are recorded in her account. There is also evidence to suggest that Lamb's narrative does not always assume male agency and female passivity. However, as with *haremlik* literature, it is actual experience (enabled by access to Afghan women), albeit heavily mediated, as much as any sense of personal solidarity with Afghan women that seems most likely to interrogate the narrative of universal female oppression. Divergent gendered positionings also play a role in some of the differences between Kremmer's and Lamb's modes of representation. The assertion of Lamb's narrator that she has a different (female) vision provides some hints as to the possible consequences of women's different relationship to travel. However, this conclusion may be tempered by remembering that, while Kremmer's narrator does not question his right to travel, his narrator is subject to crises of masculinity that cause him to interrogate that which Lamb's narrator characterises as the *Boy's Own* adventure plot.

As I have suggested, it is misleading to privilege gender over other salient factors such as genre and the influence of anterior writings, which (as Parts One and Two have shown) powerfully promote, if they do not determine, particular modes of representation. Neither can subversions of inherited tropes and myths about Afghans be automatically attributed to political intent. This is apparent in Lamb's textual tug-of-war over egg-fighting, where anthropology's in-built theoretical and ideological contradictions manifest themselves in her narrative and undermine the warlike Afghan study.

Again, evidence of textual negotiation creates the possibility that travel writers and journalists alike might gain from attending to the insights of ethnographers wrestling with similar dilemmas of representation. As I have discussed, adhering to particular principles such as providing unedited textual space, curbing narrative supremacy, drawing attention to the limitations of their insight and to the account's unreliability are a means of negotiating the minefields of cross-cultural representation. I have suggested that North's report on Afghan poppy-growing is an example of a report that plays to the strengths of ethnographically-inspired journalism, thereby conveying competing understandings of democracy and choice, Afghan piety and notions of Islamic duty.

Nevertheless, I qualify this note of optimism with the observation that such negotiations leave other, fundamental principles unaddressed, for example, Talal Asad's insistence that 'in order for [cultural] criticism to be responsible, it must always be addressed to someone who can contest it' (in Clifford and Marcus:158). Crucially, too, narratives about Afghanistan are subject to global market forces and, following September 11th, have been increasingly turned to and marketed not as a 'story about some stories', but as sources of insight. In this sense, textual productions such as these accrue particularly heavy responsibilities to be self-reflexive regarding their status as sources of knowledge. Finally, although Kremmer's and Lamb's narratives make no explicit claims to be ethnographic, I have suggested that the counter-influence of classical ethnographies has caused them to inherit its ethical and methodological baggage.

Journalists' attraction to ethnography was equally apparent in news media coverage of Operation Enduring Freedom in 2001. As Hannerz has suggested, both journalists and ethnographers are in the business of reporting exchanges from 'transnational contact zone[s]' (3). It is the parallel nature of these professional activities that partly accounts for the counter-influence of classical ethnographies on contemporary journalism. Other explanations pertain to the pressures on journalists to deliver insight to news audiences, a pressure that only increases the temptation to taking ethnographically-inspired shortcuts to knowledge. This has important ramifications, since it frequently entails adopting 'Afghan culture' as a means of providing the illusion of depth. This has a further advantage, namely providing an escape route from reporting more controversial international dimensions to wars waged in Afghanistan. Recent deployment of the *buzkashi* metaphor was in part a means to this end. Consequently, at critical junctures in news media coverage of Operation Enduring Freedom, anthropological totalisation (Brightman 1995: 517) indeed became journalistic totalisation. Overuse of the explanatory narrative of 'Afghan culture' meant that a causal relation was frequently implied between socio-religious attitudes and Afghanistan's frequent experience of conflict. Bearing in mind the persistent inattention of classical ethnographies to geo-political contexts, it is disappointing that journalists by and large did not venture where ethnographers have failed to tread.

While ethnographic writing has benefited from the insights of interpretative communities whose critiques have made a striking impact on its form and content, journalism and travel writing about Afghanistan have yet to be subjected to sustained critical scrutiny.

Part Three:
Retailing insight: reporting Operation Enduring Freedom.

Travel writing and journalism: a meeting on the road

On the 4 of December 2002, *The Observer* carried an article about Rory Stewart, 'Afghanistan's first post-Taliban trekker'. The article flits between past and present, characterising Stewart as 'fearless[ly]' following 'in the footsteps of [a] Mogul emperor' and describing his journey as 'post-Taliban'. After Operation Enduring Freedom, journalistic and political realities inevitably impinge on 'timeless' travel along the routes of emperors and conquerors of old. As Stewart's own travel narrative *The Places In Between* (2004) illustrates, travel writing about Afghanistan has for the first time become inflected with a profound sense of belatedness. Stewart's preface notes that Afghanistan is 'now' at 'the centre of the world's attention' (x), recognising how his travel account comes not so much after the emperor *Babur*, as after intense media focus on the country during the first phase of the War on Terror. It is not his journey's homage to Babur but its association with the 2001 coalition attack on Afghanistan that stands behind its perceived relevance and newsworthiness.

The inside cover of Stewart's *The Places In Between* notes that he 'walked from Herat across Afghanistan to Kabul via the mountains of Ghor, a route taken five centuries before by the first Mughal Emperor of India, Babur the Great' (29). The walk's relation to earlier journeys is a salient theme of the narrative itself: 'After lunch we walked on. At the outskirts of town, we passed one of the traditional junctions for the Silk Road, where the caravan route turned north to China or south to India' (29). This passage exists in tension with Stewart's consciousness of the impossibility of removing post-9/11 travel narratives from the ideological coordinates of the War on Terror. This awareness is signalled by the rude interruption of his traditional mode of travel on foot by the arrival of a highly significant figure - a journalist:

> I was just beginning to feel that I had left Herat and started on my journey. Then a jeep clattered up and stopped beside us. It was David from the *LA Times*, who had run out of stories and wanted to know if he could interview me (29).

In this encounter with the *LA Times* reporter, two travellers, each journeying at distinct speeds and with apparently dissimilar purposes, find that their paths unexpectedly converge. Each appears in the other's writing as though in acknowledgement of some kinship – albeit mutually suspicious - of genre and purpose. Stewart's narrative thereby dramatises the encounter between parallel genres as his travel narrative takes up a critical commentary on journalistic writing. The meeting on the road develops into a critique of journalism's mode of fast travel (note the clattering jeep), its rushed glances at the world and its infidelities made manifest by the problematic framing of its subjects:

> He asked me whether I didn't think what I was doing was dangerous. I paused. I had never found a way to answer that question without sounding awkward, insincere or ludicrous. 'Surely you can understand', I said, 'the stillness of that man Qasim. The Prussian blue sky – this air. It feels like a gift. Everything,' I said warming to my theme, 'suddenly makes sense. I feel I have been preparing for this all my life.'
>
> But he wrote none of this down [...] 'Have you read *Into the Wild*...that book about the wealthy young American who headed off into the Alaskan Wilderness [...] It's a great piece of journalism' (30).

This attack on the journalist's editorial supremacy (albeit illusory), her or his power to omit what is considered superfluous, voices concerns about the prioritisation of style over substance. Apparently indifferent to its faithlessness, the desired end product of the reporter's encounter with Stewart is 'a great piece of journalism'. In this sense, the travel narrative promises to expand confined journalistic spaces, both literally and metaphorically, with the implied objective of reinserting what news professionals deem unnewsworthy.

Maintaining the focus of this study on established patterns of representation, Part Three edges towards an understanding of travel narratives' potential for combating news priorities and resisting savage editorial processes. As both travellers and war correspondents recognise, Afghanistan's subjection to decades of warfare has led to increasingly narrow purposes of travel so that, in recent years, war correspondents have had a virtual monopoly on British writing about Afghanistan. As travellers such as Danziger (1988) have implied, the sub-genres of travel writing associated with the region (such as 'art-travel') have, one by one, become either ethically or literally unsustainable. This journalistic monopoly should not detract from the paucity of reporting from Afghanistan before Operation Enduring Freedom, which contrasts sharply with the media's concentrated interest in the region throughout the recent military campaign at the end of 2001. Crucially, journalists' long absence required that audiences in Britain be re-familiarised with Afghanistan's geographical, historical, socio-cultural and geo-political terrain. In the stages leading up to the conflict, correspondents with experience of reporting during the Soviet occupation were recruited to re-acquaint British news audiences with the region's military and socio-cultural history. These commentators were occasionally joined by ex-SAS sergeants, academics and even Red Army veterans. However, as I will argue, among the leading agents of the re-familiarisation process were nineteenth-century commentators such as Kipling. Part Three minutely examines that process, concentrating on its key themes, emphases and preoccupations throughout the period of combat.

Reading news media coverage in times of war

As I argued in Parts One and Two, journalism is a transgeneric form[133] that feeds off the parallel genres of ethnography, literary fiction (particularly that of Kipling) and travel writing. Part Three explores this inter-generic dependency and considers its implications. Drawing from evidence provided earlier in the study, I argue that, despite the huge variety in journalistic modes and conventions of news reporting, there are some striking continuities between the British tradition of travel writing about Afghanistan and news media coverage of Operation Enduring Freedom.

The following discussion is based upon UK mainstream television news reports on the ITV early evening news, BBC1's early and late evening news and BBC2's 'Newsnight' programme, although 'Channel Four News' receives occasional mention. Also conducted was an extensive survey of British radio and print media published and produced within the specified period, although some reference is made to news reports and documentaries produced after 2001. The rationale for incorporating radio and news articles into the analysis is threefold. First, though television news is widely consumed, it does not exist in a vacuum. In a spirit of inter-referentiality mirroring the recycling of literary texts outlined in Part One, journalists themselves are heavy consumers of newspapers and radio programmes with relatively small audiences, such as *Radio 4's* 'Today' programme. As radio journalist Celia Udden explains, her punishing schedule, which involves producing two news reports seven days a week, means there are often days when she never leaves the office and instead studies four newspapers, watches television and reads a number of magazines (Hannerz 2004: 210). These practices account for the derivative nature of much reporting; broadcast and print media tend to feed from, and bleed into, one another. Second, as Philo and Berry suggest, monitoring sources that parallel television news is a useful means of mapping the range of differing positions in the public domain (95). Lastly, a multi-faceted approach means that attention can be paid to the relative roles of agency and determinism in news reports on Afghanistan, allowing the work of individual journalists to be traced across different mediums. It also leaves open the possibility of pinpointing those conventions that are most conducive to possible future reworking. Television news reporters such as Lyse Doucet and John Simpson habitually make television documentaries and contribute newspaper articles or reports to radio programmes such as 'From Our Own Correspondent' or 'File on Four'. Newspapers surveyed include *The Independent*, *The Scotsman*, *The Times*, *The Sunday Times* and two tabloids: *The Daily Mail* and *The Mirror*. In addition, my survey of one hundred radio reports from BBC *Radio 4's* programme 'From Our Own Correspondent' allows investigation into the pitfalls and possibilities of a radio programme that is, according to its website description, anthropologically inspired. Finally, a number of recent television documentaries are incorporated into the discussion to establish whether documentaries use radically different techniques to (re)familiarise audiences with Afghanistan.

Central to the ethics of reporting is a consideration of its likely impact, not merely on news audiences but on decisions from grassroots to governmental level. This effect has been called the 'feedback loop' by Jake Lynch, which he defines as follows: '[e]very time journalists report something, it [...] add[s] another layer to the understanding of what is likely to be reported in future [...] That understanding then becomes the basis for governing or influencing people's behaviour'. If, for example, news professionals prioritise violent civil protest, violence is more likely to become a tactic for engaging media attention next time around. Lynch argues that the strategies of governments, organisations and citizens alike are frequently based on 'calculations about how particular facts will be reported – calculations, based, in turn, on an understanding derived from experience of previous reporting.' To illustrate journalists' responsibility regarding their role as inadvertent actors in conflicts such as these, Lynch relates the 'parable of the plastic bottle':

> Once, in industrial economics, the environmental impacts of manufacturing could be set apart as 'externalities'. A maker had only to ensure that, say, a plastic bottle would perform satisfactorily the job for which it was designed. What happened after it left the factory gate, or after the contents were consumed, was none of his responsibility (28).

He suggests that, although the feedback loop cannot be quantified in the way the damage caused by plastics can, news priorities have a definite bearing on future events (2002: www.Reportingtheworld.org). The 2001 attack on the twin towers perfectly illustrates the feedback loop phenomenon because those who launched it fully understood that the attacks' status as a media spectacle was assured from the outset. Indeed, only an act of such enormity could guarantee sustained international news coverage and analysis.

There was some acknowledgement of the feedback loop phenomenon by journalists covering Operation Enduring Freedom. Alan Johnston, reporting on General Dostum, notes how the General arrived with his troops on horseback. Johnston interprets Dostum to be 'orchestrating what amounted to a grandiose photo-opportunity' and he goes on to comment that '[h]is fighters had had some success, and he wanted to make sure that the BBC and the outside world knew about it' ('An Encounter with General Dostum', 'From Our Own Correspondent', Friday 26 October, 2001). Similarly, in BBC2's 'Newsnight' programme, Tim Whewell suggests that the BBC camera crew are presented by Commander Qazl Kabeel, (described as an 'Alliance warlord') with 'a whirlwind tour of photo opportunities [with...] sound bites to match' (15 October 2001). Foregrounding the possibility that the presence of the cameras determines the approaches of key military players such as Dostum and Kabeel may partly be accounted for by journalists' professional fear, expressed here in BBC Controller Stephen Whittle's words, of being 'led by the nose' by parties to the conflict.[134] Nonetheless, both reports clearly consider the possibility of camera-consciousness on the part of strategic actors in the conflict, in this case two Northern Alliance leaders associated with the anti-terror coalition. Other reporters express concerns about the power of media imagery to mobilise support (or not) by rendering scenes of suffering invisible. In a report for BBC1's early evening news, Fergal Keane summarises the worries of aid workers about the absence of television pictures of Afghan refugees:[135] 'There's a feeling that just because the world isn't seeing vast numbers of refugees flocking across the borders, the crisis can't be that acute' (17 October 2001).[136] Keane here adopts a tactic that Lynch himself recommends by alerting news audiences to scenes and people that 'li[e] outside the frame' (101) and pointing to its possible consequences vis-à-vis the international response.

The question of media effects remains a highly contentious one. Greg Philo and Mike Berry argue that, for the majority of the British population, television news 'remains the main source of information on world events'; a survey by the Independent Television Commission of viewing habits found that, in 2002, 79% of the UK population regarded television news as their main source of world news' (200).[137] Moreover, Philo and Berry's own study of British news reports on Israel suggests that television news is a source of public misunderstanding of the basic facts of the Israeli-Palestinian situation. For example, in their main sample of British University students carried out in 2002, only 11% in 2002 knew that the Israelis were occupying Palestine or that the settlers' nationality was Israeli (217). The study concludes that key absences in public knowledge 'very closely parallel the absence of such information on the TV news' (218). Precisely because they are the most popular television channels attracting large audiences,[138] ITV's early evening news and the BBC late evening news form the main focus of interest for television news throughout Part Three.

All-powerful media models have received many critical modifications, however. For the purposes of this discussion, the most relevant critical revision entails rethinking varying levels of audience expertise on the places reported (Hannerz 2004:13). British news audiences may be far more familiar, and thus more 'expert', on cultural and political issues connected to, say, presidential elections in the United States, than those associated with a country like Afghanistan. Media depictions tend to be authoritative in direct proportion to the prominence and availability of alternative sources of information about the region (136), including personal experience (albeit highly mediated) of place, habitual association with its peoples or even consumption of its products. Assuming that public knowledge of the history and geo-politics of Afghanistan is at least no more extensive than that of Israeli-Palestinian relations, it seems highly probable that television news was a central source of information about Afghanistan for the British public during Operation Enduring Freedom.

The days are long gone since academics straightforwardly asserted that news reports tell audiences what to think. 'Hypodermic syringe' models of media effects have long been discarded by theorists unwilling to dismiss audiences' intelligence so readily. Paralleling contemporary thinking on literary texts, neither are scholars prepared to allow that news coverage could ever be univocal. Since Part Three focuses on news content rather than audience consumption, these debates are not rehearsed here. There is broad agreement, however, that television news is successful in setting the agenda for what audiences think *about* (Carruthers 2000: 8).[139] Furthermore, as Susan Carruthers points out, there is 'substantial evidence to suggest that media coverage of foreign events closely follows the interpretative norms offered by political elites', although Daniel Hallin suggests that dissent among those very elites grants the media a degree of autonomy, even in matters of foreign policy where 'state actors have the upper hand in setting and framing the news agenda' (36). Exacerbating this tendency is a striking uniformity (uniformity rather than univocality) of news coverage, which is partly due to the pressure to mimic the coverage of leading news networks. As British journalist Mark Huband protests: 'newsgathering is becoming a cut-throat competition to follow up the same angles as everyone else' (in Lynch:25). Journalists, too, routinely have their agendas set for them. While travel writers struggle to write something 'new', news organisations routinely scramble to follow news leaders.

The following discussion of news media coverage of Operation Enduring Freedom removes itself from the arena of value judgment about 'good' and 'bad' journalists by taking all these variables into account. Emphasising particular news reports as though they proceed from journalists' individual consciences in an unmediated fashion risks overlooking crucial economic, editorial and structural aspects of news production. As Chief Correspondent of 'Channel Four News', Alex Thompson, suggests: 'there's a lot of profit in our industry',[140] while Mark Pedelty suggests that it would be 'politically naïve' to argue otherwise. Pedelty holds that, to 'a significant degree, the ideological content of news texts is representative of the world view of the stockholders, executives, owners and, especially, advertisers who produce, manage and profit from news production' (1995: 6). The first part of Part Three's title, 'retailing insight', therefore acknowledges the extent to which news content is bound up with corporate processes, which are the preconditions for news reporting, production and distribution. Robert W. Chesney notes that, in late capitalist societies, news production has been increasingly 'consolidated into the hands of a very small number of enormous media conglomerates'. Since global news accounts for such a tiny proportion of the income of profit-led conglomerates, the significant down-sizing of the corps of international correspondents has set up a tension between the 'legitimate informational needs' of an informed citizenry and corporate needs for profit (2003: 99). British journalists, too, have noted that journalism's commercial realities increasingly hamper their ability to produce quality international news coverage (McLaughlin 2002: 17).

Over the last ten years, that which Brian McNair has called the 'brutal logic of the free market' (2003: 46) has meant that BBC news programmes have felt the need to battle for ratings with commercial news outlets. Commercialisation of the news environment means that journalists' responsibility to foster understanding tends to buckle under intense pressures imposed by the need for commercial gain or, in the case of the BBC, the need to remain competitive. In such an atmosphere, audiences on both sides of the Atlantic have become increasingly accustomed to 'the two-minute, sound bite culture' of television news that results in what Lynch calls 'abbreviated coverage', whereby surface events are privileged over underlying processes or causes of conflict (2000: 99;13). Indeed, the pressures exerted by technological advances and the likely future prominence of rolling news channels means that the imposition of one or more deadlines a day places intolerable pressure on international correspondents. As a consequence, 'more' becomes 'less' (Carruthers: 204) and news becomes a simplified product for public consumption (DelZotto: 143). While much research about the impact of commercial pressures on news content is based on the experience of the States, a recent gathering of senior British journalists, analysts and news decision-makers concluded that the difference in pressures and outcome between US and British news outlets is a matter of degree rather than of kind (Lynch: 8). Indeed, as Christina Lamb points out in a recent interview (see appendix six), non-specialist correspondents have little time to grapple with the complexities of Afghanistan because they are obliged to rush back to base and file their reports. As I explore later, these pressures increase the temptation to simulate insight by means of shortcuts to 'understanding' often derived from the methodologies of classical ethnographies.

Quality international news is in many ways antithetical to commercial profit. However, to concede this point creates a predicament that is further explored in the conclusion to this section. Correspondents in semi-permanent residence are extremely expensive and area specialists are thus becoming a relative rarity. Both journalists and commentators have expressed concern over the increasing prevalence of non-specialist reporters, or 'parachutist' journalists, who are sent to conflict zones at very short notice. Because archival research and on-the-street newsgathering is so time-consuming, correspondents' background research frequently consists of reading news clippings, often written by other non-specialists (Pedelty: 123). In her book, *In The Hands of the Taliban. Her Extraordinary Story*, Yvonne Ridley describes her last-minute researches the night before she travels to Afghanistan, which consist of 'check[ing] out a few websites' on the Taliban (2001: 83). This sort of haste explains the prevalence of errors in reporting, such as Ridley's own claim that Pashto is 'the [sole] language of Afghanistan' (2001: 27). Indeed, gaffes and factual errors were a common feature of television news reports on Operation Enduring Freedom. In the space of a single news programme, Asia correspondent Adam Mynott called Mazar-e-Sharif 'Mazar-e-Shara' while Herat was called 'Heret' by John Soper (BBC1 *Six O' Clock News*, 8 October 2001). Basic errors continued well into the conflict: even as late as December 2001, BBC correspondent Tim Ewart was referring to Afghan fighters as 'Afghani fighters' (3 December), as was Olive Stromberg, reporting for *ITV*'s late evening news (27 November 2001).[141]

It is impossible to examine media coverage of Operation Enduring Freedom without reflecting on the ethical dilemmas faced by news media professionals with respect to the political fall-out from 9/11. Of course, war correspondents are routinely subjected to intense political as well as commercial pressures. For example, Pedelty observes how reporters in the Salvadorian conflict of the early 1990s were forced to appease the United States Embassy, which correspondents habitually used as their primary source of information. As they explained to Pedelty, the consequences of pursuing reporting activities that angered the Embassy could be grave; simply scrutinising the activities of the US-supported Salvadorian government amounted to a form of professional suicide. As one correspondent remarks: '[b]eing screwed by the Embassy [...] is a big deal because then you don't really get into the press conferences; you don't get the access [...]; you can't get "the Embassy spokesman said such and such"' (on 44). In a chapter headed, 'Discipline and publish', therefore, Pedelty argues that reporting on El Salvador was 'a heavily-controlled practice' (39), whereby the two biggest constraints on correspondents and, paradoxically, on news sources,[142] during the Salvadorian conflict were the Embassy and news editors (85). Pedelty defines this discipline as 'an active, productive, and creative form of power, [a]

more subtle, sophisticated, penetrant, and effective means of control'
than censorship (6), concluding that 'most reporters are neither the
die-for-the-truth adventurists they would have us believe, nor the
lobotomised barflies of solidarity' with official versions of events.
Rather, he suggests, '[t]he truth is more complex, and in certain ways,
more disturbing' (31). Since the media are often depicted by news
professionals as 'one of the four cornerstones of democracy' (Mike
Nicholson in McLaughlin 2002: 14) or 'the eyes and ears of a public
that c[annot] see and hear for themselves' (James W. Carey in Zeliger
and Allan 79 & 80), democratic press models need to be set against
the media's track record of war coverage, which is notoriously
antidemocratic in its sourcing practices. DelZotto's study of news
media coverage of the Kosovan war, for example, found an over-
reliance on 'official' sources (such as government or military sources)
and corresponding under representation of non-state actors of war.[143]

In times of war, journalism comes under exceptional pressure from
governments of liberal democracies not to undermine official
justifications for the conflict. Governmental notions of media
management, delivered through NATO's Public Information
Officers[144], military briefings or press secretaries, are clearly hard for
war correspondents to swallow and yet because liberal democracies
require a degree of public sanction for warfare waged in the name of
citizens, governments are clearly worried by adverse coverage. Patrick
Bishop claims that, during wartime, there is little difference in western
political elites' understanding of the media's role from that of a
dictatorship when rigorous attempts are commonly made to
'transmogrify it into an adjunct of state propaganda' (in Carruthers:
129). Moreover, as Phillip Knightley argues, the British media's best
commercial or political interests lie in supporting the government
when it wages war (2000: 256). Added to this is that which
McLaughlin calls 'the seductive power of military public relations'
(5). Whether or not Bishop exaggerates this situation, recent practices
such as embedding journalists with allied troops in Iraq mean that war
correspondents have an ever-pressing need for professional autonomy
(Tumber and Prentoulis in Kishan Thussu and Freedman: 217).
Indeed, in an inversion of the anthropological taboo against 'going
native', many war correspondents' worst fear is being seen to 'go
official' (Carruthers 2000: 160). Despite this anxiety, overt

governmental interference or state censorship is rarely necessary since, for a number of reasons ranging from patriotism, governmental pressure, fear of losing franchises, access to military news briefings, or of being seen to give terrorists publicity, self-censorship is the norm (Carruthers; Kishan Thussu; Pedelty).

Before I examine British news coverage in detail, it is important to consider dilemmas peculiar to Operation Enduring Freedom itself while bearing in mind their relationship to journalistic predicaments that pre-date this period. To what extent did British news reports collapse, disrupt or support the rhetorical structures associated with Operation Enduring Freedom and how is this related to news organisations' historical response to perceived national and international crises? Mainstream British media have a long history of 'semantic complicity' with official definitions of 'terrorist' and 'counter-terrorist' acts (Carruthers: 193;194). In recent years, for example, journalists have tended to report with the grain of official versions of events by applying labels such as 'weapons of mass destruction' in a unidirectional manner. Throughout the military campaign, BBC and ITV news programmes made habitual and uncritical reference to the 'War on Terror' and the 'anti-terror coalition'. Given Afghanistan's recent political history, this is a disquieting practice. As Derek Gregory suggests, the designation of Afghanistan as a coherent space and, correspondingly, al Qaeda, which was by its nature scattered and various, as being located in Afghanistan was a performative act of 'territorialisation' (2004: 49) to which news professionals might well draw attention. Moreover, Gregory argues, since Afghanistan lacks the standard features of statehood, its designation as a legitimate target suggests 'the continuing fixation of a simple cartographic description in circumstances where sovereignty has to be simulated to render the categories of political action meaningful' (50).[145] News media coverage clearly played a part in what Gregory calls the 'extraordinary accomplishment' of persuading sufficient numbers of people that carpet-bombing Afghanistan was a viable means of capturing Osama bin Laden (50), which was the coalition's stated war aim.

Less obvious is the complicity of British news reports with official shifts in definitions and policy. Treatment of the figure of Hamid

Karzai provides a useful illustration of this phenomenon. Derogatory labels were (and are) routinely applied to key Afghan military leaders, and these were initially applied to Karzai. In November 2001, when Karzai first came to prominence on the international scene, he was described as a 'tribal leader' (BBC early evening news, 11 November 2001 and BBC2, *Newsnight*, 13 November 2001) and, elsewhere, as 'one of four top warlords now carving up Afghanistan between them' (Liz MacKean, BBC 2 'Newsnight', 16 November 2001). Derogatory descriptors were dropped once the news became generally known, by December, of Washington's decision to support Karzai (a decision made four weeks after the bombing campaign began (Rashid 2001: 3)). By December, Karzai was mentioned with increasing deference as 'a Pashtun commander' and a 'Pashtun military leader' (ITV news at 10pm, 5 and 6 December 2001), in a manner that appears to corroborate the theory that coverage of events tends to give greatest credence to the interpretative norms of political elites (Carruthers: 36).

As Pedlety found with reporters in El Salvador, official sources play a significant role in shaping news agendas. He found that reporters relied, in descending order of importance, on the US Embassy, the Salvadorian Government Press Office, opposition radio stations (the Farabundo Marti National Liberation Front), the Armed Forces Press Service and academics from the University of Central America (1995: 7). Of course, exclusive access to key actors of war is commercially and professionally desirable. Keith Morris, for example, boasts without any qualms, that Lyse Doucet's 'unrivalled contacts' meant that they both stayed with Hamid Karzai in the presidential palace (*Radio 4*, 'From Our Own Correspondent', September 7, 2002). However, the influence of official sources on news stories is rarely self-evident. The mechanics of this influence can be understood by quick recourse to two news reports on the night of 27 November, 2001 by BBC1 and ITV's late evening news. On the BBC news, Washington-based Stephen Sackur explains to the news anchor what General Tommy Franks has discussed with journalists that day:

> Well, America's top military commander [...] gave us a fascinating insight today. He said that they had found about forty Taliban and al Qaeda sites where they believe that weapons of mass destruction were being researched and worked upon. Now certain samples have been sent away [...] to

> America for testing. [There's] no confirmation at all of what substances
> have been found but the Americans believe it is distinctly possible that they
> will find evidence of chemical and biological weapons.

This is a textbook example of the overt citation of an official actor of
war, whose claims about 'weapons of mass destruction' are placed in
a relatively positive light (the General has provided an 'insight' rather
than communicated a suspicion). The ITV news report by Mark
Webster is less forthcoming about its sources, however:

> [Camera moves along a row of dusty chemical boxes in a mud-brick room
> with close-up shots of drawings of men on motorbikes attacking cars with
> guns]. American forces are carrying out checks on more than forty sites in
> Afghanistan where chemicals have been found. There are fears the Taliban
> were trying to develop weapons of mass destruction before they fled.
> General Tommy Franks: Chemical, biological or nuclear, we'll perform the
> tests that needs [sic] to be performed.

Although the General's words are included at the end of the report, the
news conference in Washington is not cited as the source of 'fears'
about 'forty sites' for 'develop[ing] weapons of mass destruction'
('WMDs'). This omission makes it more difficult for viewers to
determine the source of the claims as having a vested political interest
in pursuing the theme of 'weapons of mass destruction'. Having said
this, close attention to the apparent visual evidence to support the
'WMD' claim supports counter-interpretations on the part of the
viewer since the hand-drawn pictures clearly depict scenes of low-
level warfare. Visual narratives do not always corroborate spoken
commentaries. Janet E. Steele's study of US news organisations' use
of expert sources during the Persian Gulf War found that the news is
'peopled by well-known individuals or aggregates', 'the "usual
suspects"' drawn from lists of specialists held by programme
producers' (1995: 800 & 801). Steele found that sixty percent of all
'expert' appearances were made by former political players, public
officials and retired military personnel with credentials to support the
contention that these experts are part of a Washington-based power
elite (803 & 804).[146]

Carruthers notes that on-the-spot journalists often rely on reports from
one of the world's four main news agencies or, when reporting live to

the studio, depend on 'lines fed by earpiece from HQ in Atlanta, New York or London' (2000: 204). In a recent Glasgow Royal Television Society debate, Chief Correspondent for Channel Four News, Alex Thompson, responded to the suggestion that more Iraqi voices be incorporated into news reports as follows: 'Iraqi voices? [You] get straight into a taxi [from the airport] to the Palestine hotel, [then you're] stuck on a roof having a report fed through an earpiece' (Wednesday 29 September 2004).[147] As Hannerz argues, therefore, 'barefoot journalism' (the gathering of raw materials) is rarer than is commonly believed (163). Unlike anthropologists working in adjacent fields of cross-cultural representation, 'parachutists' in particular tend to live at a certain remove from local populations. To point this out is not to revive some anti-touristic notion that close contact alone provides the conditions for radically different forms of representation. The experience of travel writers and anthropologists has suggested that projecting a 'view from inside' can actually accrue narrative authority and a corresponding failure to be self-reflexive about the limitations of the insights on offer. However, it seems likely that the jeep-borne, city-based lifestyles of war correspondents, often contrasting so sharply with the daily experiences of local populations living through war, are bound to have some impact on representational practices.

The problem of journalistic isolation from local populations – cultural, psychological and logistical - was particularly acute at the beginning of Operation Enduring Freedom since virtually all correspondents were excluded from the actual site of warfare. As journalists from a coalition country, British reporters found themselves in much the same position as their US counterparts. They were, in Neil Hickley's words, 'denied access to American troops in the field in Afghanistan to a greater degree than in any previous war involving US military forces' (2002: www.cjr.org). As with allied reporting on the Balkans, coverage of Operation Enduring Freedom was characterised by lack of access to the fighting itself (Tumbler and Palmer 2004: 161) including the period after journalists finally entered Afghanistan. It is difficult to exaggerate the significance of these restrictions, which had direct and particular bearing on two facets of the coverage, these being the shifting themes and preoccupations of the reports themselves, and widespread reliance on the history of nineteenth-century Anglo-Afghan encounters as a major context for the conflict.

As I have suggested then, in addition to political and commercial pressures, correspondents reporting Operation Enduring Freedom were faced with grave logistical constraints.[148] Afghanistan had always been considered a tough assignment for war correspondents, who frequently express a sense of hardship over having to rely on mules to carry rucksacks and equipment (Kaplan 2001: 9). As travel writers have long pointed out, the absence of creature comforts means that travel through the region retains many of the difficulties encountered by nineteenth-century travellers. Moreover, as Robert Kaplan explains, Afghanistan presented such difficulties for war correspondents during the Soviet occupation that news professionals actually decided to tune out until the withdrawal in 1989:

> Over a million were killed, but there were no images of epic battles [...] or of mass death [...] There were major battles in Afghanistan, but the only way to get to them on short notice was to fly, which was impossible, since the only people in planes were the Communists. Instead, for nearly a decade the public was shown the same monotonous film clips of smoke billowing in the distance and of bearded, turbaned guerrillas with old rifles sniping at convoys – images that only increased the war's unreality (15).

As if the conditions of reporting were not already challenging enough, from late September 2001, journalists found themselves stranded at the North-West Frontier for six weeks after the fighting had begun (Magder 2003: 40), making the standard closure of television news reports 'This is [...] for [...] reporting from Pakistan, near the Afghan border.' With very few exceptions (notably John Simpson and Yvonne Ridley who each managed to slip into Afghanistan under *burquas*), war correspondents filed reports from Pakistani hotels. Reporters were nevertheless under intense pressure to provide live action – or a sense of live action – and so they reported the humanitarian disaster from refugee camps in Pakistan and attended Taliban press conferences. While the accusation of 'rooftop journalism' (Baker 2003: 245) is often bandied about between commercial rivals, it is nevertheless a fairly accurate description of news coverage throughout September and early October in 2001. Ridley, one of the few journalists to get an early war exclusive, writes rather smugly of television reports issuing from the roofs of the Pearl Continental in Peshawar and The Marriot in Islamabad: 'some journalists became quite inventive in making viewers think that they were in the thick of the action [...] The reality is that many of them never left the rooftops of the hotels and the majority of those with the Northern Alliance were up to seven miles away from the frontlines.' Telling a further anecdote of reporters paying the Northern Alliance '$5 a round to start firing off as the cameras rolled', she concludes: '[t]his was always going to be a war without witnesses' (2003: 249), or, we might add, without British witnesses. While journalists such as Robert Fisk, Christina Lamb and Jake Lynch have problematised the notion that the true action takes place on the battlefield itself, the restrictions had, as I have suggested, a significant impact on news reports' content, most particularly, as I will argue, on the process of (re)familiarisation. Even after journalists finally gained access to Afghanistan, correspondents were generally assigned to Northern Alliance positions or the Bagram airbase, from where John Simpson (BBC) and Julian Manyon (ITV) reported. The sole battle to be filmed was at the fort of Qali-i-Jhangi ('The House of War', Channel Four, 4 July 2002). Indeed, ongoing restrictions on access to the fighting meant that news audiences were treated to the recurring visual motifs of yet more billows of distant smoke, already familiar to older news audiences from the era of the Soviet occupation, and the 'aerial ballet' of overhead jets high above (Julian Manyon, ITV 10pm News, 24 October, 2001).

News reports tend to avoid reporting practical and political impediments to ascertaining key information or even facilitating access to television screens by parties to the conflict. Pedelty and Philo have respectively noted journalists' customary failure to report a stringent government pass system in El Salvador, and the inability of Palestinian representatives to travel to Jerusalem studios because of roadblocks during the 2001 *Intifada* (1995; 2004). This tendency was maintained throughout Operation Enduring Freedom, since this silence was rarely broken.[149] One small exception to this was a report by Julian Manyon, who explains he cannot investigate conflicting claims of casualty numbers by the Northern Alliance and the Taliban in Mazar-e-Sharif, yet he draws attention to his inability to investigate thoroughly: 'Because journalists can't get there we simply don't know which of these are true' (ITV late evening news, 2 February 2001).

Manyon and Tom Bradley, also a correspondent for ITV's late evening news, both refer to 'the refugee crisis that the world hasn't yet been allowed to see' (ITV evening news, 13 November 2001) and 'the great [humanitarian] crisis we cannot see' (27 September, 2001).

The absence of context in British news media coverage of Operation Enduring Freedom

'[In the past, Afghanistan was as] incomprehensible to outsiders as it still is today' (the *Daily Mail*, September 17, 2001).

Daya Kishan Thussu argues that the media have a central role to play in generating 'genuinely democratic' debate whereby an 'informed citizenry' gives its consent to wars fought in its name (2003: 123). However, my investigation of British news coverage of Operation Enduring Freedom corroborates the findings of Philo and Berry's study that news reports are characteristically short on context or explanation for global conflict. Moreover, their study also found that focus groups, composed of regular news audiences, generally felt journalists had a duty to provide more context or explanation than is generally the case (244). At odds with this democratic requirement, or ideal, is news editors' instructions to senior journalists to maximise live action rather than offering contexts that are conducive to some form of explanation (Philo: 2004b). The problem of lack of context is further exacerbated by news values themselves, whereby context and explanation come second to newsworthiness. In other words, for the sake of the story, the *why* and *how* is subordinated to the *who*, *what*, *when* and *where*. Moreover, since temporal sequence gives way to this requirement, news audiences are provided with a further hurdle to understanding (Bell 1999: 241 & 242). The provision of context becomes decreasingly possible in nakedly commercial settings, where journalists are subjected to editorial decisions to 'hea[t] up feeling' by emphasising 'violence, disaster and catastrophe' rather than 'chill[ing]' feeling by providing information. As Jean Seaton suggests, this is intimately related with the need to avoid rocking the 'highly profitable status quo' (in Kishan Thussu and Freedman: 51; Zelizer and Allen 2002: 11).

The Glasgow Media Group has found that omitting relevant background information can have a severe impact on audience understanding. They argue that public misunderstandings about the 2000 *Intifada* are compounded by news reports, where on the rare occasions that explanations for the conflict are proffered, these explanations are given 'in a kind of shorthand assuming some background knowledge' (in Kishan Thussu and Freedman: 136). Pedlety's study of US journalists' reporting on El Salvador also found that journalists tend to produce somewhat 'cryptic texts', which he interprets as 'fulfil[ling] an ideological role by obfuscating important realities of power' (1995: 15). Close analysis of news reports revealed that no clear correlation was drawn between occupiers and settlers, the illegality of the occupation was rarely referred to, and, when transcripts were made of television news reports, of 3,000 lines of transcript, only 17 were classified as explaining the conflict's history (136).[150] Although, as Brian Whitaker points out, Israeli occupation is the clear root-cause of the Israeli-Palestinian conflict, an internet search of 1,669 articles about the West Bank in all of Britain's national dailies published in 2000 revealed that only 49 contained the phrase 'occupied West Bank' and a further 513 mentioned the word 'occupied' or 'occupation' in the text. This meant that 66% of articles somehow wrote about the West Bank without even mentioning the Israeli occupation (Brian Whitaker in Lynch: 34). In the light of these researches it seems important to ask what type of background information news reports of Operation Enduring Freedom offered news audiences to help contextualise the conflict.

It has been claimed, with some justification, that when the Taliban destroyed the Bamiyan Buddhas in March 2001, the British media were rudely awoken from a twelve-year slumber. As Gordon Covera argues, not a great many journalists knew much about Afghanistan at the start of the conflict (in Kishan Thussu and Freedman:255). In both Britain and the United States, initial coverage of Afghanistan after September 11th 2001 consisted of old file-footage, which James W. Carey takes as evidence of television reporters' long absence (2002:77). Although the Taleban's rise provided a focus of attention for the British media between 1996 and 1997, the extent of reporting did not begin to compare with intensive coverage during the 1979 Red Army invasion (Giradet and Watters 1998:49). For most British journalists, then, the destruction of the Bamiyan Buddhas might easily be compared to arriving half way through a film and being asked for an informed opinion.[151] Establishing what has been missed is a complex business. Philo and Berry point out that where 'no single account' of recent social and political history is acceptable to all parties to a conflict – as is the case with Operation Enduring Freedom - the 'balance' principle[152] requires journalists to incorporate as wide a range of competing versions into their reports to avoid two-dimensional reporting of conflict as involving only two opposing parties (2004: 1). Two particularly contentious issues are Afghanistan's strategic importance for powerful nations and the conditions that gave rise to the Taleban, both of which have provoked national and international public debate, generating a range of possible explanations and insights to compete with those offered by the anti-terror coalition. News coverage of Operation Enduring Freedom was resolutely silent about many of these debates despite an abundance of available sources of information: competing histories and theories are even detailed comprehensively in handbooks for journalists, such as Giradet and Watter's 1998 field guide for journalists on Afghanistan, or are easily accessible by internet. Chesney argues that, for fear of controversy, establishment journalism 'tends to avoid contextualisation like the plague'. Nevertheless, despite journalistic anxiety over compromised 'neutrality' (in Zelizer and Allan 2002: 98), there are key areas of contestation that might, in the interests of the variety of 'balance' advocated by Philo and Berry, be expected to provide a relevant context for news reports about Operation Enduring Freedom. There is much to be gained, therefore, by attending to competing material histories of the region, all of which emphasise, to different degrees, a number of important geo-political conditions that foreshadowed the conflict. I briefly dwell on a small number of contested historical and geo-political factors that may or may not have had a bearing on the decision to intervene militarily, before contrasting these with the most common explanations offered by British news media during the 2001 conflict. Drawing this comparison makes it possible to see how the root causes of conflict in Afghanistan are persistently under theorised in British news media coverage.

Analysts such as Hasene Karasac have stated that Operation Enduring Freedom has a strong monetary as well as ideological element. The strategic importance, or not, of the Caspian Sea and the proposed gas pipeline running from Turkistan to Pakistan through Afghanistan has provoked a good deal of debate about the possible ulterior motives underpinning military operations. Karasac argues that international powers are engrossed in a new Great Game,[153] fought not so much over territory but over resources (2002: 18). Proponents of this view note that, at the beginning of the twentieth century, the Caspian Sea, which was opened up after the collapse of the Soviet Union in 1991, produced more than fifty percent of the world's gas and oil. Although there is some dispute over the profitability of extracting Caspian Sea oil and gas, Bulent Gokay notes that it remains a widespread belief among many in the oil industry that it is 'the world's largest reservoir of untapped' energy reserves (2002: 5). Gokay quotes Dick Cheney's comment about the importance of this unexploited resource in 1998: 'I cannot think of a time when we have had a region emerge as suddenly to become as strategically significant as the Caspian' (on 6). The discovery of natural oil and gas in Turkmenistan gave rise to a battle between two oil giants for the right to build the pipeline: the United States corporation, UNOCAL and the Argentinean company, *Bridas*. These companies spent considerable resources appealing to various factions, particularly the Taleban, with whom UNOCAL, Saudi Delta Oil and Turkmenistan signed a $2bn contract in 1996 (Voselsang 2002: 331).[154] Since Iran provided the most logical route for any oil or gas pipeline, the Iranian government interpreted UNOCAL's interest in the route through Afghanistan as a means of dominating its border region (Giradet and Watter: 22). Rashid suggests that the United States backed the Taliban between 1994-6 because they were viewed as anti-Shia and thus complied readily with Washington's prevailing anti-Iranian policy by helping to avoid an Iranian route for the pipeline (2000a: 45-6; 135). Ultimately, Gokay argues for the relevance of these facts to public debate since '[a]t stake in this contest are billions of dollars in oil revenues and the vast geo-political and military advantages that fall to the power[s] which gain a dominant position in the region' (6). China, Japan and the United States have all actively competed for dominance over the pipeline routes, which pass through Afghanistan and the Balkans. Gokay argues that this latter region is key to the competition since any pipeline from Afghanistan to Europe must pass through the Balkans (8). However, although energy security is unlikely to be irrelevant to any US-sponsored project, Karasac draws attention to the complex nature of competing interests in the 'new Great Game'. Commentators have alternately named Turkey and Iran, Turkey and Russia, or the US and either Iran or Turkey as the chief protagonists (18). Arlene Lederman likewise stresses the combined importance of multiple factors: 'the real goal [of Operation Enduring Freedom] was land, access to the oil of Uzbekistan, concealment of a billion-dollar drug business, and progress toward a central independent Pashtunistan that could be annexed to Pakistan' (2002: 55).

As news frame definers, newspapers were generally more likely than television news reports to foreground the Caspian Sea as a relevant context for Operation Enduring Freedom, notably an article by Mark Almond in the *Daily Mail*: 'Today a new Silk Road beckons strong-nerved Western investors. Modern highways and communications are widely touted as the way to open up the region's oil and natural gas deposits which rival those in the Middle East' (September 19, 2001). As I explore in due course, however, nineteenth-century Anglo-Afghan encounters were many times more often provided as a relevant context for newspaper readers. I have yet to discover a single television news report that alludes to the Caspian Sea. Whether it be the constraints of time and space or whether television news professionals were restrained by imperatives not to be controversial, this was not provided as background information for British television news audiences.

Another issue for the region, of debateable importance to Pakistan's past and recent collaboration with the United States over Afghanistan, is that of *Pashtunistan* and the Pakistani government's wariness of Pashtun separatism, which has produced militant attacks either side of the border. The issue dates back to the arbitrary Durand Line, drawn, with what Gregory describes as a 'cavalier flourish' by Sir Mortimer Durand in 1893, splitting Pashtun communities and dividing Pashtun territories between the two countries. Pashtunistan is not of obvious relevance to the United States. However, the intervention of the United States, which increased after the Second World War, drove Afghanistan towards nation-statehood by centralizing Pashtun rule in Kabul (Gregory 2004: 31). During the Soviet Occupation the United States was allied to Pakistan and their separate agendas were highly compatible. This explains how, late in the twentieth century, it was not only Pakistani Pashtuns in leadership positions who backed the Taliban (who were not sympathetic to separatist demands) but the United States itself (Butt 1998: 17). During the struggle against Soviet occupation, funds from the CIA were channelled through the Pakistan Intelligence Services to Afghanistan's most extremist parties because they pursued an Islamicist yet non-Pashtunistan agenda, satisfying Pakistan on the issue of separatism and Saudi Arabia, a major financial backer of the struggle against Soviet invasion[155], in its quest to reassure a restless populace of its commitment to an Islamicist agenda (Gregory 2004: 36). Saudi-Arabia and Pakistan thus collaborated with the United States in its aim of precipitating the downfall of the Soviet Union.

The lack of context in news reports tends to support historically amnesiac political rhetoric about the need for military intervention, especially regarding the extent to which key members of the anti-terror coalition were historically implicated in the rise of the Taleban. Not only was the political fallout and human cost of the ten-year Soviet occupation immense, but Afghanistan was, as Rambo puts it in *Rambo III*, the Soviet Union's 'Vietnam'. His words echo those of President Carter's National Security Advisor, Zbigniew Brzezinsky, who, on the day of the 1979 invasion, said the United States at last had its chance to ensnare the USSR in 'its own Vietnam war' (in Gregory: 35). The occupation of Afghanistan contributed to the Soviet Union's demise and arguably led to the end of the Cold War. Weeda Mansoor expresses bitterness at the way Afghan suffering assisted the strategic interests of more powerful nations, noting that the United States' provision of weapons and funding of training, including training camps, for the *mujaheddin* was tied to political conditions that led inexorably to the Islamicisation of Afghanistan's political landscape (in Mehta 2002: 97). Despite widespread Afghan (including mullah) support for moderate resistance parties, such as the Hazakat Inquilabi-Islami party and the Hizb-e-Islami party, the CIA and ISI[156] gave financial assistance to the more radical opposition parties (Rashid 2000: 84). CIA chief William Casey had in 1986 committed the organisation to the ISI policy of recruiting Muslims worldwide to fight in Afghanistan. After the Cold War, when Taliban fighters were thin on the ground, Pakistani *ulemas* closed down their *madrassas* in the interests of furthering its ambitions to become the Islamic leader of Central Asia, so that students would have no choice but to join the Taleban. Consequently thousands of volunteers arrived from Pakistan because Pakistan had waived all visa requirements (Rashid 2000:53). As many Afghan commentators have pointed out, when questioned about the wisdom of such a policy, Brzezinsky's response was: 'What was more important in the worldview of history? The Taliban or the fall of the Soviet Empire? A few stirred-up Muslims or [...] the end of the Cold War' (in Rashid 2000: 130)?

On the basis of their exposure to British television news reports alone, the absence of this latter context would have made it difficult for news audiences to perceive the absence of deep history in a statement by Tony Blair at the beginning of the conflict: 'there are scores of these terrorist camps in Afghanistan and they have been helped and given succour by the Taliban regime'. The same difficulty applies to Jack Straw's contention that 'the collapse of law and order [...] has caused huge hardship [in Afghanistan]' (Channel Four News, 5 September 2001). Straw's statement over-simplifies the situation to the point of being misleading, omitting the commonest explanation offered by Afghans for their initial welcome of the Taliban as guardians of law and order at a time of extreme social breakdown exacerbated, in centres such as Kabul, by the behaviour of the ruling Northern Alliance in the late 1990s. Moreover, even when Afghan interviewees' comments flagged up the relevance of this context, reports consistently failed to follow them up. For example, at the end of military operations, a report for BBC2's 'Newsnight' programme fails to contextualise a comment by a jubilant Afghan outside a cinema who says: 'I'm happy that we've got our country back from Pakistani domination' (19 November 2001). The comment is left hanging in the air, unexplained and unexplored. So, too, in an article for the *Mirror* on October 1, 2001, the words of radio Kabul presenter Mohammed Omar are left unexplained: 'If you attack us, there will be no difference between you and the Russians [...] Whatever the Americans are facing is the result of their policies' (4). However, as I argue in the conclusion to this section, greater analytical intervention (rather than less) on the part of reporters is not necessarily desirable.

A report for the Washington Institute of Near East Policy, published on 6 April 2000, diagnosed increasing tensions in Afghanistan as proceeding from the 'significant presence of foreigners in Afghanistan', misleadingly known as 'Afghan Arabs'.[157] The report reached a number of conclusions about the causes of unrest:

> Both the Taliban and local civilians are unhappy about U.S. policy toward Afghanistan. Taliban officials complain that the United States keeps Afghanistan weak and divided by always supporting the opposition. One foreign ministry official explained that when communists were in power, the United States supported the factions that later became the United Front; when the United Front took over Kabul, Washington supported the Taliban; now that the Taliban are in Kabul, they allege that the United States is supporting the Northern Alliance. Locals on the street accuse the American government of abandoning Afghanistan after the Soviets left, and blame local hardships on U.S. sanctions even when not related (Rubin and Benjamin 2000: 2).

In a report for ITV's 10pm news, Tim Ewart makes a common, generalised statement: 'in Afghanistan, violence and warfare are never far away' (27 November, 2001), while an article in the *Daily Mail* states that Afghanistan 'was always a wild country, populated by twenty-six million unpredictable and vengeful people' (Ross Benson, 'The City of the Damned', 19 September 2001). The prevalence of such claims highlight the need for the type of context offered by policy reports long in the public domain, such as this one by Rubin and Benjamin. Such reports clearly complicate statements such as Benson's, which is founded on outmoded nineteenth-century notions of Afghanistan.

As Lynch suggests, the absence of context tends to foster essentialised portraits of populations undergoing conflict (2000: 17). News media coverage of Afghanistan frequently implies a relation between Afghanistan's geographical features and its apparent cultural wilderness. This tendency is apparent in the following passage from the *Sunday Times* whereby 'Afghanistan's murderous terrain' is said to 'have helped to make [...Afghans] some of the fiercest fighters in the world' ('Our bloodthirsty friends in the north', 30 September 2001). A feature of British news coverage of Operation Enduring Freedom was persistent inattention to the political consequences of the

Cold War for Afghanistan and a corresponding emphasis on Afghans' cultural and religious predilection for illiberal versions of Islam. However, such emphases do not always go unchallenged. Yvonne Ridley records how she told her Afghan jailor that she judges the country by the quality of its prisons, which, in her words, makes Afghans 'primitive, cruel people'. However, the jailor's reply, which she also includes, resists this charge of barbarity: 'But what do you expect? This is Afghanistan. We have been at war for twenty-two years' (2001: 156).

News coverage that disrupts this line of reasoning tends to take socio-economic or psychological factors into account to produce more nuanced explanations, as with the following explanation offered by Pakistani journalist Ahmed Rashid for the ongoing prevalence of violence in Afghanistan:

> [Many Afghan fighters] were from a generation who had never seen their country at peace [...] They were literally orphans of the war, the rootless and the restless, the jobless and the economically deprived with little self-knowledge. They admired war because it was the only occupation they could possibly adapt to (2000:32).

Rashid's explanation contextualises violence by attending to the significance of war-related poverty and social breakdown. Very rarely, British news reports of Operation Enduring Freedom followed this principle, as can be seen with Ragi Omar's report for BBC1's early evening news, which took into consideration the possible psychological impact of ongoing warfare on the life in Kabul. As the cameras sweep past streets of ruined buildings the commentary runs: 'This is the result of twenty-three years of war [...] a whole generation has grown up here with a total absence of peace, the same generation that makes up nearly all Taliban fighters' (9 November 2001). Omar's report was the exception to the norm, partly because his team very likely took unacceptable risks in getting the pictures but mostly because, as Hannerz argues, 'barefoot' journalism is rarer than might be supposed.

As Gregory observes, British news media coverage tended to maintain a rather vague focus on Afghan micro politics – and, I would add, 'culture' – at the expense of the region's macro political scene (2004). Throughout the military campaign, Afghanistan tended to be depicted as culturally and geo-politically isolated, as 'cut off from the outside' (Kevin Toolis, the *Mirror*, September 15, 2001). Afghanistan's persistent depiction as 'locked in its savage past, cut off from the outside world' (the *Daily Mail*, October 1, 2001) disregards the fact that, as Edward Giradet suggests in a handbook for journalists on Afghanistan, 'no country in the modern era has been the victim of such outright foreign interference by superpowers and its regional neighbours as Afghanistan' (1998: 16). Moreover, my search of the Guardian Unlimited archives carried out on 10 August 2004, reveals that, of a total number of 21,702 articles on Afghanistan in British broadsheets, only 1,091 mention Pakistan or the United States as key players. Instead, the absence of peace in Afghanistan was most commonly plotted within the coordinates of 'culture'. It is this practice that enables Mark Urban to imply that some internal cultural dynamic is to blame for Afghan suspicions about the purpose of Operation Enduring Freedom, placing the responsibility on 'this traditional Afghan distrust of the outsider' (BBC2 'Newsnight', 19 November 2001). Similarly, a report for 'From Our Own Correspondent' entitled 'Talking, Afghan-style' begins: 'If there's one thing – other than fighting – that Afghans are good at, it's talking. Ideally they like to do it sitting cross-legged on threadbare carpets, sipping endless cups of green tea'. Even though the report hearkens back to the crucial context of the Soviet occupation, it is nevertheless able to go against the grain of well-documented evidence of sustained and deliberate policies of superpowers to encourage factionalism: 'Afghans are notoriously disunited. Even the Afghan communists were split into two bitter factions. Their *mujahideen* opponents weren't much better'. The warlike Afghan narrative has a subtle disclaimer attached to it, however:

> It's not that Afghans are particularly quarrelsome by nature. Or even that Afghanistan is composed of dozens of rival tribes, competing clans and startlingly varied ethnic minorities.

> It stems from a fundamental disagreement over what kind of society Afghans want to live in [...] [The] *mujahideen* say that they have learned from their past mistakes – but relinquishing power voluntarily isn't

something that any of them have shown themselves capable of so far
(George Arney, November 30, 2001).

This disclaimer is in many ways negated by the title, which intimates
a cultural reason underlying the absence of peace; the manner in
which Afghans talk. If Afghans are 'disunited', therefore, it is because
they disagree 'over what kind of society' they want. Even so, the
unremarkable disclosure that not all Afghans agree is then linked to a
dichotomous choice: liberal democracy or 'age old' factionalism.
Despite the disclaimer, therefore, its commitment to analysis in the
cultural mode offers little insight into the politics of factionalism but
rather fails to recognise that the form of 'disunit[y]' (as he
characterises it here) is as observable a phenomenon in Britain as in
Afghanistan. Another report for BBC1's 'Ten O' Clock News' by
James Robins on the 27 November 2001 covers the meeting at Bonn
where the interim government was appointed:

> Robins: After twenty-three years of war some real warmth [mid-shot of two
> delegates embracing] as rival Afghans face the challenge of settling disputes
> by talking, not killing. [Mid-shot of delegates talking in a lobby]. Twenty-
> five delegates for twenty-five million people. Four rival groups converging
> around the UN table. [Mid-shot of delegates sitting round a large circular
> table.] Their task: to agree a path towards sharing power for a change.

In this implicit narrative of teaching Afghans to be democratic,
cultural factors ('fac[ing] the challenge of talking, not killing';
'sharing power for a change') are blamed for the long absence of
peace, and the paradoxical study is advanced that the root cause of
Afghan violence is *Afghan violence*. Once again, heavy reliance on
well-established notions of Afghan cultural interiority ensures that
controversy is avoided.

I return, therefore, to the question of how British news audiences were
(re)familiarised with Afghanistan. As critiques of historical analogies
between 9/11 and Pearl Harbour attest, analogies are not always
insightful, and often conceal as much as they purport to reveal. Recent
news reports and documentaries about Afghanistan habitually link the
historically disparate events of the First Anglo-Afghan War and
Operation Enduring Freedom as though they were umbilically
connected.[158] In these cases, as Lugo suggests, historical analogy

becomes 'historical distortion' when two or three unrelated facts are placed in the same paragraph or commentary as though there were a genuine relation between them.[159] Hannerz similarly suggests that, in the absence of obvious explanation, storylines commonly link events in a dubious manner, so as to imply their connectedness (219). Indeed, as Lederman argues, the storyline itself is in many respects a device that allows journalists to simplify complex facts and tackle the problem of multiple realities, grouping 'seemingly random events' so as to 'give them coherence' (in Hannerz: 102). A BBC1 documentary entitled 'Panorama with the Paras' illustrates this phenomenon. Reporter David Lomax trails British paratroopers at the close of Operation Enduring Freedom:

> [Mid-shot of Bala Hisar fortress towering above British troops below].
> Lomax: The British ought to know about Afghanistan from the military adventures here in Victorian times. It was here, in the nineteenth-century, that Afghans massacred British troops.
> [Mid-shot of Sergeant Major talking to his men].
> Sergeant:: 16,000 men, women, children and camp followers [...]
> [Close-up of Victorian painting depicting scenes of terror from the 1842 massacre]
> (24 February 2002).

Following this sequence, Lomax describes the murder of British diplomats just before the retreat from Kabul and offers the following explanation: 'The killers were Afghan troops that had not been paid'. This claim is accompanied by a close-up shot of a painting depicting bloody corpses from the massacre then followed by a question on the same topic addressed to a British soldier: 'If the British were wiped out then by troops who weren't paid, what do you think of the fact that you're next door to, er, troops that haven't been paid [Laughs]'? A customary historical analogy between the two wars thereby slips into historical distortion, splicing together twenty-first century military operations with the 1842 massacre related by the British sergeant to his troops for the cameras. A related distortion occurs when parallels are drawn between the 1840s and the present in the shape of unpaid Afghan troops wreaking revenge whereby commentary and image combine to confirm the dubious analogy. First, the ever-present threat posed by military service in Afghanistan is symbolised by the towering Bala Hisar fortress, filmed from below. Next comes the historical analogy with the 1842 massacre, the credibility of which is strengthened by the impromptu history lesson to troops about their forebears, accompanied by the close-up of a Victorian painting of Afghans killing the British. Analogy becomes distortion with the claim that now, as then, murders of diplomats took place because of unpaid wages. The accompaniment of this information with another close-up of a painting of bloody corpses is misleading, since Alexander Burns and other diplomats were murdered before the massacre in separate incidents and for a variety of well-documented reasons, none pertaining to unpaid wages. However, leaving aside the fact that unpaid wages do not feature in any leading history of the conflict, the documentary's omission of the facts of Afghanistan's invasion by British India's Army of the Indus and the subsequent imposition of the much-vilified Shah Sujah on the Afghan population seems as likely an impediment to viewers' understanding as colonial claims that cow or pig fat was a major root-cause of the sepoys' discontent that spilled over into the 1857 Mutiny, or First War of Indian Independence. It is doubtful whether the historical parallel offers any insight for viewers attempting to understand the situation in 2001; the blurring of historically disparate incidents simply repeats well-established assertions of Afghans' predilection for savage slaughter following relatively little provocation. Furthermore, the documentary's concluding question and summary of the situation (early in 2002) contains a tellingly Victorian phrase: 'How to bring security without being dragged into something from which they cannot escape? Without more international peacekeepers, *the Afghan nightmare* might some day recur' (italics mine). It is my contention, therefore, that allusions to the First Anglo-Afghan war prioritise drama over understanding, ignoring the immediate social and political background to the 2001 conflict, and privileging the voices of Victorian commentators – which are ventriloquised through direct and indirect reference to Victorian paintings and writings on the subject - over those of Afghans on Operation Enduring Freedom's symbolic meanings and implications.

An important consequence of drawing parallels with the First Anglo-Afghan War is that media depictions of the 2001 conflict are infused with nineteenth-century conceptions of warfare, a phenomenon observed by Richard Wright in recent news reports on Eritrea.[160] In fact, news reports on Operation Enduring Freedom tended to consist of two incompatible and competing narratives: sustained focus on the modern machinery of warfare on the one hand, and fascination with early nineteenth-century military encounters on the other. During the 2001 coverage, the obligation to engage with geo-political realities was often negated by a persistent nostalgic return to this (now) less contentious earlier period of history. Despite the apparent wisdom of Robert Fisk's advice to younger colleagues to 'take a history book' (in McLaughlin 2002: 15), therefore, nineteenth-century literary and historical contexts held journalists in as much thrall as their traveller counterparts, causing them to inherit a peculiarly colonial and mythologised sense of Afghanistan as bloodthirsty and unconquerable.

On 23 November 2001, Mark Urban, who clearly took his history book to Afghanistan, produced a report for BBC2's *Newsnight* programme on, as Jeremy Vine introduced it: 'the strange and violent history of Britain's diplomatic presence [in Afghanistan]':

> [Distant shot of mountains at sunset. Soundtrack of Afghan woman singing.]
> Urban: This has always been an untamed land [volume of singing raised], where the gun has often ruled [close-up of antique gun] and where foreigners come at their peril. Now Tony Blair has sent in a new ambassador. [Urban walks through embassy grounds in Kabul]. This place has always been on the wild frontier of diplomacy. During the nineteenth century Kabul was Britain's frontline in the Central Asian Great Game. [Nineteenth-century sketches of Anglo-Afghan fighting. Brass fanfare and military drums.] The British waged three wars here and twice their embassy was overwhelmed with staff killed. [More nineteenth-century sketches then Elizabeth Lady Butler's painting of Dr. William Brydon, 'Remnants of an Army'.]
> Correspondent William Reeve: Historically, at the time of the First Anglo-Afghan war, the British envoy, along with everyone else, just about everybody else, was killed. Ok, that was 160 years ago. More recently at the time of the Second Anglo-Afghan war, the envoy was also killed and, ok, it's modern times, but Afghanistan is always a difficult place. [Photograph of Reeve in 1993]. One thing about Afghanistan is that things are always terribly unpredictable. Things seem calm on the surface and then suddenly...bang! [2 second shot of contemporary Afghan butcher's knife

chopping meat filmed so that the knife comes towards the camera
positioned below.]

Urban [in street]: This is Kabul's appropriately named Butcher Street.
[Close-up shot of bloody goat's head lying in a gutter. Soundtrack from
beginning of the report recommences]. That the lives of this new mission
are in as much danger as those of previous ones is clear. You only have to
think of the remnants of the Al-Qaeda network and what they might do to
see the threat. But Tony Blair, like Lord Curzon in the 1820s, thinks the risk
is worth taking. [Close-up of the British Embassy sign, then gradual close-
up shot of an iron grille through which peeps the eye of an Afghan guard.
Soundtrack ends].

Structurally neat and metaphorically rich though it may be, the report
makes a questionable contribution to audience understanding. Again,
historical analogy becomes historical distortion as past murders of
diplomats, once more divorced from the context of British conquest
and invasion, are mentioned in virtually the same breath as Tony
Blair's decision to send a new ambassador. The sense of ever-present
threat is driven by the nineteenth-century sense of 'peril' at entering
the 'untamed land' by crossing Afghanistan's 'wild frontier'. The
absence of historical explanation for Afghan 'butchery' leads to the
all-too-familiar focus on Afghan violence, conveyed by the shot of the
knife chopping meat. Furthermore, the absence of a relevant historical
context leads to the uncorrected assertion that 'the gun has often
ruled' in Afghanistan because Afghans have been the first to wield
them. The commentary draws continual parallels between past and
present, creating a dubious sense of historical continuity, reinforced
by constant switches between images of past conflict and everyday
scenes on Butcher Street or shots of the Kabul embassy. Moreover,
the descriptor 'always' strengthens a sense of continuity ('always been
an untamed land'; 'always terribly unpredictable') and is symbolically
strengthened by means of cyclical return to the original soundtrack of
Afghan singing. The report is thus caught in the circularity of its own
logic, leading inexorably to the location of violence in the Afghan
psyche, thereby precluding analysis of root causes beyond the
immediate theatre of war. Predicated on nineteenth-century memories
of Afghan-Anglo encounters, and ensnared in its own intellectual
tautology, this report merely offers the illusion of insight: again,
Afghan violence is caused by Afghan violence.

Immediately before the commencement of Operation Enduring Freedom, fossilised notions of Afghan warfare were clearly at odds with twenty-first century military realities, when –incredibly - several newspaper articles actually implied that the impending conflict had an uncertain outcome. On September 22, 2001 the *Daily Mail* ran an article by Anne de Courcy entitled 'Horsemen of the Apocalypse'. De Courcy's article underestimates the scale of change on the military landscape since the First Anglo-Afghan War by referring to the early nineteenth-century defeat as though it were of ongoing military relevance: 'In four days, 17,000 [sic] British men, women and children and their followers were massacred by Afghan tribesmen. As our troops prepare to go in again, we should remember that some of our most humiliating defeats have been in this primitive land' (44). De Courcy's inspiration no doubt comes from Sir John Keay, the nineteenth-century historian of the First Anglo-Afghan War, whose favourite phrase 'wild and turbulent country' is unacknowledged in the article, which then goes on to quote from Lady Florentia Sale's account of the massacre on retreat from Kabul. In the same edition of the paper, Tom Carew similarly casts doubt on the outcome of the present conflict: 'If it comes to a ground war now with British and American troops [...] I believe the Western forces will have a very slim chance of victory' (30). The phenomenon of implying that an equal military contest is taking place is nothing new. Frank Webster points out that, as with the Balkans war of 1999, anxieties were regularly expressed about hardened warriors even though this war, too, entailed little soldier to soldier combat and minimal risk to US and coalition forces.[161]

In *The Irish Times*, a cartoon depicts a UN soldier at the edge of a vast mountain range staring disconsolately at a huge map of a maze labelled AFGHANISTAN beside a signpost offering only three destinations: 'British graveyard', 'Russian graveyard' and 'local graveyard' (http:CartoonWeb.com). As I have suggested, during this period of reporting, news articles, documentaries and television reports frequently contained potted histories of wars fought on Afghan soil that favoured metaphorical simplicity and steered clear of complex recent political histories. Once again, one of the consequences of this approach is the persistent failure, even in the face of the journalists' desire to resist any form of perception management by coalition governments, to examine the implications of that which Shaw calls 'risk transfer militarism', with its 'new distribution of death' and 'small massacres' of local civilians in aid of minimising the political cost of operations such as Operation Enduring Freedom (2002: 346-7). While it seems justified to point out, as political leaders such as Abdul Haq and even Taliban spokespeople have done, that Afghanistan is 'easy to go in [to] but hard to get out [of]' (Doucet 2001: 3), consistent lack of 'balance', in Philo and Berry's sense of the word, leads inexorably to a brand of mythologisation whereby emphasis on an internal cultural dynamic overrides the material facts of geo-political interference while failing to recognise the well-documented relationship between lawlessness and extreme violence, the persistent experience of warfare and prolonged political instability. Depictions of murderous terrain or 'natural guerrilla genius' (Gall 1988: 23) represent a broader failure to address the issues raised by the form of militarism represented by Operation Enduring Freedom or to interrogate, overtly at least, the highly politicised nature of the rhetoric surrounding the War on Terror and the open secret of CIA and ISI intervention in Afghanistan's affairs. To return to Mark Urban's historically-inspired news report from the Kabul embassy and David Lomax's documentary about unpaid and vengeful Afghan soldiers, then, it is clear that peering through nineteenth-century lenses inhibits analysis of the justification for Operation Enduring Freedom and obstructs a serious focus on the ethics of its particular mode of warfare. There are no B42s or guided missiles in Urban's report, only antique guns. These are some of the sacrifices made on the altar of 'great journalism': historical distortion exercises a form of artistic licence that seems likely to impede audience understanding of the conflict's wider contexts. By according greater relevance to the First Anglo-Afghan war than to any other recent contexts of violence or international intervention, therefore, British news reports tended to support many of the rhetorical structures and amnesiac rhetorical justifications for Operation Enduring Freedom. Moreover, the tautological mode of analysis that seeks to explain Afghan violence as instigated by Afghan violence meant that the background to the conflict was persistently under-theorised.

As I have mentioned, news coverage did, of course, make some reference to the massive technological disparity between UN and

Taliban forces, not least because these disparities were so photogenic. An article by James Clark in the *Sunday Times*, tackles the issue in the following manner: 'For several years now, the buzz phrase in defence seminars has been "asymmetric warfare". Simply put, it means the conflict between forces of greatly different type and size: David versus Goliath' (September 31, 2001). Another instance of sustained focus on the mode of warfare entailed can be found in an article for the *Mirror*, which featured Chief of Defence Staff Sir Michael Boyce explaining an aspect of the risk-transfer principle, namely the unlikelihood of a 'massive land invasion by coalition troops' because 'the job of bayonet to bayonet' fighting' would be left to the Northern Alliance (Saturday 27 October 2001: 4). More generally, however, news reports' preoccupation with the sophistication of fighting technologies tends to reinforce a celebratory theory propounded by military and security communities, namely the Revolution in Military Affairs (RMA), which argues that advances in technology and communications have initiated a revolution that allows warfare to be conducted in cleaner and better ways. Proponents of the RMA tend to minimise talk of civilian deaths by discussing 'clinical strikes' and 'collateral damage' (Downey and Murdock in Kishan Thussu and Freedman: 70-73). RMA-fuelled narratives rarely communicate to audiences the realities of risk-transfer, tending to ignore the 'post-heroic'[162] aspects of what Frank Webster has termed 'information warfare', characterised by 'small numbers of professional war operators' who adopt aerial bombing as the main strategy (2003: 60).[163] News reports about Operation Enduring Freedom rarely reflected the 'post-heroic' aspects of this type of warfare. A news report by David Loyn for BBC1's 'Six O' Clock News' depicts the Northern Alliance as 'just spectators as the most powerful air force in the world impose their will with effortless technological superiority', and this commentary is accompanied by images of Alliance soldiers gazing skywards at US jets (31 October 2001). Other reports resolutely cling on to the heroic mode, adopting such phrases as: 'America has put 1,000 of her marines in harm's way tonight. They've been flown into Southern Afghanistan to set up a base within striking distance of the Taleban's last strongholds' (BBC1 early evening news, 26 November 2001). The same applies to Webster's commentary on the same day for ITV's late evening news: 'Until now the forty-nine day concentrated bombing campaign has avoided heavy allied casualties', implying the avoidance of coalition casualties to be a matter of good fortune rather than a relative certainty. Not one of the coalition's military personnel was lost during Operation Enduring Freedom.

Aside from a persistent lack of focus on the ethical implications of such wars, there are important consequences attached to the failure to adapt commentaries and analyses to the specific conditions that give rise to conflict. Given that the 2001 conflict in Afghanistan was generally plotted within the coordinates of 'culture', propounding the warlike Afghan study and deploying pseudo-ethnographic metaphors such as *buzkashi*, it is understandable that news coverage gives rise to what Michael Ignatieff describes as: 'one of the most dangerous cultural moods of our time – the feeling that the world has become too crazy to deserve our serious attention' (in Carruthers: 237). Afghanistan thus joins the list of 'underdeveloped' nations serving as what Carruthers calls 'representative allegories of [...] the New World Disorder' (239), whereby Afghan anarchy is implicitly contrasted with Euro-American[164] sanity. Kenyan Nobel Peace prize-winner Wangari Maathai stresses the importance of understanding that 'hungry people are angry people' (BBC *Radio 4*, 31 December 2004). Indeed, the persistent experience of war-related poverty (and poverty that leads to instability) seems a more useful starting point for contextualising Afghan conflict than assertions of some mythical warlike spirit substantiated by massacre that took place in 1842. Lynch makes a similar point, noting how '[i]nsecurity over basic needs, having enough to eat or shelter to keep warm, or being safe in one's own home drives poor people all over the world into the arms of 'strongmen' or 'warlords', especially if state authorities are so weak as to be unable or unwilling to control private armies' (13). Once again, Lynch notes the likely consequences of covering only surface events, or of assuming that the arena in which conflict takes place and the roots of that conflict are one and the same. In fact, as he suggests, such assumptions merely 'incentivis[e] intervening parties to devise remedies for the symptoms not the cause'. The danger is that when acts of violence are interpreted as random acts of insanity the need to investigate causes is restricted to the search for 'a single mad or bad perpetrator' (14 & 15).

The issue of sustained economic deprivation provided an occasional context for news reports during Operation Enduring Freedom, but these tended not to be explored thoroughly. However, one report produced before the conflict proves the exception to this general rule. In February 2001, a hijacked plane full of Afghans was diverted to London Stansted and the passengers claimed asylum. In a report for 'From Our Own Correspondent' entitled 'I want to be a hostage', Owen Bennet-Jones explores the phenomenon of wanting to be hijacked by ranging beyond the immediate context of events in London Stansted airport:

> It is often said that the world is getting smaller, but after a few days in Kabul, I have come to doubt that cliché.
>
> The gap of understanding between people in different parts of the world seems as great as ever.
>
> Within hours of arriving in Kabul it was clear to me [...] that most rational people would want to leave the city [...] There is no hiding the fact that Kabul is a tough place to live. It has been ruined by years of war.
>
> [...] So what do Afghans make of the hijack? I asked them, and the answer was almost universal.
>
> They wanted to be on board the plane [...] After twenty years of war, the Afghans are no strangers to the possibility of meeting a violent death.
>
> [...] People in Britain just could not believe it. How could anyone want to be the victim of a hijack? It was a cultural gap, and a big one.
>
> How could it be that a classic Western nightmare – being hijacked – is most Afghans' fantasy?
>
> As I struggled to elucidate the attitude of people here in Kabul, the gulf between Britain and Afghanistan seemed almost inexplicable. In some ways, perhaps, the world is just as small as the cliché suggests. People aren't so very different.
>
> Put it like this. I have little doubt that if they were trapped in a city like Kabul, most British people would want to get out as well (BBC *Radio 4*, 12th February 2001).

The anthropologically-inspired remit of 'From Our Own Correspondent' may in part underscore the commentary's apparent embrace of Huntingdonian notions of clashing civilisations and fundamental difference ('[t]he gap of understanding [...] seems as great as ever'). However, the programme's aims perhaps also have some bearing on the way in which the *how* and *why* take precedence over the *what, where* and *when* of most news reports to focus on the context of deprivation and war-related trauma to explain the apparent madness of wishing to be hijacked. Indeed, the report quickly moves beyond assumptions of difference to gesture towards that which James Clifford has called ethnography's 'allegorical project of sameness' (Clifford and Marcus 1986: 101). Though the explanation for the hijacking phenomenon is still plotted within cultural coordinates ('[i]t was a cultural gap', rather than an economic one), the report also testifies to a 'ruined' city and attends to the relevance of the real 'possibility of meeting a violent death' for many Afghans.

Lynch contends that promoting an understanding of conflict as a simple tug-of-war between only two opposing sides (moving either 'their way' or 'our way') rather than as complex and multi-faceted, as is the case with the recent conflict in Afghanistan, has a direct bearing on public understanding, and support for, any resolution proffered by international bodies (40-42). After all, as Anne Penkeith, international news editor of *The Independent* complains, journalists have a tendency to 'define 'peace' [as] a kind of UN-brokered 'solution' which had been applied from Angola to Cambodia' and is characterised by a ceasefire and the formation of a unity government, which has 'a habit of rapidly going wrong' (in Lynch: 46). Other than military intervention, news coverage generally failed to bring alternative solutions into the public domain. Fahima Vorgetts, for example, points out that the economic roots of Afghanistan's troubles are all too apparent since, for example, *madrassas* provide free education and meals in a poor country. She thus suggests non-military solutions such as remedying 'poverty and ignorance' (2002: 100). Furthermore, Riffat Hassan points out that, since, to many Muslims, 'the Qu'ran is the Magna Carta of human rights', promoting secular democracy can be counter-productive, causing some Muslims to 'rais[e] the slogan of "Islam in danger" to rally people behind them'

(2002: 144). There is much to be gained, therefore, by attending to a number of material histories of the region, all of which emphasise, to a different degree, potentially relevant factors that preceded Operation Enduring Freedom.

To summarise, news coverage of the conflict tended to avoid controversial explanations, preferring instead to focus on nineteenth-century contexts of the Anglo-Afghan encounter. Moreover, journalists' versions of the First Anglo-Afghan War themselves almost always omitted the crucial context of British invasion, tending to understand Afghan violence as an irrational and primordial response to the British presence in Afghanistan. Again and again, as with the following example of Mark Urban's claim made to 'Newsnight's' Kirsty Wark about 'traditional Afghan distrust of the outside world' (19th November 2001), the assertion of a fixed cultural trait is cut adrift from the context of resistance to invasion. These silences and omissions explain why Afghanistan seems destined to remain 'as incomprehensible to outsiders [then] as it still is today' (the *Daily Mail*, September 17 2001).

Revisiting Afghanistan: the resurgence of nineteenth-century themes in news media coverage of Afghanistan

Channel Four's documentary 'Here's One We Invaded Earlier' (31 May 2003) opens with a close-up shot of presenter Peter Osborne reading Robert Byron's *The Road to Oxiana*. The image hints at the incestuous relationship between text and screen, illustrating the power of ideas to migrate across genres and eras. This section concentrates on the media's role in (re)familiarising British audiences with Afghanistan's geographical, historical, socio-cultural aspects and (to a lesser extent), its geo-political location.

Despite Zelizer and Allan's contention that, after September the 11, 2001, journalists 'lacked a readymade "script"' to relate subsequent events (2002: 1), the British tradition of writing about Afghanistan means that the reverse is true for coverage during Operation Enduring Freedom. Indeed, there was a range of 'scripts' from which journalists could and did draw. Considerable reliance on prevalent ideas in the parallel genres of ethnography, literary fiction and travel writing is a characteristic feature of British news reports during this reporting period. James Carey points out that the use of old file-footage on Afghanistan revealed quite how long it was since journalists had visited it, necessitating an intensive period of (re)familiarisation with 'unknown cultures in barely known places' (77). In fact, the journalists' long absence had a strong bearing on their choice of sources. There is an important relationship between the lack of substantial recent news coverage on Afghanistan and reliance on much earlier narratives, a relationship best understood in terms of *which* available texts, or bodies of ideas or writing, were consulted to compensate for such neglect. As already noted, of related significance to this question is that, even while logistical and practical considerations led to a paucity of news coverage, almost twenty-five years of warfare had forced anthropologists and travellers to steer clear of the country. As I have argued, in 2001, the lack of recent travel writing and ethnography about the region considerably increased journalists' dependency on textual productions from an earlier period of sustained interest in Afghan-British relations: the nineteenth century. During the initial weeks of Operation Enduring Freedom, journalists consulted writers such as Kipling, Lady Florentia Sale or Sir John Keay as a means of (re)acquainting the public with Britain's historical association with Afghanistan.

There can be little doubt of the nineteenth century's thematic imprint on an article in *The Scotsman* entitled 'The challenge of Afghanistan's House of Warlords', about the recent Afghan elections in 2004. Armed with such frequently borrowed sources as Sir Walter Scott's High Romanticist comparison of Afghans with Scottish Highlanders and the much-cited stanza from Kipling's 'The Young British Soldier', the piece advances well-established warlike and 'unruly' Afghan tropes, reintroducing the British public to old themes of Afghan brutality and terror. I quote from it at some length:

> This is a country for social Darwinism. Here, the survival of the fittest is not biological theory. It is the first law of existence. Afghan Darwinism has produced a wiry, fighting race: men capable of great endurance, as strong in will as in body [...] The tribes throw up warlords, who win their followers' allegiance by a combination of hereditary claim, and prowess in battle. They are best compared to the Scottish clan chiefs in the [M]iddle [A]ges. Over the millennia, conflict and blood feuds have been endemic. If Afghanistan

had a national motto, it ought to be "bellum omnium contra omnes": the war of all against all. The warlords still exercise great power and territorial control. Their tribes have little taste for stability: still less, for foreign rule.

Thus successive imperialists have discovered, from Alexander the Great via the British Raj to the Soviet Union. There are passes through the mountains and plateaux on which cities have been built [...] With sufficient force, they can be captured.

Then the conqueror realises he has marched into a trap. The foes up in the rocks are only waiting for the opportunity to hurl down the mountain's wrath upon him and terminate his brief rule in blood and bones.

> *When you're wounded and left on Afghanistan's plains,*
> *An' the women come to cut up what remains,*
> *Jest roll to your rifle an' blow out your brains,*
> *'An go to your Gawd like a soldier.*

Afghan women had more fun in Kipling's day than they do now [...] the Afghan female is one of the most maltreated beasts of burden in the world.

[...] There are suggestions that the West, and Dr Karzai, are benefiting from war weariness. In the 30 years up to Operation Enduring Freedom, Afghanistan had suffered from constant warfare. It may be that even Afghans eventually tire of killing and being killed (3 July).

Of course, it is inaccurate to claim that social Darwinism is about 'the survival of the fittest'. References to Darwin and to the British Raj, however, are important indicators of the piece's Victorian underpinnings. Accounts of the 1842 British retreat from Kabul obliquely inform the image of Afghan 'foes up in the rocks', a prevalent depiction in nineteenth-century accounts of the retreat, accounts that also inspired Kipling's poem, which conveys the massacre's full horror and establishes the imaginative foundation for substantiating the article's claims of Afghans' thirst for 'killing and being killed'.

The article's inherited notion of Afghan ferocity, an agenda promoted by Kipling's poem, detracts considerably from the fact that, in 2001, coalition military operations were very far from being engaged in an equal contest. In many senses, of course, this was not lost on journalists, since, as I have argued, the stark contrast between first and third world weaponry was of tremendous visual appeal. Nevertheless, despite journalists' self-image as adversarial (Carruthers 2000; Kishan Thussu and Freedman 2003; Pedelty 1995), the article's nineteenth-century historical foundations and associated literary assertions about the Afghan character are implicated in a form of complicity with the perception management of governments heading the anti-terror coalition; as I have suggested, repeated reference to nineteenth-century Anglo-Afghan encounters tends to detract from the uncomfortable military and political realities of Operation Enduring Freedom. This is not to suggest intentional complicity on the part of individual journalists but rather to study the ramifications of their citational practices and historical references. Despite the prevalence of images of Afghan ferocity and unconquerability, Operation Enduring Freedom is a textbook example of what Martin Shaw terms '[r]isk-transfer militarism' (2002). This form of militarism exacts what Shaw calls a 'new distribution of death', whereby the risk of being killed during military operations is transferred from western military personnel to local and civilian populations. This is partly accomplished by using local allies to carry out actual fighting on the ground, as was the case with the Northern Alliance in Afghanistan, although in recent years, 'peacekeeping' forces have had to change their tactics. Of clear public concern here are 'small massacres' of local civilians. Shaw argues that 'small massacres' are "'accidental" in the sense that they are not specifically intended'. Nevertheless, they are 'a completely predictable consequence of the protection provided to Western aircrew [...whereby] reliance on high altitude bombing makes aircrews safe; but [...] inevitably leads to errors of targeting in which hundreds or thousands of civilians die in each campaign.' This enables wars to be waged with minimal human and, by extension, political cost to western powers (2002: 346-7). British news media have a critical role to play in dealing with governments' multiple strategies of perception management in order to query, collapse or disrupt official versions of what such 'risk transfer militarism' entails. As is apparent in *The Scotsman* article, re-working notions of Afghan unconquerability creates a primary focus on Afghans as perpetuators (rather than recipients) of violence, masculinising Afghanistan's population as a warrior race by making repeated reference to the British literary tradition.[165]

Men and women reporting Afghan women

'[D]rag[ing] Afghanistan's brutalised men and invisible, downtrodden women out of the dark ages' (Jonathan Miller, Channel Four website, 2004).

'The brutal Taliban regime [...] makes its women non-people' (David Williams, the *Daily Mail*, 29 September 2001).

The concealment of female bodies under the *burqua* was a major focus of attention for British reporting on Afghan women during Operation Enduring Freedom. The British fixation with the veil has a long history extending to times of colonial expansion and periodically resurfacing in response to migration to the United Kingdom from India, Pakistan and Bangladesh during the twentieth century. This recurrent preoccupation again arose at the beginning of the War on Terror. The enduring currency of the veil as a metonym for oppression has been the subject of many articles and commentaries by women from Asia and the Middle East advising that the garment be situated in its shifting historical, political and social contexts. Indeed, Nadia Wassef argues that the veil represents 'a gross essentialisation of a fabric worn by different women in different ways and in different settings to express different things' (2001: 118). Nevertheless, repeated vilification of the Afghan *burqua* during 2001 suggests how under-theorised was this garment in British public debate.

As recent news media coverage of the *burqua* shows, there is a clear need to complicate British popular understandings of the garment. On 1 October 2001, the *Mirror* carried an article headed by a photograph of a *burqua*-clad woman with a caption reading: '[a] mother in traditional Islamic dress'. This depiction may be criticised on two fronts. Firstly, it peddles what Nirmal Puwar has called 'homogenised, static readings' of the garment (2002: 65) and, secondly, it implies that Islam is, in the words of Nadia Wassef, the ultimate 'explanatory force behind women's lives' (113). One means of combating 'homogenised' readings of the garment is to historicise the *burqua's* origins and to catalogue its changing significance at different historical junctures. The *burqua* made its first appearance in the Ottoman Empire, where it was used as a curtained sedan-chair by upper-class Christian women to denote status and as protection from thieves and dust. From this period, the head-to-toe *burqua* evolved within a Christian context, making its relationship to Islam by no means as straightforward as the *Mirror* caption implies (Lederman: 51). Moreover, the garment has a more complicated relationship to political patriarchy than news media coverage generally allows. As Christine Aziz notes, during the twentieth century, Afghan women have 'slipped in and out' of the *burqua* 'according to the male dictates of the day'. Although Amanullah's rule between 1919 and 1929 was in many ways an emancipatory time for Afghan women, they had to adhere to a strict policy of forcible unveiling (1998: 54). Neither has the *burqua* been a classless garment. For this reason alone, it is important to attend to the huge variety in social position and status between urban and rural women, Hazara, Tajik and Pashtun women[166], and between upper-class women and their maids.

The actions and experiences of Afghan women hardly begin and end with their apparel. As Sahar Saba of the Revolutionary Association of the Women of Afghanistan (RAWA) argues, adopting the *burqua* as a visual symbol of women's oppression proved counterproductive, since it set the parameters of discussion within such narrow confines that some Afghan women actually declared they could even live with the *burqua* if they had the right to pursue their chosen life goals, to receive an education or have access to healthcare. However, despite the complex history of Afghan women's alternate involvement and exclusion from national politics since the early twentieth century, disproportionate news media focus on the *burqua* risks defining women as victims and precluding them as agents of change. Relatively emancipatory times, as Aziz argues, have paradoxically involved a degree of coercion, such as enforced mixed-sex education despite strong local opposition and reprisals during the Soviet invasion. Women have also been central to the armed struggle against, and occasionally for, the Soviet occupation,[167] joining the resistance, enlisting in militia and regular army units, participating in the establishment of mujaheddin organisations and sometimes using explosives and teaching young men how to use them (55-56). More recently, Herati women organised themselves into militias against the

Taliban and set up a university (59). Rashid's *Taliban, Islam, Oil and the New Great Game in Central Asia* notes that Afghan women have 'had as many roles as there were tribes and nationalities', and points to the significant role played by Hazara women both in defensive operations against the Taliban in the Bamiyan district and recounting that the eighty member Central Council of the Hazara *Hizb-e-Wahadat* party had twelve women members (2000: 110 & 69). This sort of information about women was scarce during coverage of Operation Enduring Freedom.

The complex interaction of international politics and gender politics is of central importance to this investigation because it landed journalists in an ethical quagmire. This was because Afghan women and their *burquas* featured so prominently in coalition rhetoric of political and social liberation. Despite the morally compromising alliance between the United States and the Saudi Arabian royal family, coalition leaders understood the political expediency of adopting the *burqua* as a potent metaphor of liberation (Roy: 2002). Correspondents were thus faced with the problem that feminist discourses of liberation were appropriated for the purpose of marketing western liberal secular democracy through military intervention. For commentators such as Krista Hunt, this was nothing less than 'violence cloaked' in women's rights (2002: 119). The events of September 11 saw a sudden surge of interest in women's organisations such as RAWA. As Saba relates, a RAWA film, posted on the association's website, of a woman being executed in Kabul Stadium was offered to media outlets two years previously, including the BBC and CNN, but it was turned down on the grounds that it was too shocking to show to news audiences. After September the 11, however, the Pentagon took the film from the website without permission, and brought it into the public domain to justify military action against Afghanistan.[168]

The pseudo-feminist content of coalition rhetoric depended on an astonishing degree of historical amnesia regarding US support for the Taliban between 1994 and 1996. As Rashid points out, during this period the position of Afghan women was 'conveniently ignored' until Clinton was forced to reverse his policy when he required the help of the feminist lobby to survive the political fall-out from the Lewinsky affair in 1997 (2000: 176).[169] However, as much as being a maternal/paternal quest to save Afghan women from Afghan men (and Muslim women from Muslim men), the *burqua* – or its absence - was thus co-opted as a sign of western freedom as much as Afghan unfreedom (Rogers 2003:206). The apparent feminist turn in coalition liberation rhetoric, then, was not – as Roy points out – because US soldiers were on some 'feminist mission' (2002) but was instead related to the flexing of moral and military muscle with the declared aim of restoring order amid the clamour of 'medieval' Islamic misogyny. Correspondingly, the *burqua's* vilification was intimately related to the self-image of British society as providing an emancipatory environment where women are, as Chandra Talpande Mohanty suggests, 'secular, liberated, and hav[e] control over their own lives' (2001: 481).

There is nothing new about the reduction of women's bodies to battlefields for the moral high ground. Opposing sides readily introduce the subject of women's rights as a means of discrediting the other (Hunt 2002: 120). Forcible veiling and unveiling, in Afghanistan, Egypt, Iran, Turkey and now in France, have long been used as a means of signalling identification with changing models of progress.[170] The coercive nature of forcible unveiling was very rarely touched upon in news reports such as George Arney's for BBC *Radio 4*'s 'From Our Own Correspondent', which notes an historical instance of this phenomenon at work in Afghanistan during the reign of Amanullah: '[i]n a mirror image of Taliban edicts, he forbade women to walk the streets of Kabul unless they were bareheaded' ('Talking, Afghan-style', Friday November 30, 2001). The challenge for journalists in 2001 was not only to interrogate the rhetoric of women's 'honour' as a pretext for violence but to resist – or at least question - the co-option of women's rights for the same purpose (2002: 119). The war in Kosovo had already seen the defence of female 'honour' as a strong component in the rhetoric of nations opposing the UN intervention, such as Cuba, Iran and Pakistan (DelZotto 2002: 146). Another responsibility resting on journalists' shoulders is the way in which the relentless intrusive and voyeuristic gaze of the United States and its allies has been used by Muslim conservatives as justification for curtailing women's freedoms (Fatima Mernissi in Karim H. Karim: 107). Nevertheless, news reports about Afghan women tended to blame Islamic misogyny or medieval conservatism for women's suffering, and this explanation was generally preferred to more nuanced explanations. Connections were not made, for example, between Taliban repression and the fear of being seen as a puppet government of the United States which, as Rashid contends, had a major bearing on the escalating strictness of Taliban policies on women, a policy that became the last outpost of non-compromise and the sustainer of their political morale (2000: 112). Journalists' attention to the Afghan women's 'plight' therefore ran the attendant risk not merely of complying with the coalition's moral and ethical justification for military intervention but of indirect complicity with forms of Islamic conservatism more closely related to a history of foreign domination than images of 'medieval Afghanistan' allow. Fahima Vorgetts suggests that 'fanaticism' be redefined as the forcing of one's views on others, making the point that, during the Soviet occupation, the policy of coercing village women to attend school meant that education became forever associated with 'un-Islamic and anti-Islamic' foreign domination, which was in the end counter-productive for women's rights (2002: 96).[171]

The *burqua's* prominence in the pseudo-feminist discourse of chief political players and their associates exposes a range of contradictions and hypocrisies housed within British public discourse on women's rights. On 19 November 2001, Cherie Booth's high-profile interest in Afghan women was the subject of a number of television news reports, as with the following commentary by the news anchors of ITV's early evening news:

> News anchor one: The Prime-Minister's wife showed today that Mr. Blair isn't the only one in the family working on the problems of Afghanistan.
> News anchor two: *Mrs* Blair gave her support today to a campaign to make sure the country's women get a better deal when a new government is set up. She hosted a meeting of Afghan women at number 10 [Two second mid-shot of unveiled Afghan women in Downing Street] (emphasis hers).

The commentary's implicit characterisation of British women as liberated from the structures of sexual inequality is belied by the fact that a public gesture of solidarity with Afghan women accrues prestige and credibility solely through her association with a man in power: top QC Cherie Booth becomes '*Mrs*. Blair'. The implicit alignment of power with masculinity disturbs the contention, intimated by the pictures of Booth with unveiled Afghan women, that unveiled women automatically have the political leverage to help veiled women 'get a better [political] deal'. Furthermore, implicit in the gathering of the unveiled is the conception of veil-wearers as aspirant unveiled women.[172] Moreover, the prevalence of antifeminist definitions of Afghan women according to their object status, leads to Afghan women being commonly depicted in the possessive mode ('their women'), which underwrites notions of Afghan women as passive victims rather than as active agents of their destiny. As Gloria Steinem observes, women campaigners in the United States had little influence over foreign policy when they opposed their country's support of pre-Taleban[173] elements (2002: 67). Furthermore, Lederman points out that her husband had Afghan women colleagues a full decade before he had female colleagues in the United States (2002: 50), suggesting that British and US critiques of women's position in Afghanistan are driven by men and women's self-constructions as liberators and liberated.

Channel Four News also covered the campaign's launch:

> [Backdrop of two women in blue *burquas*]
> News anchor: Cherie Blair has launched the campaign to help the women of Afghanistan. She wants them to regain the human rights that they've been losing under the strict Taliban regime. Today the Prime Minister's wife held talks with Afghan women in Downing Street explaining how Afghan women had suffered terrible injustices under the Taliban [...] But in Afghanistan, some women say they object to being dictated to by politicians from the West [...] many women in Afghanistan are still wearing the *burqua* [...] it's part of their religion and culture. Many say it's a choice that should be left to them (Zabaida Malik, 19 November 2001).

The report depicts Cherie Blair/Booth as a benevolent and politically mature spokesperson dispensing feminist help and advice to Afghan women. As Talpade Mohanty points out, however, '[a]ssumptions about 'responsibilities'' betray solidarities based on biological identity rather than 'historical and political praxis' (in Wassef 2001: 479). As this campaign illustrates, such solidarities may be more conservative than they appear, offering solutions predicated on a unidirectional model of change whereby Afghan women simply learn to rise above their object status (Talpade Mohanty: 479). Moreover, its second implied solution that Afghan women simply be granted access to power tends to filter out Afghan men and women's collective experience of war-related poverty and its relationship to the actions of powerful nations on whose continued wealth Afghanistan's own fortunes to an extent depend.

In an article about the British fashion industry's enthusiastic embrace of 'Asian chic', Nirmal Puwar points out the inherent contradiction of Cherie Blair/Booth's condemnation of the *burqua* while making frequent public appearances in Asian dress, suggesting 'the power of whiteness to play' and 'grant legitimacy' to 'items it had only yesterday almost literally spat at' (2002: 75). Moreover, the equation of high heels or make-up with Afghan women's liberation seems little more than ethnocentrism parading as cross-cultural female solidarity. Once again, there is an implicit conceptualisation of Islam as the common denominator accounting for Afghan women's oppression (Tapper in Wassef 2001: 113). As Talpade Mohanty implies, alliances predicated on *women* as 'a coherent, already constituted group' are rarely able to straddle the vast social, economic and cultural fault lines that separate the global south from its northern counterpart (2001: 480). Superficial solidarities are apt to disintegrate, though perhaps not so dramatically as when Yvonne Ridley refuses to enter a cell with two Afghan women prisoners sitting cross-legged inside: 'I am not going into that cell. I don't do squalor: I am a British journalist and you cannot treat me like this' (2001: 142). This last statement illustrates power's shifting and context-specific nature since, just as colonial women's alignment with power was implicit in the orders they gave, so does Ridley evoke her rights as a 'British journalist' rather than as a woman.

A further consequence of the broad failure of news commentary to interrogate the self-forgetful premises on which many public displays of solidarity are founded leads to the historically amnesiac implication that 'injustices' committed against Afghan women begin and end with the Taliban and can be swiftly resolved by the Taleban's expulsion. Moreover, it complies with a form of strategic re-historicisation on the part of the anti-terror coalition regarding ways in which key coalition players are implicated in the rise of the Taleban. Again, there is a failure to recognise the political orthodoxies underpinning public displays of feminist Anglo-Afghan solidarity. Nevertheless, if the Channel Four report is somewhat vague about the contexts surrounding the *burqua*, attributing its wearing merely to 'religion and culture', it at least gestures towards the possibility that injustice to Afghan women is no recent phenomenon and has no single or simple origin. Importantly, too, the report bears traces of dissenting voices, mentioning, albeit in a non-specific manner, that Afghan women 'object to being dictated to' and implying, without providing details, that the *burqua* is not to be simplistically linked to Taliban rule but has a longer and more complex association with Afghanistan.

More generally, however, news coverage tended to read the *burqua* as a straightforward metonym for women's oppression under Taliban rule, illustrated by the following report by John Simpson for the BBC1 *Six O' Clock News* towards the end of Operation Enduring Freedom:

> [Close-up shot of an elderly man being shaved.]
> Simpson: Shaving is a way of demonstrating your liberation.
> [Mid-shot of a woman's unveiled face.]
> So is showing your face in public if you're a woman.
>   And there's one more thing. Children can fly kites again. Freedom is in the air.
> [Close-up shot of a kite. Mid-distance shot of a woman in a blue *burqua* walking behind the kite-flyer] (13 November 2001).

Clearly, the presence of a 'post-Taleban' Afghan woman in a *burqua* complicates and undermines both the simplistic narrative of liberation. The same is true of an ITV news report on the same day by Julian Manyon:

> Manyon: But it was women who suffered most from the bigotry of the Taliban who forced them to wear the veil [close-up shot of a woman wearing her *burqua*.] Against the objections of men standing nearby, I asked this woman about life under the Taliban [close-up of interviewee]. They were cruel, she told me. They beat us (Early evening news).

Once again, the objections of the very men who are at that moment celebrating the Taleban's departure and the fact that the woman remains in her *burqua* put paid to Manyon's suggestion that the

Taliban are the source of all 'bigotry'. At least within the commentary's narrow terms, the interviewee does not fit the mould of a newly liberated woman. An interview on the same day with correspondent Kate Clark for the BBC1 'Six O' Clock News' reveals an equally unnuanced understanding of the *burqua*. The commentary runs: 'in a few days' time [...women] will be taking off their *burquas*, uncovering their faces and that will be the most visible sign of the end of Taliban rule here'. The lack of impact of journalists' gender on reporting the *burqua* again suggests male and female journalists' shared investment in preserving their self-image as non-sexist men and liberated women. In the case of this report at least, it is not true that a woman correspondent's access to Afghan women leads to a better understanding. Very occasionally, television news reports problematised notions of 'post-Taleban' liberation, as can be seen with Alex Thompson's report for 'Channel Four News' on the same day: 'But the vast majority of men here, the Northern Alliance included, prefer to keep their beards. Just as many women will still prefer to wear the *burqua*' (13 November 2001). However, suggestive though these comments are, the reasons remain unexplored.

Media interest in the campaign to facilitate Afghan women's access to political power quickly waned; relatively little attention was paid to Afghan women's right to be present at the talks in Bonn, Germany (Hill and Aboitiz 2002: 145). Coverage of the Bonn talks was problematic from this point of view and James Robin's report for BBC1's late evening news suffers from the kind of oversights and omissions that typify that day's coverage of the Bonn talks:

> [Close-up of female Afghan delegate seated at the round table]
> Robins: And one other positive sign: two women at the negotiating table for a change. Afghanistan could emerge from years of suffering as a more inclusive society (27 November 2001).

This represents the report's sole mention of women's presence at the Bonn talks in ways that are fairly representative of celebratory reconstruction stories common towards the end of the military campaign. Moreover, the degree to which the presence of only two women is likely to effect genuine change at a structural level is left unexplored. The recent antifeminist endorsement of legal forms of wife-beating by a female member of the new Iraqi Shia government suggests that structural violence against women is not merely countered by female figureheads.[174] Neither, as Saba points out, has anyone been brought to account in Afghanistan for crimes against women committed between 1992 and the fall of the Taleban.[175] Not only does this erase strong traditions of political participation by Afghan women at various junctures, but it ignores feminist voices calling for more substantial representation by women at Bonn. Even when, in the 2004 election campaign, Channel Four paid some attention to Masouda Jalal's candidacy for the Afghan presidency, the mode in which such coverage is written can be problematic; an article on the Channel Four website by Jonathan Miller represents her campaign as having 'mobilised girl power' ('First Lady', 3 September 2004).

Equally problematic is the construction of Afghan women's liberation as past to western feminism's present, as illustrated by a rather maternalistic statement by Ridley about 'start[ing] a bum-the-burkha [sic] campaign just as women had burned their bras in the sixties' (2001: 105). Aside from the customary reduction of the *burqua* to a symbol of oppression, the statement contains many ironies in the face of unrelenting emphasis in the west on women's social duty to be attractive while commercial markets rapidly expand to target teenage women. The need for women to resist such practices is counselled against by political opposition movements such as the Iranian Council for Resistance.[176] In 2001 more open readings of agency beneath the *burqua* were adopted under two very particular and restricted circumstances. The first was when Afghan women were depicted as would-be western women hiding make-up or high heels under their *burquas*. The second circumstance was when garments were 'donned' in a form of cultural transvesticism, by British female, and occasionally male, correspondents. When Ridley first wears the *burqua* she expresses regret at the way she 'went from being a Western woman in charge of a project to someone who had no significance at all' (2001: 91). However, as with Victorian women travellers such as Lady Wortley Montagu in Turkey, she also recognises the power of being 'invisible' to give her heightened powers of observation (95), a common claim by *burqua*-wearing journalists, a claim that is only rarely extended to *burqua*-wearing

Afghan women. By contrast, focus on the garment's subversive potential for Afghan women tended to be restricted to its ability to conceal make-up or high heels. Once worn by western journalists, the garment does not automatically efface her or his presence but rather tends to liberate an undercover, trickster spirit capable of fooling Taliban border guards, and Afghans in their own market places.

One important consequence of journalists' wearing of the *burqua* is the tension set up between empathetic identification on the one hand, and its power to qualify her or him to speak for and on behalf of Afghan women on the other. This is apparent in Ross Benson's account of wearing the *burqua*:

> I know what it feels like because last time I was here [in Afghanistan], I had to disguise myself as a woman in order to avoid the Soviet border patrols.
>
> I was forbidden to speak because in Afghanistan women are allowed no voice. For several hours my only sight of the world was through the fretwork of my enshrouding *burqua*.
>
> It was a terrible view from the inside of how women were subjugated ('Into the War Zone', the *Daily Mail*, October 1, 2001).

Benson's act of transvestism might be classified as a form of empathetic identification. Even so, when it comes to cross-dressing, acts of identification are rarely straightforward, since they accrue power as readily as they relinquish it. The reasons for this are twofold. Wearing the *burqua* in many senses acts as a verifiable marker of an indigenised 'view from inside' – an 'apparent acquisition of "double consciousness"', leading to a powerful knowledge-claim ('I know what it feels like') (Fowler 2004: 213). It is this position of apparent knowledge and insight that permits Benson to speak. This apparent indigenisation (Goldie 1989: 210), of which cross-dressing is a tangible sign, tends to detract from the asymmetrical power relation – in representational terms - between journalists and the *burqua*-clad women that are the subject of their articles. This is not to deny the existence of empathy. Rather it is to temper over-optimistic readings of cross-dressing by recognising its built-in elements of voyeuristic theatricality, its tangible demonstration of having 'boldly gone where no reader has ever gone before' (Fowler 2004: 213). Empathy, therefore, does not necessarily lead to insight. As is so often the case, Benson's manipulation of the clothing register is not accompanied by self-reflection on the part of the journalist on his article's acts of narrative exclusion. Despite the claim that Afghan women 'are allowed no voice', Benson's account of his 'several hours' as a woman receives absolute primacy, while the implied experiences of his fellow *burqua* wearers are ventriloquised through his commentary.[177]

Caroline Wyatt's report for 'From Our Own Correspondent' points to a common self-image of British journalists as agents of, or advocates for, Afghan women's liberation. This is conveyed by a metaphor of Afghan women as 'silent shadows': 'Their husbands insist they wear the burqua. Not to, they tell me, would bring shame on their family and insults on the streets [...] They give me a last wry smile and then the veil comes down on their faces and the lively women I've spent the day with turn back into silent shadows' ('Afghan women's life in the shadows', Tuesday 16 October 2001). This symbolism clearly pertains not merely to the women's social eclipse but to the power of the correspondent to rescue them from obscurity by bathing them in the light of non-Afghan attention and concern before they slip back once more into Afghan gloom. In this sense the narrative cannot shake off the connotations of Afghan damnation and western (possibly feminist) redemption.

The *voiceless women* claim falls in easily with the myth of universal male dominance and female subordination with little regard to important variations in experience from man to man, woman to woman, region to region and historical moment to historical moment. As Saba argues, Afghan women were 'the first to [...] work for democracy' in Afghanistan.[178] Moreover, coverage of war tends to heighten an already well-established sense of female victimhood. War reporting tends to exacerbate women's portrayal as victims since, as DelZotto found with coverage of Kosovo, women's commentary is sought only within restricted roles denoting passivity: women tend to feature as 'passive refugee[s]' and 'waiting wi[ves]' (where – contrary to all statistical evidence – 'men die and women mourn') (145-146).[179] News professionals' sustained focus on the *burqua* tended to be narrowly confined to the oversimplified and restrictive dichotomy of victimhood and liberation. As Amanda Cornwall and Nancy Lindisfarne point out, however, throughout Central Asia and the Middle East, there is an entire spectrum of male responses to ideals of male honour, a spectrum along which 'many nuanced masculinities are created' and to which women respond differently according to personality, class and a range of political and economic circumstances. Like femininity, masculinity is plural and negotiable (1994: 86 & 10). Moreover, it is subject to all sorts of variable social conditions. As Rashid points out, by contrast with even the most conservative of Pashtuns where male and female relatives mixed relatively freely, segregation was the norm for youthful Taliban brought up in *madrassas*. Indeed, so diverse a nation has never had a 'universal standard' for women's social role (2000: 33 & 110). Nevertheless, Jonathan Miller's characterisation of Afghanistan as a nation composed of 'brutalised men and invisible, downtrodden women' is by no means untypical of news media coverage during 2001 ('First Lady. Elections', Channel Four website, 2004). There was no sustained, internal critique of Afghan women's portrayal as helpless victims. Moreover, Sima Wali calls for journalists to resist demonising Afghan men, pointing out that many have supported Afghan women and advocated their rights. Wali advises that Afghan men also be regarded as part of the solution (2002: 5). President-elect of the Iranian Council for Resistance, Maryam Rajavi even calls for 'male emancipation'.[180]

There is a clear correlation between assumptions of Afghan women's subordination and the exclusion, or muting, of their voices. The commonly applied descriptor 'invisible' is at least as performative as it is descriptive. The danger is that the metaphor of invisibility executes its own form of exclusory agency, providing a pretext for conjuring women off the news scene. This is apparent in Robert Kaplan's claim that Pashtun women 'simply don't exist' to the extent that, after some time as a journalist near the North West Frontier, 'you forg[e]t about Pathan women altogether' (2001: 50). During Operation Enduring Freedom, Afghan women were commonly portrayed as literally unreachable, removed to another century, be it the Middle Ages or 'the dark ages' (Jonathan Miller, Channel Four website, 2004).

While the quest for any single, 'authentic' female Afghan voice is by
definition doomed to failure, I have found that, despite the prominence
of women's liberation in the British news agenda during the 2001
conflict, the prevailing norm of coverage was to deny Afghan women
access to media spaces during Operation Enduring Freedom. The
overwhelming tendency was to exclude them as commentators on
their own 'plight'; for example, I found only two television news
reports where an Afghan woman was asked directly about the *burqua*
('Channel Four News', 13 November 2001; ITV evening news, 13
November 2001). Most markedly, however, Afghan women were
typically excluded as commentators on the conceptual and ethical
premises of Operation Enduring Freedom and the War on Terror.
They were commonly portrayed as 'non-people' (David the *Daily
Mail*, 29 September 2001) or referred to as possessions by female and
male reporters alike ('their women' or 'mere chattels', Kevin Toolis,
The Daily Mirror, September 13 2001). This supports Hannerz's
suggestion that, while women journalists have frequently commented
on the *machismo* of male colleagues, a range of professional
constraints mean that there is often little real difference in outcome
(2004: 94). In the case of reporting on Afghan women, I would also
add that, aside from professional careers, what is at stake in reporting
on Afghan women is British reporters' self-image as neither
oppressors nor oppressed which, I have argued, has a clear bearing on
correspondents' approaches. Ultimately, however, since women make
up sixty percent of Afghanistan's total population and represent one of
the world's highest concentrations of female-headed households, the
practice of privileging minority male voices over the explanatory
narratives of their female counterparts in newspapers, radio and
television news reports alike reveals the profoundly antidemocratic
tendencies of British news coverage during Operation Enduring
Freedom.[181] Celebratory coverage of the Taleban's fall from power
was thus rarely countered by critiques, such as the following by
Waeda Mansoor:

> Yes, music has returned to Kabul. Yes, men are shaving, cinemas are
> reopening, and women can be seen on television. [...But] these [the
> Northern Alliance] are the same people who closed the cinemas, banned
> women from appearing on television, forced women into *burquas*, called
> schools "gateways to hell" and the television a "devil's box" [...] the

Taliban's place has been taken by a group of fundamentalists of a similar, if not the same, mind-set (2002: 82).

Furthermore, during this period of reporting, women's persistent under representation clearly restricted audiences' exposure to, and Afghan women's critical intervention in, the range of viable 'solutions' pursued, whether these be economic, military or social.

There remains a strong ethical imperative to scrutinise exceptional or unrepresentative reporting that disrupts or negotiates representational trends and exclusory practices during Operation Enduring Freedom. Bearing in mind the pressing need for constructive conclusions, it is fruitful to identify those conceptual or methodological features of news coverage that suggest journalists can and do exercise a degree of agency, working creatively and self-reflexively with an eye to the inherent dangers of reporting on Afghan women. The examples set out below typically attempt, at the very least, to foreground the limitations of insight imposed by reporting restrictions such as lack of access to local women, which was a genuine, and persistent, cause of exclusory reporting practices. This led a small proportion of journalists to foreground this absence as a way of acknowledging its significance, as occasionally happened, such as with Sean Langhan's remark in a documentary that his gender represents a serious impediment to understanding since women's experiences are effaced due to his lack of access to them ('Langhan Behind the Lines: Tea with the Taliban', BBC2, 27 February 2001).

Peter Beaumont's article for *The Observer* entitled 'Tyranny of veil is slow to lift' (30 December 2001), is fairly typical in its conception of the *burqua*, which adheres to established tendencies to under historicise and under theorise the garment by overemphasising its Talebanesque association and equating *burqua*-shedding with women's liberation. The opening sentence complies with the metaphorical over-simplification of the article's title: 'Nouria Anwari took off her burqua yesterday [...and now] she will no longer wear the all-encompassing veil the Taliban prescribed for all women' (1). However, because Beaumont gains access to the headquarters of Anwari's organisation, the article's rare inclusion of women's voices allows some attention to be paid to the psychological aspects of shedding *burquas* from three women's points of view. Beaumont's account of the meeting is relatively self-reflexive about the limitations of the 'encounter', conveying a sense of its 'awkward[ness]': 'most of the women are embarrassed to make eye-contact with the male journalists who have intruded on their meeting' (1). In this sense, anxiety is expressed about male journalists' voyeurism, and there is an oblique confession at their attempts to make eye-contact, which 'most of the women' try hard to avoid. The following passage quotes the words of three women interviewees:

> 'If women remove it, men stare at them and the women feel somehow exotic. NO one wants to be the first.'

> It is the same answer that we get from all the women that we interview. They would like to take off the veil, they tell us, but five years of the Taliban make them too self-conscious to do it.

> [...] Rezaye tells us she tried to take off the burqua last week, but felt too intimidated to continue with the experiment [...] 'I took off the burqua and put it in my purse. But then after ten minutes I felt that people were looking at me and I felt too exotic, so I had to put on the burqua again.'

> [...] But [...Wahib] draws a social distinction. 'It is more difficult for women who do not have access to a car to take off the burqua. If you are forced to walk about the city, you feel more exposed' (Sunday, 15 December 2001).

While the article only partly addresses the question it sets out to answer (if the Taliban are gone why are women still wearing their *burquas*?), women's voices nevertheless permeate the article, drawing attention to the psychological experiences of wearing the garment and making distinctions between the experiences of women from differing socio-economic backgrounds.

A radio report for 'From Our Own Correspondent' by Andrew Harding takes Afghan women as its central theme by way of a discussion with some young male Afghans. As Harding describes walking along a path with his male interviewees towards the end of the piece, the commentary draws attention to the 'absent presence' of

Afghan women: 'Almost hidden behind their second floor balcony, three teenage girls watch our progress silently' (Saturday 27 April 2002). It is not that the report's attention to the non-verbal utterances of three teenage girls can be read as a straightforward renunciation of narrative authority. In a similar manner to Mary Kingsley's description of the silent audience at the edge of an African verandah in *Travels in West Africa* ('if you stole out onto the verandah, you would often see it crowded with a silent, black audience listening intently' (77)), Harding conjures the teenagers out of thin air, producing himself – as did Caroline Wyatt - as a keen observer capable of directing the listener's attention to alternative sources for seeking insight into female experiences of life in Afghanistan. In this sense he positions himself at the edge of patriarchal perception, foregrounding his empathy with Afghan women and indicating his desire to mediate between male and female experience. Crucially, however, he does not presume to understand the observing consciousness of the three teenagers, the silent narratives that parallel those spoken, and the existence of these parallel narratives is acknowledged and given priority placement in report's final sentence. He is unable to read or interpret their thoughts yet he does not render them invisible. The report is thus sensitive to notions of untranslateability, suggesting that this seemingly insurmountable problem need not impede good reporting. In the end, foregrounding the limitations of the correspondent's ability to understand is preferable to retailing an illusion of understanding.

Conclusion

The purpose of Part Three has not been to heap blame upon war correspondents but to trace the history of British ideas about Afghanistan right up to the present. This section has explored a range of factors that helped create the preconditions for heavy reliance on well-established notions of Afghanistan. Excluded from the theatre of war, frequently placed at a remove from Afghans (especially Afghan women), and under constant pressure to produce uncontroversial news, reporters commonly resorted to historical analogies with the First Anglo-Afghan War. Such analogies tended to inhibit coverage of a range of late twentieth-century contexts that might have rendered Afghan scenes and settings less incomprehensible to British news audiences or at least, in the words of Hannerz, as 'a little less foreign' (233).

Part Three has contested Zelizer and Allan's contention that journalists 'lacked a readymade "script"' for reporting on Afghanistan. I have instead argued that British ideas about Afghanistan had an important bearing on coverage during Operation Enduring Freedom. In fact the range of 'scripts' from which journalists could and did draw meant that news media coverage was neither informed about contexts, nor particularly informative.[182]

If it seemed to me back on the train in 2001 that 'cultural portraits' were not the province of British news media, it has become apparent during the course of this study that, in 2001, news media professionals frequently drew from well-established notions of Afghan cultural interiority. Commentaries pertaining to 'Afghan culture' often amounted to the sum total of news reports' explanatory content. I have argued in this section that widespread media focus on cultural phenomena was largely the result of intolerable pressures on reporters to retail insight with minimal time for reflection. To what extent, then, can anthropological critiques be legitimately applied to the agents of news media coverage, who operate on radically different timescales to anthropologists? The scope of anthropological theory is decidedly limited in respect to time available for 'self-reflexivity', or even self-reflection. Nevertheless, anthropologists have made invaluable contributions to resolving problems such as excessive interpretative authority. On this last point, foregrounding the fact that the insights of news coverage are necessarily partial may not always be possible, but it seems desirable at least to minimise as far as possible war correspondents' analytical presence. This conclusion has not been widely adopted by critics of news media coverage. Although Philo and Berry have pointed out that the most important implied critique of British coverage during the *Intifada* came from Palestinian interviewees themselves, and while, as they explain, journalists frequently fail to elaborate on the possible meaning of these interviewees' comments, I would argue, as anthropologists have done, that it is *less*, and not more, reporter-centred analysis that stands the best chance of accommodating a range of competing commentaries.

Time constraints do not wholly preclude the substitution of unidirectional commentary with a degree of dialogue and exchange.[183]

Throughout Part Three, reports produced for 'From Our Own Correspondent' have also illustrated the pitfalls and possibilities presented by journalism's anthropological leanings. Ethnography's potential for cultural critique by relativist means has occasionally been exploited in this programme to subvert or disrupt familiar tropes about Afghanistan. This was the case with Kate Clark's report on the 22 September, 2001, which imaginatively transports an Afghan scene to the British social landscape:

> "They're alright aren't they," one journalist said to me, "the Afghans, they're really nice people, very courteous."
>
> What could I say? Afghans have such a savage reputation, these days, in the West [...] I and the other two members of the BBC team sat on a roadside one night, surrounded by luggage – three foreigners in a strange town with a broken-down car.
>
> Every single person who drove or walked by stopped to see if we needed help or wanted a bed for the night.
>
> Unimaginable that a tired group of Afghans might receive the same treatment in Britain.
>
> ('Afghanistan veers towards chaos').

Although the report wrongly implies that the notion of savage Afghans is a recent phenomenon, and while she disregards the relevance to this anecdote of her status as a journalist, Clark here uses a similar device to Elliot's travel narrative, which visualises a group of Nuristani men reading papers in the London Underground and finds no harm in them. In this way, Clark's report intervenes in tropes of savagery, pitching personal experience against expectations that are, as I have argued throughout, fuelled and bolstered by the British tradition of writing about Afghanistan. Leaving aside the problem of positing direct personal experience as an antidote to expectation (as though the latter cancels out the former), her commentary demonstrates the possibility of challenging entrenched modes of representation. Another report for the same programme by Andrew North entitled 'US ambition in Afghanistan' picks up the theme of cross-cultural encounter and adopts a similar strategy by divorcing Afghans from the very cultural and geographical landscapes that are so charged, for the British at least, with traumatic and savage associations. The report features US soldiers distributing gifts to Afghan villagers in south-eastern Afghanistan: 'If I was in the position of those villagers, I would try to get everything I could [...] I tried to imagine it the other way round, Afghan soldiers turning up unannounced at a small town somewhere in the desert of Arizona' ('US ambition in Afghanistan, 22 November 2001). In both reports, then, these analogies pre-empt ready judgements about Afghanistan in the minds of potential news audiences.

As I noted in Part One, travel writers such as Jason Elliot and Rory Stewart have discovered the effectiveness of drawing attention to tropes and representational habits. Elliot details his predecessors' depictions of murderous Nuristanis, and, recalling earlier descriptions of traffic in Herat, Stewart notes that he 'had read five different travel writers on traffic policemen' (21). This foregrounding device will become increasingly useful to travel writers dealing with the problem of belatedness in 'post-Taleban' Afghanistan. Correspondents did not generally use the device during the (re)familiarisation process. Aside from its ethical desirability, however, it might usefully be adopted by journalists as a means of implying that a fresh eye is being cast over (by now) already-familiar news scenes. Irrespective of conscious or unconscious strategy, however, contemporary travel writing has in particular shown that journalists might deploy this tactic as a means of intervening in established patterns. Such a tactic, however, would require training in site-specific awareness for correspondents or else depend on individuals' commitment to be conscientious.

Stewart's roadside encounter with the reporter from the *LA Times* raises important questions about journalism's kinship with travel writing. Travel writing, Stewart implies, has the supreme advantage of 'space', whether this be textual space (a book can literally say more than a newspaper article) or discursive space (travel narratives allow a different quality of experience to be communicated). However, while space is of obvious relevance, 'more space' as a potential solution

does not necessarily reach the heart of the matter. As I hope Part One
has shown, travel writing's spatial leverage has not as yet managed to
counter effectively the powerful narrative drift of British ideas about
Afghanistan. Moreover, television and radio documentaries, which by
definition allow for greater contextualisation and complexity of
analysis, often medievalise Afghanistan or draw on the warlike
Afghan study. Peter Osborne's documentary 'Here's One We Invaded
Earlier', for example, suggests that Herati governor Ismael Khan
provides 'a fascinating sense of what it must have been like to be a
medieval king' (Channel Four, 31 May 2003). Having said this, the
principle of 'more space' clearly assisted documentaries such as John
Simpson's 'Afghanistan – the Dark Ages' (despite its title) to examine
those contexts that his television news reports consistently lacked,
such as the political fallout from the Cold War and the Pentagon's
favouring of extremist groups of fighters and politicians in
Afghanistan ('Panorama', 7 October, 2001). Other documentaries
have provided war as an important context yet shifted their focus to its
aftermath. Documentaries are not under the same pressures as news
media coverage to provide 'live' action and therefore have some
licence to focus on war's causes and socio-psychological effects. For
example, Mike Wooldridge's 'Breaking the Silence: Music in
Afghanistan' (BBC4) follows Afghan musicians back and forth across
the North West Frontier. The musicians detail their efforts to maintain
a strong musical tradition in the face of constant hardship and social
upheaval. A Channel Four documentary, produced by Carla Gara with
Saira Shah, 'Lifting the Veil' (10 November 2002) (again, despite its
title) shows the potential of 'more space' for promoting Afghan
commentaries. 'Lifting the Veil' begins with the now infamous
footage of a woman being executed in Kabul stadium and sets out to
investigate the sequence of events that led to her execution. With the
exception of Tajwar Kakar, the Afghan Minister for women's affairs,
the story is taken up by non-official actors and includes interviews
with six children, two Afghan men and seventeen Afghan women. The
documentary's length indeed facilitates the emergence of conflicting
accounts of the executed woman's act of murder through the voices of
uncles, daughters, neighbours and female prison guards. Importantly
too, Gara and Shah's documentary counters the belief, implicit in
journalists' customary selection of interviewees 'inside' Afghanistan,
that only English-speaking Afghans, or members of the expatriate

community, have anything insightful to say about the country's affairs or its human dramas.[184] In the words of Bruce Williams, the documentary clearly had room to '[j]uggle multiple viewpoints, like the reader of a novel with several unreliable narrators' (in Kishan-Thussu and Freedman: 179). For war correspondents, then, I would suggest that the problem goes deeper than simply this, since it is not merely 'more space' but 'more time' that is required in order to produce quality news coverage of Afghanistan. Since such coverage is antithetical to both commercial profit and prevailing hard news formats, this predicament cannot be resolved overnight by individual journalists.

While Part Three has stressed the importance of attending more closely to the controversial international causes of conflict in Afghanistan, anti-war coverage by independent journalists such as Robert Fisk and John Pilger reproduces many of the representational practices found in mainstream coverage despite its points of ideological divergence. This is the case with Pilger's characteristically polemical documentary entitled 'Breaking the Silence: A Special Report by John Pilger' (ITV, 22 September 2003). Pilger's powerful analytical presence often precludes Afghan commentaries on Operation Enduring Freedom, focusing largely on Afghans' expressions of grief or loss. Likewise, while Fisk's article 'Blood, Tears, Terror and Tragedy' goes against the ideological grain of unidirectional understandings of 'terror', the article's 'dark ages' parallel is nevertheless familiar: 'I [...] wondered at the battle I had watched for twenty years: a swaying host of eighth-century black turbans and, just behind them, the contrails of a B-52 heading in from Diego Garcia. God against technology' (*Counterpunch*, November 26, 2001). Once again a metaphor, that indispensable tool of journalism, produces the customary essentialised reading of the Taliban as a throwback to an earlier century. Despite the implied relation between the 'eighth-century' Taliban and the technology owned by wealthy nations, the neat analytical summary ('God against technology') negates the substance and suggestiveness of such links. Later in the same article, context is sacrificed to a form of poetic licence as he encounters the victims of an attack on a village: 'They came out of a blizzard of sand, these people, each with their story of blood.' The sole context for the utterances of 'these people' (whose stories are conflated into the single phrase 'their story of blood') is the direct violence of a single attack. Independent/mainstream dichotomies can thus prove unhelpful, since more politically conservative productions, such as Sean Langhan's 'Langhan Behind the Lines: Tea With the Taliban' have provided relatively contingent and nuanced readings of the Taliban by focusing on the movement's lack of internal ideological consensus (BBC2, 27 February, 2001). There is no indication that anti-war coverage had a radical impact on correspondents' relationship to the history of British ideas about Afghanistan.

Despite the massive hurdles faced by correspondents, there are, as Lynch argues, a number of 'first principles' that war correspondents may follow (5) in order to close the gap between 'value' in the economic sense and 'value' in the ethical (Pedelty: 277). The ultimate dilemma for correspondents is how to assist audience understanding of complex issues without resorting to gross over-simplification. Lynch suggests that journalists make audiences privy to the questions and confusions necessarily encountered on the road to journalistic discovery (17). Rejecting the two-dimensional model of conflict implied by the 'balance' principle, he calls for journalists to adopt a 'cat's cradle model', whereby the allocation of space to 'many parties with interdependent needs and interests' assists news audiences' assessment of 'the likely consequences of any particular intervention' (56).

Finally, Lynch has suggested that reporters, producers and editors be 'fortif[ied] in overcoming self-censorship and the constraints of consensus and inertia' (5). The problem, for example, of setting Afghanistan in an earlier era might be tackled by means of sustained focus on the interconnectedness of the apparently disparate 'worlds' of twenty-first century Afghanistan and Britain. As Lynch points out, an example of this type of journalism is found in Mark Phillip's report on the recent war in the Democratic Republic of Congo, when he travelled to an area controlled by the forces of the Rally for Congolese Democracy to observe col-tan being mined. Col-tan is a mineral indispensable to the manufacture of electronic equipment such as computer game consoles. The report intersplices images generated by a Sony Playstation with col-tan miners at work with picks and shovels, stressing the interrelatedness of two apparently distinct lifestyles by describing the relationship between the explosion in demand for coltan and the mineral's increase in value to $200 a pound, thereby initiating armed struggles to secure control of the mines (59 - 61).

It is crucial to be realistic about the extent to which news media coverage is capable of delivering self-reflexive portrayals of Afghanistan's multiple and conflicting realities. Nevertheless, focusing on points of cultural, economic and political interconnection gestures towards a form of social critique that raises provocative questions about what it means to be a British news audience consuming media coverage of Afghanistan.

Conclusion:
De-mining the terrain of Afghan-British encounter.

'Landmine use has become ever more indiscriminate, with little central control over deployment, and scant effort made to map or mark minefields, or to clear areas no longer of tactical value' (Timothy Weaver, 'Landmines/Part 1: An Enduring Legacy' in Girardet and Walter 1998: 68)

I cannot now hope to ascertain the knowledge-status accorded Jason Elliot's travel book by the woman on the train back in September, 2001. As it turned out, *An Unexpected Light* is relatively forthcoming about the limits of its interpretative abilities and communicates a degree of ambivalence towards its relationship to the production of knowledge about Afghanistan. Indeed, by foregrounding its own relation to patterns of representation perpetuated by earlier narratives such as Robert Byron's *The Road to Oxiana* and Eric Newby's *A Short Walk in the Hindu Kush*, Elliot's narrative seems at least partly committed to an ethic of de-authorisation. The temptation, therefore, is to let the matter rest with the woman reading quietly to herself in the corner of a train carriage. However, this study has explored the ethical dimensions of travel writing about Afghanistan, which, like any writing, has never been produced in a political vacuum. In late 2001, travel narratives were involved in the process of (re)familiarising the British public with Afghanistan. The act of reading Elliot just days before the coalition forces were due to attack cannot be deemed timeless or innocent. The prominence of this particular travel narrative was not merely evidence of Picador's successful marketing of 'topical' reading material following 11 September 2001. Regardless of this particular reader's political stance towards Operation Enduring Freedom, Elliot's travel book was, at that instant of reading, profoundly implicated in the acquisition of knowledge about a place that had so recently been designated a legitimate target in the War on Terror.

Academic work is routinely judged according to shifting trends and changing currents of thought in the field. In recent years, critics of travel writing, wearying of the apparently tireless (and possibly tiresome) ethical interrogation to which these narratives have been subjected, are instead turning to widespread evidence of experimentation in travel writing past and present. Modernist travellers have become a particular focus of attention since, as has been convincingly argued, travel writing from this period reflects a loss 'of confidence in the western gaze'[185], signalled by an altered attitude to the act of travelling that has possibly had abiding consequences, initiating more 'radical styles of writing' thereafter (Hammond 2003: 184). I have no quarrel with the desire to rescue travel writing from the charge of being always and already unethical. In fact, this scholarly change of tack has generated terms such as 'conventional travel writing' (Youngs 2004: 73), a term implying that travel narratives have the capacity to be less culturally arrogant and less complicit with earlier representations or prevailing political orthodoxies than ethical critiques have hitherto supposed.

Despite its ethnographic leanings, travel writing does not profess to be 'ethnography' and cannot be judged according to anthropological strictures. Nevertheless, Andrew Hammond's contention that modernist narratives provide evidence of a 'self-reflexive turn' in travel writing written during the interwar years (2003: 184) is clearly inspired by anthropological responses to the 'crisis of representation'.[186] This study has drawn attention to a number of dangers associated with ethnography's kinship with both travel writing and journalism, noting the tendency of explanatory metaphors to slip into synecdoche, whereby the whole is emphasised at the expense of multiple, conflicting realities. I have also focused on the way in which Afghanistan's persistent experience of conflict is frequently explained in terms of an internal cultural dynamic.

Given the recent scholarly impetus to attend to innovation and self-reflexivity (or at least to legislate for its possibility) and, given Schiffer's objection to 'fervent ideological loyalties' in studies of travel writing (1), the question arises as to whether a different scholar (probably one without a background in postcolonial studies) might have argued that there has been a 'self-reflexive', or even ethical, turn in travel writing about Afghanistan. My findings so far make me unwilling to concede that there has been anything resembling a 'turn'. There are two main reasons for this. As I have argued, a number of narrative passages contain self-reflexive elements. Only by privileging such instances, however, would it be possible to assert that travel narratives have produced anything like a sustained critique of entrenched British ideas about Afghanistan. The second reason relates to the paucity of narratives produced in recent years. There is not as yet a sufficient body of post-Operation Enduring Freedom narratives about Afghanistan. It therefore remains to be seen whether future travel writing will further the goals of its ethnographic counterpart, which is charged, in the words of Deborah Battaglia, with 'undertak[ing] its own ongoing self-analysis within sight of the dialogic, inherently contingent enterprise' on which it has embarked. Whatever the legacy of nineteenth-century travel narratives about Afghanistan, I would welcome future studies examining the capacity of future travel writing to investigate, *The Places In Between* or, in Battaglia's words, 'the slippages, ambivalences, aporias, and generally speaking, the ambiguities [...] which adhere in its own and others' ideas and practices' (1999: 15).

Scholars are increasingly exploring the capacity of travel narratives to engage in sustained socio-cultural critique. It seems to me that this is an interesting and potentially fruitful line of enquiry. If contemporary ethnography can, as Marcus proclaims, 'break out of generally acknowledged genre constraints' (1998: 36), it follows that travel writing about Afghanistan also has this potential. Even though the legacy of certain generic dependencies and strategies of representation is very weighty, it is no straitjacket. Studies of travel writing by writers such as W.H. Auden (Smith 2004; Youngs 2004) and D.H. Lawrence (Michelucci: 2004) have shown that travel writing is a relatively flexible genre capable of supporting and sustaining experimentation and self-interrogation. Moreover, ethnography's influence, its tutelage even, opens up some encouraging possibilities. There are a number of strategies that anthropologically-inspired travel narratives might further develop and refine in order to contribute to 'situationist, constructivist' understandings (Hannerz: 123) of what it means to travel or to live in Afghanistan. These include strategies to curb or to problematise the traveller's analytical supremacy, to promote Afghan agency by providing unedited textual space for a range of voices (especially female voices), and to draw attention to the account's unreliability or its relationship to earlier narratives.

I would like to add a final word of caution. Irrespective of travel writing's broader potential to support 'self-reflexive turn[s]', the shifting imperatives associated with different modes and purposes of travel have a strong bearing on travel narratives about Afghanistan. The country remains relatively inaccessible to regular travellers. This means that, for some time to come, journalism will remain in the ascendant. As Hulme and Youngs have argued, 'journalists [...] have a deep investment in maintaining their credibility' (2003: 10), and these professional imperatives have tended to intensify, rather than to resist, the pressure brought to bear by the counter-influence of classical ethnographies. The tendency to accrue, rather than problematise, narrative authority, militates against any 'self-reflexive turn'. Ultimately, however, it has not been the purpose of this study to berate travel writers or journalists for producing material that does not conform to new ethnographic directives. Its remit has been to examine the history of British ideas about Afghanistan, which has been traced through its various generic forms at different historical and political junctures.[187] I have shown that, even if these travellers have ceased to travel as 'representatives of Britain' (Hammond 2003: 186), their writing has, in representational terms at least, remained deeply British. Timothy Weaver's description of minefields was chosen as an epigraph because it provides a constructive analogy with contemporary accounts of Anglo-Afghan encounter. It may not be possible to make these minefields safe, yet I hope this study facilitates concerted and informed efforts to map, mark and negotiate them.

Despite the obvious legacy of nineteenth-century Anglo-Afghan encounters to the 2001 news media coverage, this period of intensive media focus has opened up unexpected discursive possibilities. As I have argued, until now, travel writing about Afghanistan has tended to be written in a more corroborative tenor than is generally the case with contemporary narratives of travel simply because the relative paucity of writing about Afghanistan reduces travellers' sense of belatedness, which is not nearly so intense as it is for travellers who write about frequently visited locations such as Greece, Turkey or India. A cause for cautious optimism, therefore, is Britain's first post-Operation Enduring Freedom narrative by Rory Stewart, which registers a keener sense of belatedness than has hitherto been the case. In this respect, Afghanistan may henceforth provide more fertile ground for writers to subvert inherited ideas. Even so, this note of optimism must again be qualified with a reminder that journalists are likely to remain prominent on the travel writing scene for some time to come.

Part Three noted the way in which news media coverage is premised on the need to minimise risk by being uncontroversial. Again, unless they are journalists, travel writers need not minimise controversy and can engage in a form of productive risk-taking. Charles Forsdick has explored how the writing of travellers such as Edouard Glissant entails a very real sense of risk. Forsdick suggests that Glissant repeatedly questions the primacy of his own journey, which is frequently interrupted by competing journeys self-evidently more urgent than his own.[188] Rory Stewart likewise undermines the premises on which his own journey is founded: '[my] sense that I was on an adventure seemed self-indulgent in the context of war' (52). This consciousness of the faultlines dividing bourgeois travel from necessary journeys is nothing new to British travel narratives about Afghanistan; the 'art-travel' sub-genre petered out with much the same ethical question. However, by juxtaposing British journeys with those of Afghans fleeing war and starvation, Stewart casts a retrospective judgement over earlier narratives, hinting at an emerging critique that reflects upon the legitimacy of walks through the Hindu Kush and post-Taliban hikes in the footsteps of Babur.

Since travel writing is so undeniably pleasurable to read, what are the roles and responsibilities of the reader? I make one recommendation with regard to Afghan agency. However faint and mediated their voices, those Afghans who feature in travel writing or indeed news reports about Afghanistan are, as Ong has argued, 'active cultural producers in their own right, whose voices insist on being heard and [who] can make a difference in the way we think about their lives' (in Behar and Gordon: 354).[189] Critical readers might, with some commitment, enter into a form of subversive collaboration with the voiced and unvoiced statements of Afghans, which house a host of conflicting perspectives, claims and counter-claims (Battaglia: 141).

I wish to address one final issue. As I have argued, 'more space' has not as yet led to radical diversions from established British notions of Afghanistan. Nevertheless, I return for one last time to Rory Stewart's roadside encounter with the journalist from the *LA Times*. As I have suggested, this scene makes an implicit claim that travel writing opens up certain discursive possibilities that journalism necessarily shuts down. To an extent, *The Places In Between* testifies to this possibility, allocating occasional textual space to a small number of counter-commentaries that compete with Stewart's construction of his journey's meaning. On one occasion a villager compares Stewart to a twelfth-century traveller: 'I was thinking about you last night, Rory. You are like a medieval walking dervish' (24). This intervention turns the medieval trope inside out by positioning Stewart himself as medieval in a way that captures some of the ironies of 'being modern'. To this Afghan at least, it is baffling that an emissary from a technologically-advanced society prefers to walk when he has, in Afghan terms, access to comfortable means of transport. The inclusion of such remarks increases the possibility of these ironies being suggestively and self-reflexively explored. Stewart later notes how he dresses 'a little ludicrous[ly] in my Afghan clothes' only to see his guard 'wearing neatly pressed camouflage trousers' (27). As I have argued elsewhere, reflections on one's choice of clothing or purpose of travel have the power to generate moments of productive confusion. These moments can temporarily disorientate narrators and readers within the narrative, laying bare the desire to 'become Afghan' and allowing reflection on the assumptions and premises that underpin both the journey and the writing itself (2004:220). Stewart's roadside encounter provides a powerful sense that, for all its representational pitfalls, travel writing about Afghanistan at least provides the opportunity to attend to that which news coverage inevitably leaves out. With time on their side, travel writers can attempt to compensate for journalism's mode of fast travel and its rushed glances at the world. Contemporary anthropological theories about dilemmas of representation cluster around a particular brand of self-reflexivity, stressing the need to explore the ironies of 'mutual entanglements' (Battaglia: 116). Despite the weighty history of British ideas about Afghanistan, Stewart's narrative suggests that these ironies might be suggestively and productively explored.

Endnotes

[1] *The Observer*, 4th December 2002. Note that I have standardised the spelling of 'Taleban'. The original spelling in *The Observer* was 'Taliban'. The former spelling is generally preferred by Afghans.

[2] Dyserinck observes that one of the best example of this longevity related to the French image of Germany throughout the nineteenth and twentieth centuries that could be traced back to Charles de Villiers (2003: 6).

[3] The coinage of this phrase is often wrongly attributed to Rudyard Kipling by British travel writers. Kipling popularised the phrase, using it thirty-six times in his novel *Kim*, but Peter Hopkirk argues that its originator was Captain Arthur Conolly, who used it fifty years earlier (2001: 6 & 7).

[4] Useful decade-specific analyses can be found in Charles Burdett and Derek Duncan's *Cultural Encounters. Travel Writing in the 1930's* (2002).

[5] The inverted commas acknowledge an historical tendency among European travellers to discount the relevance of non-European familiarity with a given region.

[6] I am grateful to Angela Smith for suggesting the term *familiarise* as an apt description for recent representations of Afghanistan.

[7] First published in December 1888 in *The Phantom Rickshaw*.

[8] I am grateful to Stephen Penn for pointing out the disparity between academicised and popular understandings of medieval society. The latter is frequently based on stereotypical notions of a torture-happy society.

[9] See the back cover of the Phoenix 2001 edition of *On Alexander's Track*.

[10] Despite Murphy's Irish nationality, her narrative conforms to many features of the British tradition. I do not wish to narrow the discussion unnecessarily by being overly prescriptive about the boundaries of my classification 'the British tradition', which does not after all exist in isolation from travel writing by travellers from other nations.

[11] By the late twentieth century, women's travel writing had become a strong focus of critical attention. In the academy at least, this resurgence of interest was related to ongoing concerns about women's absence from historical and literary archives. As Sara Mills suggests, the establishment of a substantial body of women's travel narratives was an important means of reclaiming historical periods, especially the Victorian period, for women (1992: 27). As Robert Young also argues, sustained focus on writing by women was partly

driven by the need to produce new feminist histories and theories to re-evaluate women's role in colonialism (2000: 361).

[12] At the forefront of debates over women travellers' relationship to colonialism is Mills' seminal 1992 study entitled *Discourses of Difference*. Also important are the works of Karen R. Lawrence (1988), Jayawardena Kumari (1995) and Indira Ghose (1998), all of whom have written extensively and influentially about the travels of colonial women.

[13] As Mary Maynard suggests in her essay '"Race", Gender, and the Concept of "Difference" in Feminist Thought' (in Juschka 2001: 440) there is an ongoing need to 'challenge the homogeneity previously ascribed' to the category 'female'.

[14] For examples of this type of approach, see Mary Russell (1986) and Mary Morris and Larry O'Connor (1994).

[15] See Linda Anderson 2001: 132 & 133

[16] From the late 1970's, too, women's travel writing had increasingly become a focus of interest for publishers. In the first instance, the re-publication of women's travel writing was spearheaded by Virago, which began its Reprint Library in 1977. The Library is described on the Virago website as being 'dedicated to the celebration of women writers and to the rediscovery and reprinting of their works [that was] hugely guided by the influential *A Literature of their Own* by Elaine Showalter' (www.virago.co.uk/virago/home.asp). In 1982, Virago extended its range, initiating the Travellers Series, which published works by writers such as Isabella Bird (*A Lady's Life in the Rocky Mountains*) and Mary Kingsley (*Travels in West Africa*). More recent initiatives such as the Exploring Travel series for Manchester University Press signal an acute degree of self-reflexivity vis-à-vis the politics of recuperation, particularly regarding the reassessment of women's role in colonialism, since the project of rediscovering lost travel narratives (especially in a celebratory mode as feminist or proto-feminist) becomes easily confused with the desire to achieve positive interpretative closure on women's colonial narratives (see Mills 1992).

[17] As Mills argues, 'gender structures texts in both their production and reception' (1992: 198).

[18] Mills cautions against celebratory approaches to women's travel writing (especially those that adopt a biographical approach) by stressing the point that 'texts are determined by elements other than the author's personal wishes or actions' (1992: 196).

[19] Mills adopts the term 'negotiation' in her 1992 study.

[20] Butler's point was originally made in the context of autobiographical writing by women.

[21] It seems prudent to avoid applying terminology too loosely. Concepts such as *patriarchal imperialism* loom large in analyses of travel writing by colonial women yet the habitual use of such terms might occasionally mislead. I do not wish to deny that, as Elleke Boehmer argues, colonialism is 'usually accurately represented as a male institutional practice, involving the feminization of colonized peoples, the sexual and economic subjugation of native women [...] and the reification of white women as symbols of race purity' (x). However, the overuse of this term risks downplaying the significance of class, ethnicity, race or sexuality to colonial women's travel writing. Furthermore, one has to wonder about the compatibility of words such as *straightforwardly* with either *colonial* or *patriarchal*. Elspeth Probyn observes that personal experience often brings into question the universal applicability of discursive categories such as *patriarchy*. Recalling an incident where her father is chastised by a park-keeper for picking bluebells in the park with his daughter, she argues that personal stories often contradict the 'generalized account of the centrality of the father's role within the family and culture' (Probyn in Anderson 2001: 112).

[22] The unstable nature of imperialist discourse has been attributed to a whole host of factors. Critics sometimes speak of colonial anxiety, or imperialism's unease with itself. As Ghose argues, 'power is inextricably coupled with a sense of its own precariousness' since power's corollary is 'anxiety about the instability of power' (160 & 161). Homi Bhabha speaks of the 'deep psychic uncertainty of the colonial relation itself, its split representations stag[ing] the division of body and soul that enacts the artifice of identity, a division that cuts across the fragile skin - black and white - of individual and social authority.' (1990:44) Other explanations pertain to colonial fears that its authority is never total or complete. Ghose observes how 'colonial rule was frequently haunted by a sense of insecurity, terrified by the unknown, the unknowable, by the obscurity of 'the native mentality', overwhelmed by the natives' apparent intractability in the face of government' (15). In 1902, the historian J.A. Hobson famously defined imperialism as being 'based on a persistent misrepresentation of the facts and forces chiefly through a refined process of selection, exaggeration, and attenuation, directed by interested clichés and persons so as to distort the face of history' (in Boehmer xxiii). Instability, then, is the inevitable consequence of persistent imperial distortions and misrepresentations that fly in the face of multiple, competing realities. Indeed, travel writing embodies the tension between ideological misrepresentations and colonizers' actual experience. This tension provokes 'a kind of despair' because 'the space and social entity of the colony [...] were constantly untrue' to imperial representations of it (Nicolas Thomas in Mills 1992: 119). Further tensions derive from ways in which imperial rhetoric was, as Boehmer argues, 'ceaselessly [...] unsettled by

countervailing perceptions and impulses' (xvii). This latter point is taken up in this study, where I examine the tension between textually mediated expectations about Afghanistan and actual lived experience of that place.
[23] *The Bookseller of Kabul* is ethnographic in flavour. Sierstad has since been held to account by the man (to whom she gives the pseudonym 'Sultan') whose household she lived in while writing the book, which features her experiences of living in his family home. In an article entitled 'Bookseller of Kabul: She said, he said', web logger 'Kevin' quotes *The New York Times* on the plans of 'Sultan' (whose actual name is Shah Mohammed Rais) to sue Sierstad's publisher:

> [S]hortly before the book's publication in Britain, a set of the English-language galleys reached the bookseller, Shah Mohammed Rais. Outraged by what he said were lies, distortions and dangerous indiscretions, he flew to Oslo last month to denounce Ms. Seierstad and to prepare a lawsuit against her and her publisher, Cappelen (The book will be published in the United States on Wednesday by Little, Brown).
>
> [...] Mr. Rais said that when he read *The Bookseller of Kabul* he was 'terribly, terribly' shocked. 'There were lots of misrepresentations of me, my family and my country,' he said from Frankfurt. 'She did not understand who I am. The host for her, I very kindly accepted her, I gave my hospitality to her, without any contract, without any financial expectation, without anything. She doesn't understand how shameful it is to write such things on paper.'

Mr Rais sought libel action against the publisher and announced his intention to take a share in profits from the book.
[24] As pointed out in Part Two, Laura Ahearn notes that agency need not be intentional and cannot always be attributed to deliberate strategy. John Simpson's news report about the bombing campaign is a case in point. Although his commentary states that the UN bomb-targeting is effectively 'leaving the Afghans alone', a later mention of cluster bombs at the end of the report casts doubt on the claim that Afghan civilians will not be maimed or killed (BBC1 *The Six O' Clock News*, 23 October, 2001).
[25] I found five television news reports for BBC1 and ITV that featured women correspondents. The correspondents were Lindsey Hillsen, Catherine Marston, Liz McKean, Jackie Rowland and Caroline Wyatt. Rowland and Wyatt also produced reports on Afghanistan for BBC *Radio 4*'s 'From Our Own Correspondent'.

[26] In Internet discussions, Shah has repeatedly expressed a belief that her documentary was co-opted by political elites as moral justification for attacking Afghanistan in 2001.

[27] Belief in the gendered nature of journalistic productions is not confined to journalists. In his review of Lamb's *The Sewing Circles of Herat*, Paul Clammer states that the book is 'enlivened by a rare female perspective' (2004), although he neither defines a 'female perspective' nor specifies what it offers.

[28] Access to Afghan women was not always a serious impediment to 'balanced' news coverage by male reporters. As Rashid points out, in the mid-1990's, reporters could talk to women in the streets, shops or in offices (2000: 109).

[29] For more on this shift see Michael Cronin 'The Empire Talks Back: Orality, Heteronomy and the Cultural Turn in Interpreting Studies' in *Translation and Power* edited by Maria Tymoczko 2002.

[30] Lyall's phrase is not theorised as an originary source here, but as the most likely source.

[31] That is, by the British.

[32] Lord Salisbury, letter to Edward B. Lytton, Governor General of India 1876-1880 (in Heathcote 1980: 91). Salisbury was referring to those politicians who backed the Masterly Inactivity Policy towards Afghanistan and who were not in favour of a second military intervention. Salisbury terms this group of politicians 'men who in their youth have seen the Afghan ghost and have never lost the impression'.

[33] 'Mutiny' is the most familiar term used to describe the events surrounding the siege of Lucknow. Historians have subsequently pointed out that the name implies that the fighting resulted from religious grievances over cow and pig fat used to grease the Lee-Enfield rifle. Alternative names have been offered as a means of connecting the events of 1857 to India's conquest and colonisation together with its associated cultural and religious oppression. The 'Mutiny' has thus also been termed 'The First War of Indian Independence', 'The Sepoy War, or Insurgency, of 1857' and the 'Sepoy Rebellion'. See Jain (ed) 1998, *Indian Mutiny of 1857: An Annotated and Illustrated Bibliography*.

[34] As a 16 year-old schoolboy Kipling proposed the following resolution: 'That in the opinion of this Society, the advance of the Russians in Central Asia is hostile to the British Power' (Wilson 1979: 69).

[35] The aim of Britain's 1839 invasion of Afghanistan was, according to T.A. Heathcote, 'not so much to keep the Russians out [of Afghanistan] but to let the British in, and to install a British puppet', Shah Shujah, whom Afghans had previously rejected at Kabul in place of Amir Dost Mohammed. Capable and popular though Dost Mohammed was, negotiations for British control of

Afghan foreign policy had broken down over the issue of Peshawar, which was then ruled by British India's ally Ranjit Singh, which Dost Mohammed wished to be restored to Afghanistan (1980: 209). The British did not wish to jeopardise nearly 30 years of treaty with Ranjit Singh, ruler of the then-independent Punjab (Macrory 2002b: xiv). Though Dost Mohammed had for some time been willing to negotiate with the British, he was deposed to make way for the ever-unpopular Shah Shujah. As a result of the deposition, Dost Mohammed's son refused exile in India with his father and instead remained to wreak revenge on the retreating army. The 1838 Simla Manifesto promised the Army's withdrawal from Afghanistan once Shah Shujah was established on the throne, but it became quickly apparent that the detested Shah could not survive without substantial military support and so cantonments were established at Kabul (Macrory 2002a: xvi). (The full title of the Simla Manifesto was 'Declaration on the Part of the Right Honourable Governor-General of India' and it was published on 1st October. As Macrory explains, the Manifesto was an attempt by Lord Auckland and his advisors to persuade the British public of the need to invade Afghanistan (2002a: 78)).

The cantonments' design and location contributed to a number of key military defeats and were later condemned by serving officers. Lieutenant Vincent Eyre later wrote: 'it must remain a wonder that any government, or any officer or set of officers, should in a half-conquered country fix their forces in so extraordinary and injudicious a military position' (Eyre in Macrory 2002b: xvii). Moreover, a series of misjudgements were made by key players in the War, such as General Elphinstone and Sir William MacNaughten, Chief Secretary of the Calcutta Government, who consistently underestimated the strength of Afghan resistance to the British occupation. Another mistake was to trust and meet Dost Mohammed's son, Akbar Khan, at the height of anti-British tensions, which led to MacNaughten's death, allegedly at Khan's own hands. Perhaps the most serious of MacNaughten's mistakes was to send for his wife and family and to encourage the sepoys to do the same. This drastically increased the number of civilian deaths during the 1842 retreat. Furthermore, a change from the Whigs to the Tories in Britain meant that the new government came under pressure from the British public to curtail the occupation's escalating costs by making expenditure cuts that were instrumental in the army's downfall. A payment of £8,000, traditionally made each year by Afghan rulers to the Ghilzyes (who controlled the mountain passes along the main trade routes) to ensure travellers' safe passage through mountain passes, was halved. The Ghilzyes responded by blocking the most direct route to India from Kabul through Jelalabad and the Khyber. Further problems related to excessive baggage, animals and servants that encumbered the invading British Army of the Indus on its advance and, more fatally still, upon its retreat. One brigadier took 60 camels to carry his personal belongings, while General Keane was reported to have as many as 260 for himself and his staff (Macrory 2002a: 86). As Kipling later explored in his poem '8 Ooonts', the 30,000 camels brought by the British to Afghanistan represented a major mistake since camels from the Indian plains could not adapt to the mountainous conditions of Afghanistan and 20,000 camels were therefore lost en route (Heathcote 1980:33; Macrory 2002a:87). In addition, Baluchi robbers managed to carry off huge amounts of baggage and cattle (Macrory 2002a:90) and, on 6th January, 1842, the first day of the retreat, Lady Florentia Sale recorded that 'the origin of [that...] day's misfortunes [...] involved the loss of nearly all the baggage and the greater part of the commissariat stores' at a footbridge (96).

[36] Moreover, as Bart Moore-Gilbert points out, *Kim* depicts the border as a site of perpetual warfare, reinforcing the sense of the sheer force required to maintain British India's hegemony (1996:120) and hinting at the constant danger posed by Afghanistan's unpacified state.

[37] I refer to Marquis Richard Wellesley's warning against occupying a land of 'rocks, sands, deserts, ice and snow' (in Keay 1951: 363).

[38] The painting was originally entitled 'The Remnants of An Army'. It is readily viewable on the web. The popular title heightens the painting's dramatic effect yet is historically misleading since some Indian sepoys survived the massacre.

[39] I am grateful to James Procter for making this point.

[40] While Kafirstan is commonly translated as 'land of the unbelievers', I am indebted to Payam Shalchi for pointing out that this translation does not convey the term's insulting force, which implies wilful disbelief in the face of all evidence to the contrary. The word's origins are the subject of some debate. The derogatory Arabic term 'kafir' also means 'denier' or 'concealer' and was directed towards non-Muslims by Muslims. The term was later adopted by Afrikaaners (spelt 'kaffir'), who used the word in a similar sense to the North American 'nigger', referring to black Africans. 'Kaffir' is likely to be derived from the Dutch word for 'beetle' and the Arabic word (http://encyclopedia.thefreedictionary.com/kaffirs).

[41] According to one reviewer's account of an audience's response to being read the story, 'there was not heard in the whole of the vast audience a sound, a whisper, a breath. In dead silence it was received; in dead silence it concluded [...] perhaps the storyteller himself took it for applause' (Lancelyn-Green 1971: 255).

[42] See Hopkirk (1996) *Quest for Kim. In Search of Kipling's Great Game.*

[43] By this I mean that the phenomenon of absentee authority is not unique to travel writing about Afghanistan because much authoritative colonial writing was produced *in absentia*.

[44] Marx argues that Kipling set his story slightly retrospectively in order to disregard the accounts of his contemporaries since he preferred a Kafirstan unexplored by Europeans (56).

[45] Peter Levi also mentions 'the strangely persistent rumour', associated with Goes and other Jesuit missionaries, and relying on what Levi terms 'meagre evidence' that 'the Kafirs had once been or might easily become Christian'. Levi dismisses this claim as relying too heavily on 'their hatred of their Moslem [sic] neighbours and the fact that they drank wine and had European looks' (165).

[46] Shortly after the publication of Kipling's story, the region was conquered by the Afghan Amir, who took advantage of Britain's policy of non-interference. The inhabitants were forcibly converted to Islam and, Edward Marx contends that the region thenceforth began its 'slide into archival obscurity' (1999: 60). This latter point is not strictly accurate, however. Contemporary travellers continue to produce narratives about the region and rumours that Nuristan has provided a hiding place for Osama bin Laden did nothing to diminish this fascination.

[47] In fact, as Marx points out, the 'hair-rope bridges' were an embellishment of Yule's, since his sources make no mention of them (52).

[48] A more subtle interpretative possibility is hinted at by Dravot's metaphorical description of the actual fall: 'turning and twisting in the air like a penny whirligig that you can sell to the Amir' (260). In the context of the failed Second Afghan War, the 'penny whirligig' never bought by the Amir immediately brings to mind Afghanistan's eventual rejection of British proposals to control Afghan foreign policy during the decades of non-interference.

[49] I am grateful to James Procter for observing the sinister connotations of the word 'swarms'.

[50] In Kipling's story the implications of Nuristanis' apparently indeterminate racial identity (clearly triggered by this Aryan association) have been explored by Marx (1999), who notes the relevance of potential kinship to public debates over the question of whether to intervene in 1896 when Amir Abdul Rahman brought the region under his control in 1896.

[51] While serious discussion of the legend has been a prominent feature of travel writing since the nineteenth century, the impression in Kipling's story that Nuristanis have more in common with their Muslim than their British counterparts confirms Marx's sense that, although the legend was not absent from public debates over whether to intervene with the Amir's 1896 subjugation of Nuristanis to Islam, it was not compelling enough to justify British military intervention (1999: 60). The following letter to *The Times* appealed to the legend as way of urging intervention on behalf of 'Kafirs': '[they] are a race of brave warriors [...] who love us and call us their

European brethren [...] they being white like Europeans' (in Marx:52). However, such appeals were to no avail. Marx also points out that the story's ambiguity about the racial identity of 'Kafirs' had certain political advantages. Part of the success of Kipling's story, he argues, can be explained by its appeal to both the Anglo-Indian audience and the British audience at home. The former tended to favour intervention in Afghanistan's international affairs, and, following the 1857 'Mutiny', stressed the need for tougher rule and racially separate spheres. By contrast, the British audience, which had been uneasy about the cost and justification for the First and Second Afghan War invasions, favoured more liberal policies after 1857. By drawing on the myth of Alexander, the story appealed to the Anglo-Indians' preoccupation with the boundaries of race while containing a critique of harsh or irresponsible colonial rule (61).

[52] Levi also notes that it was widely believed that Nuristanis were Christians or were at least amenable to Christianity. According to Levi, this rumour was spread by a Jesuit expedition in the seventeenth century, founded on the 'meagre evidence' of 'their hatred of their Moslem [sic] neighbours and the fact that they drink wine and have European looks' (165).

[53] Although Jonny Bealby does not specify to which anthropological writings he refers, the work of Sir George Grierson, which appeared in 1900 in the *Journal of the Royal Asiatic Society*, argued that 'Kafirs' had indeed preserved an early branch of the Indo-European language family (Levi 165). Peter Levi also adds that '[t]he truth about the racial origins of the Nuristanis is that they do have close affinities tribe to tribe and dialect to dialect' (233).

[54] Andrew Lycett, 'How Kipling created the Afghan myth', *Sunday Times News Review*, September 30th, 2001.

[55] Of course, a reverence for the writings of Kipling is by no means confined to British journalists but is also shared by many of their US counterparts. For example, in *Soldiers of God. With Islamic Warriors in Afghanistan and Pakistan*, Robert Kaplan writes: 'Kipling's writing offered the only sure guide to this [Afghan-Soviet] war' (2001: 24).

[56] Kipling and British historians are indebted to the various nineteenth-century translations of *The 1001 Nights* since the tales, depicting Arabo-Muslim civilisations over ten centuries, were quickly deployed as a means of venting nineteenth-century fears about the perceived Afghan threat to British India. As Eva Sallis points out, each competing translation of the *Nights* reflected the tastes and prejudices of the day, and different versions of the *Nights* were drawn on as an imaginative resource by nineteenth-century commentaries on Muslim societies, which were invariably 'dominated by the prejudicial mode' (1999: 68). According to R.A. Nicholson, the *Nights* were also used as an historical resource. Readers of the *Nights* knew the figures of famous caliphs and viziers solely, or primarily, through the tales (1969: 292).

As Melman records, the *Nights* structured discourses about the Orient (1992: 64), and, in the case of Afghanistan, provided a ready resource for depicting an Afghan predilection for violence, especially violence with knives and involving limb-amputation. Though only the frame story of the *Nights* (Scheherazade) could be said to be set in Central Asia, the tales' focus on Muslim civilisations nevertheless provided writers and historians with a fictive repository from which to build up a picture of Afghan vengefulness and brutality, partly as a means of expressing the trauma of the 1842 massacre and partly as a means of demonising Afghans in the face of persistent political threat from the North. Although Kipling's indebtedness to the *Nights* is largely unacknowledged in his stories and poems, reference to Harun-al-Raschid is made at the beginning of 'The Man Who Would Be King' (247). Appropriating the tales for renderings of Afghanistan is ideologically significant, not least because the translated tales are a plentiful source of scenes of brutality. Bodies of the victims of male wrath are frequently cut 'in two pieces' or 'chopped [...] to pieces' (Dawood 1954:67 & 104). Kipling's story 'Dray Wara Yow Dee', which features an Afghan horse-trader, clearly borrows its excessive violence from the *Nights*: 'she bowed her head, and I smote it off at the neck-bone so that it leapt between my feet [...] and I hacked off the breasts' (117).

[57] This is not to assert that *Kim* straightforwardly endorses British colonial values.

[58] This claim is patently untrue. As John Wood noted over 100 years before, the mountains had long been given a name by inhabitants of the Oxus region.

[59] Despite recent insights on Wild West film genre transformation, all five extracts appeal to popular rather than academicised understandings of the Wild West. For more on film genre transformation, however, see Tom Collins 'Genericity in the Nineteen-Nineties. Eclectic irony and the new sincerity' in Graeme Turner, ed., (2002) *The Film Cultures Reader*, London, Routlege.

[60] These lines, from 'The Amir's Soliloquy', were quoted by King Abdur Rahman Khan in his 1900 autobiography, *The Life of Abdur Rahman Khan, Amir of Afghanistan*.

[61] I leave it to area studies scholars to determine the extent to which this instance of temporal translocation conforms to, and deviates from depictions of comparable regions.

[62] Narratives enter more fragile terrain by depicting Afghans as medieval monks and nuns. Afghan women are repeatedly represented as resembling 'some austere religious order' (Murphy: 206), their veiled faces being 'medievally framed in white muslin' (Stark: 70). Subsequent slippage from medieval Christianity to contemporary Islam thus seems inevitable: 'I was suddenly alerted at two in the morning by the most beautiful music. It lasted

for about an hour. It was like the chanting of monks on a medieval abbey, but with the shrill edge of Islamic harmonies' (Paine 1995: 196). As I examine in Part One, this slippage was a salient feature of contemporary journalistic discourse about Islamic practices in Afghanistan. Related to this representational practice is the superimposition of Chaucerian pilgrimage onto Afghan scenes, although this practice has a different ideological outcome. Once again, examples are legion, but the narratives of Newby and Stark are useful examples: 'Our first Nuristanis [came] pouring out of the bothy [...] They were extraordinary and their clothes were extraordinary too. All [...] wore the same flat Chitrali cap that Hugh had worn [...] only theirs were more floppy [...] worn at the back of the head the effect was Chaucerian' (Newby: 191); 'Chaucer and his pilgrims might have come riding over the Afghan uplands, less surprising in the landscape than our Land-Rover, for we were back in the world of their time' (Stark: 37). One consequence, of course, of depicting Afghan as contemporaneous with Chaucerian times, is to present Afghanistan as being in an arrested stage of social evolutionary development. Indeed, this cognitive consequence is apparent in the following statement in Finlay's narrative and again indicates some slippage between medieval Christianity and contemporary Islam: 'The place was literally in the fifteenth century. According to the Muslim calendar it [the year 2001] was the year 1420' (2002: 314).
[63] Descendants of Alexander, Timurlane and Genghis Khan make regular appearances in contemporary depictions of Afghan settings. Here are just a few examples:

> With their stone bows and wild air it was not difficult to imagine that Timur himself might appear at any moment (Newby 1955: 230).

> In Balkh, Mother of Cities, I asked a fakir the way to the shrine of Hadji Piardeh. "I don't know it," he said. "It must have been destroyed by Genghis" (Chatwin:1998 [1989]: 287).

> I noticed an old man with a look of Genghis Khan (Somerville-Large 1991: 13).

> ...the driver [...] was clearly a descendant of Genghis Khan himself (Osar Chavarria Aguilar, *The Tico Times*, Costa Rica, 22 November, 2002).

In the third of these extracts, by Chatwin, the claim of Afghanistan's ever-present ancient past is apparently no figment of travel writers' collective imagination, but once again, in the self-authenticating manner of many classical ethnographies, a view to which Afghans themselves subscribe. Nevertheless, contemporary travellers' quests for the descendants of Alexander or, in Paine's case, for costumes from the times of his army's invasion do not appear so strange to a British audience as might a search for Boudicea's living descendants in East Anglia or a hunt through Britain for modern day remnants of King Arthur's costume. Furthermore, the claim that Afghanistan is contemporaneous with its ancient past obscures the abiding significance of Anglo-Afghan relations during the Victorian era.

[64] Nevertheless, the practice of drawing parallels between gothic ruins and a lack of civilisation is by no means straightforward to analyse. The uncivilised charge is almost as often levied on Afghanistan's past as its present. Murphy writes of 'huge, square mud fortresses, straddling hilltops, recall[ing] the cruel valour of this region's past' (72). In another passage by Bowie-Shor, ancient forts testify to Afghanistan's past civilisation: 'In the evening we reached the mountain fastness of Pigash, where we found out first evidence of ancient civilisation, a ruined fortress set atop a one hundred-foot mound near the town' (194).

[65] Privately communicated by the author.

[66] Literally speaking, of course, Afghan landscapes can hardly be more 'ancient' than English ones.

[67] Nielsen/Netratings Survey (Hupprich and Bumatay 2002: www. nielsen - netratings.com/pr/pr_030220.pdf).

[68] Afghans have a life expectancy at birth of 45.88 years (Voselsang 2002: 2).

[69] This figure is from the United Nations High Commissioner for Refugees in Pakistan, May 6th, 2001. Available at www.un.org.pk/ unhcr /Afstats-stat.htm, accessed 28th November 2004.

[70] The 'time warp' relates implicitly to perceived religious and cultural insularity in ways that ignore wider issues such as the politically-related significance of the influence of Wahaabism.

[71] Privately communicated by the author. Lugo writes: '[j]ust as in the past, technological development nowadays is at the core of the political narrative since it reinscribes colonial notions of progress in a decontextualised form that reinforces a sense of modernity as a universal and unavoidable social construction. Popular authors such as Toffler (1990), Drucker (1995) and Tapscott (1995) have indeed used this discourse for the past two decades [and it is] based primarily on the development of what is called Information and Communication Technologies [ICTs] to justify this paradigm. Technology – according to these authors – is at the core of progress and comes hand in hand with liberal democracy and capitalism'.

[72] As Lugo points out, in information societies, leisure time is characterised by the consumption of ICTs: in Britain, 13% of leisure time is spent consuming ICTs as against 2% playing sports at Leisure Centres.

[73] I am grateful to Sudanese documentary-maker Mohammed Naguib for pointing this out.

[74] Privately communicated by the author by email 24th November 2004.

[75] John Gray argues that calling al-Qaeda medieval detracts from those very geo-political circumstances that he argues are the driving force behind its activities. To control Saudi Arabia, for example, is to hold oil-fuelled economies to ransom because their financial markets are premised on the myth of infinite natural resources (2003: 85).

[76] The charter was only written between 1987 and 1988 and, according to Gray, 'fuse[s]' Islamic themes with European anarchist ideas. The charter was drawn up by Dr. Abdullah Azzam, who, following the ideas of his immediate forbear, Egyptian Sayyid Qutb, saw the need for a Bolshevik-style revolutionary vanguard. Azzam's anti-rationalism smacks of Neitzche (2003: 24 & 79).

[77] See Hugo Dyserinck (2003) 'Imagology and the Problem of Ethnic Identity' in *Intercultural Studies* 1 Spring.

[78] I am grateful to Tim Youngs for making this point in response to a paper I gave on this subject. ('Borders and Crossings 4', Ankara, Turkey, 2-4 July 2003).

[79] Howard Booth points out that Robert Byron's influential *The Road to Oxiana* received little critical attention at the time of publication because of the genre's low status in the nineteen-thirties. As Booth also notes, to this day there is little scholarly writing about Byron's travel writing despite the narrative's continued popularity (in Derek Duncan and Charles Burdett, eds, 2002: 14 -18). See also Youngs (2004) on critics' sustained efforts to categorise W. H. Auden's 1937 *Letters From Iceland* as anything but travel writing.

[80] I use this term reluctantly, and in a pluralized form. The term *classical ethnography* has been deployed by ethnographers as a euphemism for 'bad' or outmoded ethnography. As a result of this label, contemporary ethnography tends to distance itself (perhaps unadvisedly) from its earlier incarnations. This gives rise to two concerns. I have no wish to suggest that contemporary ethnography has successfully divorced itself from its colonial roots. Neither, however, is it desirable to privilege the self-construction of postmodern critiques of ethnography as having provided *the* defining moment of the crisis. Postmodern critiques stand accused of airbrushing out instances of ethnographic innovation and experimentation, especially feminist innovation (which was often formerly unacceptable to the academy) that predates the declaration of a 'crisis'. I therefore pluralise *ethnography* to *ethnographies* to acknowledge the diverse range of studies that predate the increasing prominence of discussions about ethnographic dilemmas of representation in the late nineteen-eighties. Not only does this plural convey

genuine diversity but it also acknowledges ethnography's amenability to disciplinary modification and textual fashion. This complicates my discussion of counter-influence, since, while it is my belief that it is classical ethnographies have had the most insidious effect on travel writing about Afghanistan, it is also important to recognize that classical ethnographies have also been an evolving and unstable form.

[81] Also see Graham Huggan, 'Counter-Travel Writing and Post-Coloniality' in Liselotte Glage (ed.), *Being/s in Transit. Travelling, Migration, Dislocation*: 57.

[82] Whitney Azoy's *Buzkashi, Game and Power in Afghanistan* contains epigraphs from Sir Alexander Burnes, while Nazif Shahrani cites travel writers such as Marco Polo and Sir Aurel Stein in his chapter entitled 'History and Demographic Process' in *The Kirghiz and Wakkhi of Afghanistan. Adaptation to Closed Frontiers and War.*

[83] This said, cultural relativism is nothing new to travel writers: the proto-ethnographic travel writing of Mountstuart Elphinstone, for example, contains numerous culturally relativist moments. Reduced to its simplest terms, this guiding principle of sameness is neatly summarized by John Monaghan and Peter Just as follows: 'People are everywhere the same except in the ways they differ' (2000: 145).

[84] I confine my discussion to social anthropology, (associated with British anthropology) and cultural anthropology, its counterpart in the United States.

[85] A series of short essays about the crisis appeared in the *Journal of Contemporary Ethnography* in 2002. The essay titles range from Norman K. Denzin's 'Confronting Ethnography's Crisis of Representation' and 'The Sky is Not Falling' to Michael G. Flagherty's 'To Postmodern Hell and Back'. David A. Snow writes of the '[p]resumed' crisis, the profundity of which was, he argues, is greatly exaggerated by James Clifford and other postmodernist critics of ethnography. Peter K. Manning's essay insists that, crisis or no crisis, the disciplinary 'centre [still] holds', while Michael G. Flagherty expresses grave concern over the importation of literary critical theories into the discipline and the subsequent 'turn towards indeterminacy'. Flagherty finds this turn politically disabling since, as he argues, it has become impossible to 'establish any form of unchallenged authority' for ill or, more to the point, for good (Flagherty, M.G., 'The Crisis in Representation: A Brief History and Some Questions' *Journal of Contemporary Ethnography* Vol.31, no.4, August 2002: 480). In a similar vein, Denzin laments ethnography's increasing political impotence and links it to the abandonment of three fundamental notions: validity, reliability and generalisability. George E. Marcus' recent edited volume entitled *Critical Anthropology Now. Unexpected Contexts, Shifting Constituencies, Changing Agendas* (1999) recognizes the political ramifications of ethnographic de-

authorization. Stressing the need to emerge from anthropology's temporary discursive paralysis, he suggests that there is a pressing need to avoid complicity with political conservatism. For cultural anthropologists at least, he calls for a shift in site of anthropological study through the 'repatriat[ion]' of one's research interests into US society (25). His collection contains ethnographic essays on the Waco Siege and the Bhopal Disaster.

[86] For a full description of the precise details of these debates, see Robert Brightman's wide-ranging discussion of debates over the culture concept, 'Forget Culture: Replacement, Transcendence, Relexification' *Cultural Anthropology* 10(4): 509-546.

[87] Once again, I have no wish to privilege Clifford and Marcus' seminal collection of essays over earlier discussions of ethnographic responsibility. However, it is impossible to omit *Writing Culture* from any discussion of anthropological crisis, since the collection generated responses from a wide spectrum of thinkers. Despite the fact that Clifford's own introduction warned against 'imposing a false unity' on the essays it contained (3), it is difficult to conceive as the book as anything other than a coherent critique of ethnographic strategies of representation that has had a lasting impact on anthropological historicisation and debate.

[88] 'Introduction: Partial Truths' in James Clifford and George E. Marcus:3.

[89] Many of the essays in *Women Writing Culture* consider significant omissions from *Writing Culture*. Bell hooks suggests that an essay on Hurston's *Mules and Men*, which she argues was 'postmodern before its time', might have lent itself to a more inclusive historicisation of ethnography's past: '[i]n many ways', hooks argues, 'Hurston was at the cutting edge of a new movement in ethnography and anthropology that has only recently been actualized' (19). Behar argues that this significant exclusion is symptomatic of the 'as yet unwritten history' not merely of feminist anthropologists, but of minority women who have historically been relegated to the intellectual margins of the discipline (17).

[90] In her essay 'Works and Wives: On the Sexual Division of Textual Labour' in *Women Writing Culture*, Barbara Tedlock examines the phenomenon of the unpaid labour of ethnographers' wives such as Rosemary Firth and Rosamond Brown (whose husband was Edward H. Spicer). Tedlock argues that wives' writing was often subsumed into their husband's work while their husbands remained silent about their presence in the field (270-2).

[91] See Henrietta Moore *Feminism and Anthropology* and Stoetzler, M., and Yuval-Davis, 'Standpoint theory, situated knowledge and the situated imagination' *Feminist Theory* vol.3, no.3, December 2002.

[92] See appendices for more detailed commentaries on Doubleday, Mills, Shahrani and Tapper.

[93] *Buzkashi* is the Persian name for a game that has traditionally been played by Turkoman and Uzbek Afghans from the North. Since *buzkashi* is the most widely recognised label I adopt Azoy's practice of using the Persian name merely to avoid confusion. See appendix one for a detailed discussion of this dilemma.

[94] www.indiana.edu/~anthro/faculty/nazif.html

[95] Delayed publication has specific repercussions vis-à-vis the ethnographies' status as sources of knowledge. One consequence has been the evocation, by publishers, reviewers or, in Tapper's case, within the ethnography itself, of that which Clifford describes as 'the theme of the vanishing primitive'. Clifford contends that, while accepting the facts of actual migration and extermination, the trope is evoked so frequently as to demand an examination of its narrative structure and effect, that is, its use as a 'rhetorical construct' to legitimize the textual salvage (crucially, the ethnographic salvage) of an ostensibly coherent set of traditional practices (in Clifford and Marcus: 112). This trope has been mobilized in relation both to the delayed publication of Tapper's ethnography and to the republication of Shahrani's. In her preface, Tapper offers her book as a 'memorial' to the Maduzai 'way of life' (xx). Because of Maduzai dispersal at the time of the Soviet invasion, Tapper argues, the book 'offers a unique account of a world that has disappeared' (xvi). Bahram Tavakolian's review of Tapper's work concurs with the notion of salvage, stating that the scattered refugees might consult Tapper's book as a means of 'making decisions appropriate to the society they would like to construct for their future' (Tavakolian, B., *International Journal of Middle East Studies* Vol.25(1), February 1993: 125). Although Shahrani's republished ethnography makes no explicit reference to this aim, it is described on the back cover as 'an account of a people that are now virtually inaccessible to anthropological enquiry' (*Journal of Asian Studies*).

[96] Book review, *International Journal of Middle Eastern Studies* 16(2) 1984:270-272.

[97] Once again, protecting sources is a key ethical tenet of journalism, suggesting further links between journalists and ethnographers.

[98] This applies to anthropology from Europe and the United States.

[99] See Graham Allen, *Intertextuality*: 103. A paratext exists at the text's 'threshold' and consists of a peritext (title, subtitles, chapter headings and so on) and an epitext (reviews, interviews, blurb and so on).

[100] Tension between the text and its peritext is nothing new. Despite Mountstuart Elphinstone's attempts to foreground the possible limitations of his 1815 account ('I have seen but a part of the countries I am about to describe'), Olaf Caroe's introduction declares 'Elphinstone knows of every tribe, its ways and location', thereby attributing an omniscience that the narrator does not claim for himself.

[101] Concise Oxford Dictionary, 9th edition, 1995: 1413.
[102] Synecdochic metaphor is not confined to writing about Europe. On the contrary, Said has noted how Orientalist thought 'rose from the specifically human detail to the transhuman one [...so that] an observation about a tenth-century Arab poet multiplied itself into a policy towards [...] the Oriental mentality in Egypt, Iraq, or Arabia' (1979: 96).
[103] The metaphor has also been adopted as a comic comparison with U.S. baseball.
[104] Azoy writes in the Wabash magazine (Fall/Winter 2000): '[I] found my notion of "game as metaphor" appropriated a decade later as journalists struggled to describe the shifting forces of Afghanistan's jihad against the Soviets' (1). In the same article he abnormalises Afghan responses to political crisis by attributing widespread Afghan rejection of the Taliban to 'the topsy-turvey dynamic of Afghan impression management politics' (3).
[105] This is no isolated instance of *temporal deixis*. It is strikingly evident in the following account of informants' speeches about preparing for a *buzkashi* match: '"We are all friends of Hajji Aziz Khan (or, alternatively, all Uzbeks, Kunduzis, Khans, Moslems, whatever) and we must work together to make our tooi [game] great and famous"' (46). The conflation of many preparation speeches into one is ('alternatively [...] whatever') is symptomatic of the narrative's powerful organising and harmonising orientation.
[106] This is a recurrent theme, even in experimental ethnographies, such that by Paul Stoller and Cheryl Oates, where Stoller claims to 'understand the Songhay [of Niger], perhaps better than they understand themselves' (1997: 100).
[107] In her review of Azoy's ethnography, Nancy Tapper adopts Sir Alfred Lyall's phraseology: 'this unruly and competitive political environment' (213) RIC1,5.
[108] Robert Brightman has described in his article 'Forget Culture: Replacement, Transcendence, Relexification', how critics of the culture concept have tended 'to reconstruct an essentialised and overhomogenous concept as the target of their criticisms' and have, in the words of Timothy Fitzgerald, 'selectively ignor[ed] the considerable criticisms of concepts (and revisionings) by anthropologists themselves since the 1920's' (2000: 239).
[109] One of the most problematic consequences of slippage from the literal (*buzkashi*;carpets) to the symbolic (Afghan culture;politics;wars) is the way that it authorises the narrator to generalise about cultural practices. In an essay tracing the emergence of ethnographic knowledge, Sarah Winter notes that the moral and philosophical thrust of liberal and Utilitarian understandings of culture during the Victorian era impelled the elaboration of 'general laws' as the practical outcome of any social investigation. Importantly, Winter insists that this drive towards generalisation acted upon

ethnographies throughout the twentieth-century (Winter, S., 'Mental Culture: Liberal Pedagogy and the Emergence of Ethnographic Knowledge' *Victorian Studies* 41: 431). In ethnographic writing, synecdoche and the culture concept are two major tools of generalisation that render various lifeways as systematically readable (Winter:429). The impetus towards generalisation is apparent in the titles of ethnographies about Afghanistan. Despite Shahrani's disclaimer ('this book does not pretend to be a comprehensive ethnography of either the Kirghiz or the Wakhi of Afghanistan' (xxiv)), his title *The Kirghiz and Wakhi of Afghanistan,* supplies, through the use of the definite, rather than the indefinite article, an illusion of totality which belies his claim. Furthermore, the title of his 2002 preface, 'Afghanistan, the Taliban and Global Terror, Inc.' (ix), is premised, not upon his self-professed minimal knowledge of two groups, but upon the unspoken assumption of expertise on Afghanistan's national entirety. From a study of three hundred Kirghiz households and 6,000 Wakhi, (xxxvii), Shahrani hopes that the ethnography 'will shed some light on [...] the dynamics of state and social relations in general, and those of *Afghanistan in particular*' (xxviii, emphasis added). Margaret Mills' introduction contains a similar disclaimer, despite the fact that a single evening's storytelling by two men near Herat becomes, not even 'Rhetorics and Politics in Herati Traditional Storytelling' but *Rhetorics and Politics in Afghan Traditional Storytelling.* (Could a study of a single storytelling session in the Orkney Islands legitimately bear the title *Rhetorics and Politics in Traditional British Storytelling?*) The ongoing value of studies' general applicability is apparent in their reception. For example, Tapper's review of Azoy's study describes it as: 'a sensitive and instructive book [...useful] for the wider insights it offers into recent events in the Great Game in Asia' (Tapper, N., *Man* 18:1, March 1983: 213). Tapper's statement creates an ever-widening circle of generalisation from the Kunduz province in Northern Afghanistan, to an entire continent.

[110] I am grateful to Fiona Darroch for suggesting that this focus on children's games strengthens the implied theory of Afghan cultural pathology.

[111] In a recent article, Tariq Ali describes a kite festival in Basant, 'when the Lahore sky is filled with different colours and shapes as old rivals seek to tangle with and cut down one another's kites' as 'the millenium-old product of Hindu mythology (7). See also www. the-south-asian.com/ March2002 and www. pakaviation.com/PVA/Experimental/Ex_Kites.

[112] As mentioned in the Introduction, it is my contention that the 'warlike Afghan' study is not primarily derived from generalised notions of Islamic militancy. On the contrary, notions of 'warlike Afghans' stem from precise Anglo-Afghan historical encounters, while notions of Islamic militancy act in a secondary role to confirm and support those impressions.

[113] Dupree uses the phrase 'the essence of Afghan culture' (218).

[114] This can be found on the cartoon section of RAWA's website.

[115] I have adapted this phrase from Charles Forsdick's conceptualisation of the genre of travel writing, which I feel applies equally to journalism. Privately communicated by the author.

[116] The term 'pseudo-ethnographic' is used here to indicate an absence of ethnographic responsibility. Most particularly it depicts the journalistic borrowing of ethnographic techniques of representation, which are, consciously or unconsciously, applied with varying degrees of analytical rigour and without any strict adherence to the ethical codes associated with the crisis of representation.

[117] A notable exception to this rule is Norwegian war correspondent Asne Seierstad's *The Bookseller of Kabul*, who, tired of 'weeks amongst gunpowder and rubble' (1), spent hours listening to bookseller Sultan's conversation and decided to move in with the family to provide a detailed portrayal of an Afghan family: 'I said to myself: "This is Afghanistan. How interesting it would be to write a book about this family"' (2). Her period of fieldwork involved an extended stay with this family, which implies that the book is synecdochic in the sense that it 'evok[es] [...] a social whole through representation of its parts' (Webster in Richards: 221). In line with contemporary ethnographic sensibilities she stresses: '[m]y family is not even typical'. In this sense her book problematises her account's status as shedding some light on wider Afghan society. However, the paratextual elements of her book again militate against this qualifier; a testimonial on the front cover describes the book in synecdochic terms as 'An intimate portrait of Afghani [sic] people'.

[118] Communicated by email by Jim Latham, secretary for the BJTC, 1st December 2004

[119] www. news.bbc.co. uk/hi/programmes/from our own correspondent/ 3143512.stm, accessed 5 October 2004.

[120] There are, of course, crucial differences. As Michael Massing indicates, journalists in Kabul 'tend to hang out with one another, eat together, party together' (2002:3).

[121] As Larry B. Lambert writes: 'The price of trained horses range [between] 20,000 Afghanis and 100,000 Afghanis in pre-jihad Afghanis. If one was to pay in a more valuable international currency, they could be had today for between $700.00 and $2,500.00' (www. afghan-network. net/ Culture/buzkashi.html), accessed 30 December, 2004.

[122] A significant exception to this general rule was an event held in April 2002 by the RAWA, where women were encouraged to participate in a variety of Afghan games, including a *buzkashi* match.

[123] I am grateful to Bethan Benwell for pointing out that this is a common device of television news reports. The camera often offers a visual summary

of commentaries' metaphorical content. On the 13 November 2001, for example, Tom Carver's report for the BBC's 'Newsnight' programme contains a mid-shot of huge, golden doors opening for Putin and Bush to walk through. As they pass between the doors the commentary runs: 'The doors of opportunity have unexpectedly opened. The Taliban have vanished' (2001). In another report, a mid-shot of a Taleb unwinding his turban is accompanied by the commentary: 'The power of the Taliban is unravelling quickly' (BBC2 'Newsnight', 22nd November, 2001). This device serves as a witty play between camera and narrative, offering a satisfying visual summary of metaphorical language.

[124] As Lynch argues, news reports that focus exclusively on 'exchanges of direct violence' rather than exploring those conditions that give rise to that violence often means that 'stock' explanations 'prevail by default' (39). Talking above sounds of distant gunfire, David Lomax reports: '[i]n the last few days there have been signs that Afghanistan's ancient rivalries are breaking out once more' (*Panorama* with the Paras, BBC1, 24 February 2002). On BBC2's 'Newsnight' programme, Jeremy Paxman groups together Afghanistan and Yugoslavia using the 'ancient hatreds' theory popular with many correspondents: 'there are parallels between the two places, both in terms of the ethnic tensions and the force of international pressure brought to bear' (29 November 2001). Talk of rival factions implies that sectarianism is an established part of Afghanistan's history, whereas sectarianism is a recent phenomenon resulting from two recent massacres and Taliban drives against 'bad Muslims', which many Afghans felt were a means of oppressing and killing non-Pashtuns. Rashid believes that the massacres of Hazaras by Masud's forces in 1995 and of Uzbeks and Hazaras by the Taliban in 1998 were key to the destruction of 'age-old Afghan tolerance and consensus' (83). He points out that sectarianism is unprecedented in Afghan history because religious extremism was not a feature of Afghan society before the Taliban because ninety percent of Afghans belong to the Sunni Hanafi sect, which is the most liberal of the four Sunni schools of thought (83).

[125] Ahearn's observation that it is customary for feminist theorists to equate agency with resistance is particularly pertinent to this discussion (112). Citing Sherry Ortner, she notes that 'there is no such thing as pure resistance [...since] motivations are always complex and contradictory'. While agency may entail some resistance, resistance is not synonymous with agency. It is perfectly possible, for example, simultaneously to resist, submit, oppose and accommodate (in Ahearn:116).

[126] See George E. Marcus's Introduction to *Critical Anthropology Now. Unexpected Constituencies, Shifting Contexts, Changing Agendas.*

[127] Robert Byron, in *The Road to Oxiana*, acknowledges his text's relation with antecedent writing by naming the books stacked on the table beside him.

These range from Maud Diver and Khanikov's *Journal Asiatique* to work by
the historians A.C. and C.E.Yate, which he literally transfers to his lap (92).
[128] See Augusta C. Del Zotto, 'Weeping Women, Wringing Hands: How the
Mainstream Media Stereotyped Women's Experiences in Kosovo' *Journal of
Gender Studies* Vol.11(2), 2002.
[129] The same was true of nineteenth-century men's writing about harems and
zenanas, which substituted 'citation' for 'first hand information', although
women travellers also drew extensively from the harem literature of their
predecessors. However, women's actual experience allowed alternative
discourses about harems to develop that facilitated a degree of textual
manoeuvre within the symbolic space of the harem.
[130] Although, as I have argued, the culture concept's widespread
problematisation by anthropologists makes such generalisations inadvisable
irrespective of the writer's gender.
[131] As I have mentioned, Kremmer and Lamb's books were published in the
same year by Harper Collins and cover similar themes, yet Kremmer's book
is categorised as 'History', while Lamb's is 'History', 'Biography' and
'Travel and Holiday'. This confirms Sara Mills' sense that women's writing
tends to be read biographically (1992: 13). The categorisation process
favours Kremmer's text by aligning it with an academic discipline.
[132] This term is borrowed from Mills, who writes that 'gender structures texts
in both their production and reception' (1992: 198).
[133] I am grateful to Charles Forsdick for this term.
[134] Stephen Whittle speaking at a public debate entitled 'television – the new
weapon of war?' hosted by the Royal Television Society, *Oran Mor* in
Glasgow, Wednesday 29 September 2004.
[135] Radio documentary maker Naomi Fowler suggests that the absence of
spectacular photographs of prisoner abuses in the Bagram airbase partly
accounted for the sparse media coverage compared with that of the abuse
perpetuated in Abu Ghraib (privately communicated by email). This
possibility was also expressed in BBC *Radio 4* news bulletins on 21 May,
2004 when the news broke that Hamid Karzai had expressed grave concerns
about prisoner abuses in Bagram.
[136] At this early stage of the conflict refugees were literally inaccessible to
British camera crews who were waiting, in some cases for weeks, by the
closed Afghan border.
[137] Philo and Berry's study found that, for 80% of the population television
news is the main source of news on the Israel-Palestine conflict.
[138] See Philo and Berry:100.
[139] News agencies are of course key agents of the agenda-setting process;
there is broad agreement that two Anglo-American news agencies, Reuters
and Associated Press, dominate the global news scene. Even so, the theory of

all-powerful news agencies has been disputed by Graham Chapman, whose study of main evening news programmes on a single night from all global regions suggests that 'local and regional forces' are as significant to news content as macro-politics (Carruthers: 33).

[140] Alex Thompson, Presenter and Chief Correspondent of 'Channel Four News' speaking at a public debate entitled 'television – the new weapon of war?' hosted by the Royal Television Society, *Oran Mor* in Glasgow, Wednesday 29 September 2004.

[141] The label 'Afghani' was in widespread use by activists and reporters alike, including two interviewees who appeared on Channel Four to talk about their Muslim faith (Channel Four News, 27th September 2001). Afghani is the name of Afghanistan's currency.

[142] I am grateful to Naomi Fowler for pointing out this paradox.

[143] DelZotto defines non-state actors as direct or individual participants in war who do not represent official voices.

[144] See Philip M. Taylor in Kishan Thussu and Freedman:104

[145] According to Howard Finerman, *Newsweek's* chief political correspondent, President Bush said in a meeting with New York and Virginia Senators on September 13th 2001: 'When I take action, I'm not going to fire a $2 million missile at a $10 empty tent and hit a camel in the butt. It's going to be decisive'.

[146] Steele found that experts from think tanks represented 30 percent of the total number of experts interviewed, of which category forty percent of all appearances were from two Washington-based institutions: the Centre for Strategic and International Studies and the Brookings Institution (803 & 804).

[147] Wednesday 29 September 2004.

[148] Hannerz points out that Japan is too expensive to receive extensive coverage, while Jerusalem is convenient and accessible because it is within reach of the settlements, and so on (2004: 54).

[149] A recent exception to this is Sorious Samura's documentary for Channel Four, 'Twenty-First Century Wars', in which he makes it clear that the Muslim custom of rapidly burying the dead makes it hard for him to know the number of those killed after a Kandahar shooting (15 December 2002).

[150] Lynch points out that a scarcity of resources is almost always at the root of conflict yet, as the Glasgow Media Group found, though water resources were a key issue of the 2000 *Intifada*, it was scarcely mentioned in British television news reports (in Thussu and Freedman: 136).

[151] I am grateful to Colombian journalist Manuel Hernandez for this analogy.

[152] Implicit in Philo and Berry's argument here is a critique of the ideal of balance, which has tended to retain its professional currency among British journalists. The usefulness of the principle has however been called into

question by academics and journalists alike, perhaps most compellingly because it implies that there are generally only two sides to any given issue when the range of contesting perspectives is likely to be more complex. To frame a topic as having two sides can thus distort through simplification; apparent even-handedness can itself become an act of exclusion. For more on this last objection see Lynch 2000. See also Pedelty 1995.

[153] This phrase is widely used and seldom attributed to Ahmed Rashid, who points out that it was he who coined it (2000: 34).

[154] Iran eventually won this battle by signing an agreement to channel oil through Iran.

[155] Saudi Arabia contributed $500m for each year of the struggle against the Soviet occupation (Gregory 2004: 36).

[156] The Pakistani Intelligence Services.

[157] In this case the term is misleading because, as the report notes, many of the foreigners were from Pakistan or the Philippines.

[158] This phrase is borrowed from Gregory 2004: 38.

[159] Privately communicated by email.

[160] Paper given at the Centre for Commonwealth Studies, University of Stirling, Scotland, 20 April 2004.

[161] Margaret Atwood's article in *The Guardian* reiterates this fear, pointing out, as though of enduring significance, that 'neither Alexander the Great nor the British in the nineteenth century had stayed in the country long because of the ferocity of its warriors' ('Taking the Veil', 17th October 2001).

[162] This phrase, offered by Edward Luttwak, is cited by Webster in the same article (60).

[163] Some modifications must be made to this definition in relation to Operation Enduring Freedom, where the RMA study does not describe adequately the way in which risk was transferred to Northern Alliance ground troops, which fought a low-technological war while planes bombed from the air and where, at one stage, US personnel participated in a cavalry charge, which Donald Rumsfeld described as 'the nineteenth-century meet[ing] the twenty-first'. John Downey and Graham Murdock also suggest that Webster overstates his case, since his case-study of the First Gulf War as the first example of such warfare overlooks the fact that it saw the largest deployment of military personnel since World War One and dropped less tonnage of bombs than in World War Two (see Downey and Murdock 2003:73).

[164] Ludmilla Kostova objects to the category 'Euro-American', arguing that there are crucial differences in the colonial history and imperial self-image of Eastern and Western Europeans (communicated by email).

[165] In the light of the coalition's overwhelming firepower, Tom Carew's article in the *Sunday Times News Review* expresses a faith in Afghan military

prowess that flies in the face of the facts: 'If it comes to a ground war, I believe the western forces will have a very slim chance of victory [...] The Afghans are a formidable enemy' (30 September 2001). Since 'risk-transfer militarism' had become the norm long before the article was written, such a conclusion seems at odds with Carew's probable knowledge of military affairs. Nevertheless, reminders of the disastrous 1842 retreat and to Alexander being Afghanistan's last successful conqueror commonly accompany expressions of doubt as to the military outcome of Operation Enduring Freedom.

[166] Hazara and Tajik women have traditionally had a great deal more political leverage than Pashtun women.

[167] According to Christine Aziz, many women joined the Soviet side because they were afraid of losing their rights to education and other associated freedoms under Communist rule (56).

[168] Communicated by Sahar Saba at the Women Against Fundamentalism and for Equality (WAFE) conference in Paris, 25-26 February, 2005. Members of RAWA declared themselves to be suspicious of the motives behind the sudden interest in the film and also concerned that as a result RAWA might be seen to support military intervention.

[169] Rashid suggests that the role of the Lewinsky affair in the formulation of international policy illustrates how frequently such policies are pursued with an eye on domestic agendas (2000: 176).

[170] As John L. Esposito points out, regimes have used the veil as a means of displaying westernised identity. To this purpose the veil has been banned by Reza Shah Pahlavi of Iran, Attaturk of Turkey and Bourghiba in Tunisia (2002: 131).

[171] This means that statements in news reports, such as that by Rebecca Milligan, noting that '[u]nder the Taleban, women are barely allowed out of their homes' ('Afghanistan: Through veiled eyes', 'From Our Own Correspondent', Saturday 8 January 2000) suffer from a lack of context, both of well-documented confinement of women by Durranis that undermines the designation of women's oppression as post-Taliban and of the historical variation in women's political agency and fortune in Afghanistan (Rashid 2000; Tapper 1991).

[172] Women's agency is not automatically directed in ways audiences might wish or expect: Afghan women may be agents of conservatism as well as of change. There were very few news stories about women who force the *burqua* on other women. Anthropologists such as Nancy Lindisfarne have generally been more successful than journalists at examining the role of women in promoting patriarchal practices.

[173] The term 'pre-Taleban' generally refers to those disparate political groups and individuals who would shortly join forces to form the Taleban.

[174] www.wafe.org.
[175] Communicated in a panel discussion at the Women Against Fundamentalism and for Equality (WAFE) conference in Paris, 25-26 February, 2005.
[176] For more on this see the text of a speech by president-elect, Maryam Rajavi, at Women Against Fundamentalism and for Equality conference, Paris, 25 February, 2005 available at www.wafe.org.
[177] In a similar act of identification, Rebecca Milligan describes her experience of tripping downstairs while dressed in a *burqua*: 'I had a sense of what it must be like for Afghan women to wear them. They are claustrophobic and isolating. In them you lose all sense of yourself' ('Afghanistan – Through Veiled Eyes', 'From Our Own Correspondent', Saturday 8 January, 2000).
[178] Comment made during panel of a session convened by Women Against Fundamentalism and for Equality, Paris, 25-26 February, 2005.
[179] Of course, Afghan women are not the sole recipients of this treatment. There is a clear correlation not merely between gender and exclusion, but between exclusion and people's status as unofficial actors of war, whether female or male. Nowhere is this principle more apparent than in news reports about refugees. Matt Frei's report for BBC1's the 'Six O' Clock News' during the refugee crisis at the beginning of the conflict is a case in point. Standing near the border, he describes the refugees as 'a swarming throng of humanity' and then, combining a close-up shot of an Afghan mother's face with his commentary, narrates her thoughts: 'you can see the will to live draining away'. This is followed by a broader claim: 'everyone fears [the conflict's] repercussions' (27 September 2001). The implicit anti-war stance of the piece in no way obviates the exclusions of those same refugees as commentators on their own fortunes.
[180] Speech given at Women Against Fundamentalism and for Equality conference, Paris, 26 February, 2005.
[181] This gender imbalance is due to war, famine, landmines and economic migration. For more on this see www.fao.org/News/2002/020105-e.htm.
[182] This alludes to Said's claim that news coverage of Islam is neither 'informed nor informing' (1997: 11).
[183] This last statement parallels Said's suggestion in his introduction to *Covering Islam*: xlviii.
[184] I am grateful to Naomi Fowler for pointing out this common implicit criterion behind the selection of 'local' sources. I am also aware that journalists' use of trained and untrained interpreters (or not) is a complex issue of pressing concern that I have not examined in this study. The issue deserves sustained attention and would merit further study in its own right.

[185] As Ludmilla Kostova points out, notions of a 'western gaze' can be unhelpful with respect to travel writing by Eastern Europeans (communicated by email).

[186] Hammond's evidence is compelling and I accept it with one reservation. There is a danger, inherent in before and after scenarios, of forgetting that even travel narratives written during the period of high imperialism are often anything but 'assured' (Hammond 2003:185) but rather tend to trail ambiguity in their wake.

[187] As I stated in the introduction, this study has not been about Afghanistan but about those notional Afghanistans most prominent in the British popular imaginary. It has not been my purpose to discuss Afghanistan's micro politics or even to explore in any depth its relation to major political powers with whom its fortunes have been so bound up. Both these tasks would require a separate study to do them justice.

[188] Talk for the panel on travel writing and ethics at the European Society for the Study of English conference, Zaragoza, Spain, September 9 2004.

[189] This point was originally made by Ong in the context of the ethnographic reader, but I feel that her point is equally pertinent to readers of travel writing.

Appendix One

Buzkashi in **Whitney Azoy's** **2003** *Buzkashi. Game and Power in Afghanistan.*

In his ethnography Azoy quotes a governmental leaflet about *buzkashi*, which describes the game as 'exclusively Afghan [...] reflect[ing] the boldness and fierce competitive spirit of the Afghan people' (109). However, a complaint by a Turkmen reader of Azoy's manuscript challenges the neutrality of the phrase 'exclusively Afghan'. This objection is relegated to a footnote, in which Azoy is urged to 'report the Kabul government suppressions of Turkoman and Uzbek *buzkashis* in the countryside' (108). Indeed, identifying the game as generally 'Afghan' is bound up with Pashtun quests for dominance and the suppression, or in this case, the strategic appropriation, of non-Pashtun identities and cultural practices.

Azoy describes the Turkmen's objections as 'marginal notes' and the footnote represents the study's sole mention of such suppressions. As anthropologist Nazif Shahrani points out, *buz kashi* is the Persian, rather than the Turkic or Uzbek name. Shahrani refers to *buzkashi* as a 'traditional kirghiz game of *olagh tartish*' (106). Azoy thus fails to address directly the charge that persistent use of the name *buzkashi* risks complicity with such acts, acts in which this study is also implicated. Azoy's ethnography could not be described as counterintuitive, therefore, since it endorses, rather than investigates, this nationalist construction by drawing parallels between the game and 'Afghan culture'. By playing down the significance of the game's contested meanings, the ethnography thus goes with the grain of these acts of historical amnesia in order to facilitate its synecdochic analysis.

Appendix Two
Veronica Doubleday's *Three Women of Herat* (1988)

As with Marjorie Shostak's *Nisa. The Life and Words of a !Kung Woman*, published two years earlier in 1981, Veronica Doubleday's *Three Women of Herat* emerged at a critical juncture in feminist theory and politics. During the nineteen-seventies, ethnographers had noted an overwhelming bias against female 'informants'. Edwin Ardener noted how anthropologists were analytically predisposed to accept dominant versions of socio-cultural organization provided by men (in Moore 1988: 4). Doubleday's observations about Herati marriages clearly problematise assumptions of male agency, however. She writes: 'I realized how difficult it was for [Herati] men, needing sex and companionship, yet having to marry without even seeing the woman. Men were reliant on the goodwill and careful discrimination of their female relatives to find them wives' (73). Henrietta Moore characterises the early corrective response to the problems of assuming universal female oppression and privileging male informants as the '"add-women-and stir" method', which directed an intimate and exclusive gaze upon female informants (3). This attempt at empirical correction generated a number of studies that concerned themselves with raising awareness about women's experiences worldwide, often aiming to generate cross-cultural solidarity and even collective action (Clifford in Clifford and Marcus: 107). Later questions over the validity of the category 'woman' problematised depictions of cross-cultural solidarity characterized by Shostak's *Nisa*. This was largely due to a growing realization of the need to cast off or rework imported notions of gender (Moore: 192 & 2). Oyewumi Oyeronke notes how gendered identity became essentialised in the west because these identities pervaded each and every encounter: women could not vote on the basis of anatomy, and so on. By contrast, she argues, in pre-colonial Yoruban society, identity shifted according to social context and was not rigidly bound to anatomical differences. As a consequence '[those who] write about any society through a gendered perspective [...] necessarily write gender into that society [since] [g]ender, like beauty, is in the eye of the beholder (1997: xi-xv).

Studies such as Doubleday's are regarded by contemporary feminist ethnographers as problematic for a number of reasons, not least because of her focus on the lives of three women situates her work in the "add-women-and stir" phase. Her study is therefore implicated in the over-simplified construction of gender difference, which, it has been argued, sometimes endorses the misleading rhetoric of women's sameness. However, Doubleday might justifiably defend her study on the basis that its detailed nature counteracts this tendency by revealing considerable variation in the experiences of the three women she studies.

Doubleday's study is experimental in the sense that it openly mixes scholarly writing with experiential writing and even unreliable narration. Its skewed position in relation to classical ethnographies serves as a salutory reminder of the impossiblity of drawing neat pre- and post-crisis dividing lines. Until recently, many feminist anthropologists had to disassociate themselves from experimental writing in order to prove their professional credentials. In recent years, however, there has been renewed interest among anthropologists in the mixing of genres (Abu-Lughod in Behar and Gordon: 14). Doubleday's narrative style explores the genre's kinship with travel writing, as her arrival scene attests: 'several shops were still open, raised above street level, like treasure caves stocked to the ceiling and lit by magical lamps' (2). Unlike most ethnographies of its time, Doubleday's text does not banish smells but writes of 'the scent of pines' (a scent mentioned in most travelogue about Herat) and 'the stench of stale urine' (6). Recent reassessments of the sub-genre's mix of together with the recognition of its deauthorizing potential have also caused the sub-genre to be taken more seriously (in retrospect).[1] However, as with the proto-professional work of nineteenth-century women travellers on the Orient, which happened outside the academic sphere or on its fringes, this sub-genre of

---

[1] See Tedlock, B., 'Works and Wives: On the Sexual Division of Textual Labour' in Ruth Behar and Deborah Gordon: 277

ethnography traditionally lacks prestige (Melman: 9). Nevertheless, Doubleday's focus on the lives of three women tackles the inadequacies of the culture concept. Her study represents an early fulfillment of Abu-Lughod's call (ten years later) for an anthropological focus on 'particular individuals and their changing relationships 'as a means of 'subvert[ing] the most problematic connotations of culture: homogeneity, coherence, and timelessness (Brightman: 515).

Appendix Three
Margaret Mills, *Rhetorics and Politics in Afghan Traditional Storytelling*

Margaret Mills recalls in a footnote that 'the main thesis' of her *Rhetorics and Politics in Afghan Traditional Storytelling* was 'rejected for presentation by the American Anthropologist Association's annual program committee in 1980' because 'it was "not anthropology"' (15). By the time the book was published in 1991, however, its approach had become anthropologically fashionable. The inside cover of Mill's ethnography describes it as 'an ethnopoetic translation and an interpretation of an evening of storytelling which took place in rural Afghanistan in 1975'. In fact, of all six ethnographies about Afghanistan to which this study refers, Mill's is most self-consciously written up with an eye on the insights of the late nineteen-eighties and early nineteen-nineties. Like Clifford, Mills believes in the birth of the reader, and in the redemptive power of new, critical 'reading styles', to which she attributes the power to 'detec[t] and rejec[t] monologically authoritative interpretations […] even when they are attempted' (17). Moreover the stories, together with the listeners' interjections appear in full, both as a direct transcription and in translated form. The principle behind 'genuine polyphony', as Clifford calls it, is that it militates against the narrative totalitarianism of which ethnographers (and travel writers) are so regularly accused. Mills cites Clifford's recommendations in her introductory chapter: 'My intention in this volume is to provide that "sufficient length"' in order to 'giv[e] the storytellers' words "autonomous textual space"' (p17) Her study also attends to '[s]ilential relations' (20) in an attempt to remove the disadvantage conventionally experienced by subordinate interlocutors.

Appendix Four
Nazif Shahrani, *The Kirghiz and Wakhi of Afghanistan. Adaptation to Closed Frontiers and War*

Nazif Shahrani states that he is keen to resist a tendency, observable in anthropologies about Afghanistan, to 'ignore' the 'painful and pervasive sociopolitical issues' of 'wars (colonial, anti-colonial, nationalist, revolutionary, and interventionist)' (www. indiana.edu/~afghan/ nazif_shahrani. htm). He conceptualises his study, *The Kirghiz and Wakhi of Afghanistan. Adaptation to Closed Frontiers and War* as counteracting the what he sees as the imperialist bias of most ethnographies about Afghanistan. Shahrani's narrative is careful to place the Kirghiz and Wakhi in the context of these incursions by mapping colonial missions, border crossings and contacts between these groups and non-Kirghiz or non-Wakhi people.

Shahrani's introduction suggests that his study is caught up in very specific contexts of power:

> During my third and last trip in late August 1973, I was fortunate enough to travel in the company of Wakeel M. Ismail Pamiri of Khandud, then the Wakhan deputy to the Afghan parliament who was making a tour of the upper section of Wakhan and the little Pamir [...] I found it both interesting and fruitful to observe a politician among his constituents (xxxiii).

When Afghan, specifically Pashtun, governments are repeatedly described as perpetuating a form of 'internal colonization', it is difficult to understand how Shahrani's association with a government official differs markedly from, say, Evans-Pritchard acting as an agent of the very government that was oppressing the Nuer (Rosaldo in Clifford and Marcus: 91). Elsewhere, the narrative conveys the honorary status accorded to him as an outsider (to the region) and which his association with agents of power confers upon him: 'I was placed next to the [Kirghiz] khan (a high honor), and treated as an elder despite my age.' (157) As is often the case, his narrative reflects on these tensions elsewhere. Shahrani's narrator states that the khan has 'tremendous economic power' and that 'Kirghiz political organization has gradually given way to an increasingly centralized, mildly authoritarian and "feudal" structure in which the khan figures prominently' in which the government '[quoting Owen Lattimore] make him [the khan] their go-between [thus] reinforc[ing] the power of the chief over his people' (184).

There is much evidence to suggest that, like other anthropologists such as Nancy Tapper (neé Lindisfarne) and Margaret Mills, Shahrani struggles to keep his ethnography from accruing excessive narrative authority. As with Tapper's work, however, Kirghiz/Wakhi voices tend to be conflated into an overarching ethnographic commentary. The following example is in keeping with much of Shahrani's narrative: 'Despite long-time trade relations between the two groups [Kirghiz and Wakhi], I found less than a dozen Kirghiz who claimed to have permanent Wakhi partners for exchange of their goods' (188). Shahrani does not here record the precise number of these interviews and, most significantly, the substance, context and nature of these denials. He thus exercises a degree of prejudicial agency. The informants' denial has doubt cast upon it, not merely by the marker of subjectivity ('claimed') but because it is dwarfed and contradicted by a pronouncement that very likely seems derived from written documentation ('long-time trade relations').

Shahrani was born and brought up in Afghanistan and describes himself as 'a "native" anthropologist'. 'Native' credentials are a powerful means of aggregating, rather than refuting, authority to accounts of life in Afghanistan. A review from the *Journal of Asian Studies* is cited on the back cover: 'Shahrani's work is […] significant', it states, because, 'it is a work by a local or native anthropologist.' The reception of Saira Shah's award winning documentary 'Beaneath the Veil', reveals the same tendency to mobilize the insider/outsider trope in ways that raise the status of the account, or documentary. In a CNN.com internet chat, Shah terms herself: 'an Afghan in Afghanistan' (2002: 2), while a CNN press release claims that it was her half-Afghan status that gave her 'unprecedented access' to Afghanistan (9 July, 2002:1).

Appendix Five
Nancy Tapper, *Politics, gender and marriage in an Afghan tribal society*

In a thinly veiled accusation of textual and theoretical conservatism, Nancy Tapper's *Bartered Brides. Politics, gender and marriage in an Afghan tribal society* has been described by Akbar S. Ahmed as 'a straightforward traditional anthropology familiar in the Middle East literature (her acknowledgements are a who's who of Middle Eastern anthropology).'[2]   Indeed, Tapper's study is conventional in many respects. It tends to orchestrate and synthesise informants' voices into a relatively coherent expression of Durrani belief. Despite Tapper's having taped over one hundred hours of conversation and interview (12), Durrani voices tend to be subsumed by the ethnographic commentary (the first direct quotation from an informant appears on 59).   Interviewees' statements are generally quoted to support ethnographic claims:

> As one of the sons of Hajji Ibrahim said:
> "Those people of Upper Sinjit are not good people; they say all sorts of things. We don't give women to them. We gave one of my sisters there and how much we regretted it. We have not given any other woman to those people, nor will we give any."
> Unfortunately I did not record any detailed statement from Chimar [from Lineage A] making the same point about marriage within Lineage A, but I know that factionalism there is conceived of in the same way (92).

The act of foregrounding a lack of conclusive evidence might be described as a de-authorizing strategy. However, Tapper's opening statement ('[a]s one of the sons of Hajji Ibrahaim said') lends weight to her conjecture about factionalism among Durranis in general, rather than her informant in particular. Even so, Tapper's stated aims in the introduction show a strong awareness of the need not to supress

---

[2] Ahmed, A.S., Book review *Modern Asian Studies* 28:1, February 1994

conflicting voices among ethnographers by declaring her 'ambition [...] to present marriage from as many perspectives as possible' (8). As one might expect, therefore, Tapper's study cannot be labelled as straightforwardly classical (as if such a state were possible).

Tapper's introduction ensures that her study is distanced from Doubleday's exclusive focus on gender, by arguing that it is no longer possible to 'justify accounts which rely exclusively on only male or female informants' (20). In addition, close attention is paid to what she describes as 'the non-verbal discourses of subordinate men and women' as a means of attending to conflicts between men and women's versions of reality to balance moments of general verbal agreement between them (12). The study demonstrates a strong awareness of ways in which '[f]eminists and anthropologists have very properly raised doubts about the universality of female subordination' (20). In fact the study is attentive to the fact that 'male prestige is heavily dependent on women', who have the 'capacity to undermine male ambitions and damage male prestige' (22).

Appendix Six
Interview with Christina Lamb (CL) by Corinne Fowler (CF).

Corinne Fowler (CF): I know you're reluctant to categorise *The Sewing Circles of Herat* but would you agree that travel writing has particular appeal for journalists because there isn't necessarily the space or opportunity to write everything they want in their news reports?

Christina Lamb (CL): Yes, indeed. It's very difficult when you know a place for a long time. There are lots of colourful details and things that you would like to convey and yet you know you can only write a thousand five hundred-word piece a week, which is usually the case. Obviously you can't get that in; those pieces are very much news-driven. I was actually talking to my editor at *The Sunday Times* yesterday and he was saying that it must be very boring in Afghanistan in the evenings. He was asking if I read lots of books and I told him I end up actually going to lots of dinners with Afghan friends and eating kebabs and stuff. So I was just drawing the scene for him as to what's it's really like at these dinners with lots of tribal leaders there and often people playing chess while people come in and out with interminable amounts of food, and he was saying, you know, you should write about this and, yes, I'd love to but it's very difficult when you're writing weekly news stories covering events. It's not easy to get all that in. I hope that because it's a country that I know very well and that I've been going to for years, that some of that comes through in the reporting. I know that when I read the reporting of my colleagues I can usually tell whether somebody has just been parachuted in or whether she or he knows the place very well and has been going there for a long time.

CF: I notice that Louis Dupree is in your bibliography. Would you say that the work of Dupree, or indeed the practice of anthropology, has had any bearing in your approach to writing about Afghanistan?

Would you be flattered or concerned by being compared to an anthropologist?

CL: Well, obviously, Louis and Nancy Dupree were real authorities on Afghanistan and when I lived there, they were also living there. I would be flattered to be compared to that kind of work, I mean their work on Afghanistan is very authoritative. I don't necessarily think their style of anthropology compares to anthropology in general, I think in their case they had a great love for the country, and so they really, you know, dedicated their lives to it.

CF: In the build-up to the Afghan elections I notice that many journalists have adopted the game *buzkashi* as a metaphor for Afghan resistance to democratic processes. Do you see any danger in using these kinds of metaphors to encapsulate what you've described as 'the whole picture' rather than 'only fragments'?

CL: I don't like using images like that. I think it's a real problem for a reporter when you see only fragments of what's happening and I think this problem should be made clear. Particularly in a country like that, so huge and so diverse. But then journalists are working within such restricted space, trying to convey something in a small amount of words and those [kinds of metaphors] are an easy way out.

CF: I've mentioned that you foreground a reluctance on your part to make any claim to see the 'whole picture', and you point out that you were always presented with multiple realities to work with. Do you find that a book like *The Sewing Circles of Herat* allows reflections and complexities that allow you to question the authority of your own observations more comfortably than if you were writing a news report?

CL: As correspondents in the past we had a lot of time to think about what we were writing. I could reflect at my leisure on what I wanted to say. Now you only have a short time and then you have to *file*. That's why I really like to write books because there is no way you can convey properly in news articles the reality of the place and it's very easy to give a very misleading view.

CF: You were saying that male reporters don't have access to Afghan women, which is of course, very problematic. Even so, my research suggests that in general both female and male reporters tend to still privilege the voices of Afghan men (although female reporters are seen to be marginally less guilty of this). I sense that you have gone to some lengths in your travel book to correct that bias and perhaps to depict Afghan women as agents of change rather than passive victims. Is that an accurate description of your rationale?

CL: A difficulty for women reporters, too, is that all the news editors – I think - in British newspapers are male, what they often want from the correspondents on the ground is sort of 'bang bang' and battles, then they get very excited and put their maps on the wall with stick-pins in, so it's quite difficult sometimes to be trying to write stuff from behind the scenes, because to them that's not the story, the story is the fighting on the ground so I think that that happens both for male and female correspondents. Sometimes it's also the case, say with the war on Iraq, in the early part we just weren't meeting any women because we weren't really able to go into towns or anything because it was still under Saddam's control and you were only meeting people out on the roads who for the most part were male. So that did make it very difficult.

CF: I've just been going through some archives in the British Film Institute and people make very telling mistakes in their news reports: *Haret* instead of Herat and *Afghani* rather than Afghan. But your book gave Marri some space to speak. Why do you think Afghan women are left out, not just from travel accounts but from war reporting?

CL: It's hard to tell but most of the reporters who are writing about Afghanistan are male and who do not have access to women and it's funny I'm always asked by people "what is it like being a woman reporting in these places?" Well actually, it's a lot better because we don't have fifty percent of the population cut off from us and actually I think Afghan men I think tend to...they don't quite know what to make of western women reporters. We seem to be some kind of de-sexualised species I think, so they often are perhaps more relaxed.

CF: I notice at one point you suggest in *The Sewing Circles of Herat* that as one of the few female correspondents it was 'different' for you and you also suggest that women might tackle war reporting differently from men. You write that 'the real story of war wasn't about the fighting and the firing, some Boy' s Own adventure of goodies and baddies.' How was it 'different' for you?

CL: I think it is very different for women because I think you, we tend to be more aware. I think that male reporters covering wars focus very much on the actual boys with toys theme; the fighting, the technology, the equipment and while that's valid, that to me isn't the real story. I think again with Iraq, you know, the story is that people there are trying to keep their lives together, keep their families together, educate their children through war. This is true of Afghanistan particularly because fighting went on for twenty-seven years, so, through that, trying to bring up, trying to educate children…and I suppose it's something I've felt more since becoming a mother, thinking of women who walk for months through the mountains scraping moss off rocks to feed their children, imagining what that must be like trying to give that to your child at the end of the day.

CF: On the subject of being a mother, you dedicate your book to your young son, which suggests a consciousness that, as a woman, extensive travel away from home perhaps transgresses certain boundaries even now. It also reminds me of Yvonne Ridley, who came under such attack for leaving her daughter Daisy behind. Very rarely do male travellers or correspondents express that kind of dilemma. Have you any more thoughts on that issue?

CL: It sort of annoys me that people ask me, you know, how can you leave your child? People don't ask male reporters. Obviously large numbers of them do have small children although I have a colleague who tells me that the only time he ever gets a good night's sleep is when he is off covering wars because he's got three children under the age of four and they're always waking him up at night. But it is difficult. I don't do such crazy things, I'm more careful because I have a responsibility to my son and it was quite hard during the war on Afghanistan when I was away all the time and when I came back when he was almost two and I was away for at least three weeks of the next eight months and in that period when he was starting to talk he used to tell people that his mummy lives on a plane. It's funny, now he's older he's fine. He accepts it. He likes to point to the places that I go to [on the map].

Bibliography of Primary Texts

Azoy, W. (2003) *Buzkashi. Game and Power in Afghanistan. Second Edition*, Illinois: Waveland Press.

Bealby, J. (1999) *For A Pagan Song. Travels in India, Pakistan and Afghanistan*, London: Arrow Books Limited.

Bowie-Shor, J. (1955) *After You, Marco Polo*, London: McGraw-Hill Book Co. Incl.

Burnes, Sir A. (1842) *Cabool: Being a Personal Narrative of A Journey To, and Residence In that City, In the Years 1836, 7, and 8*, London: John Murray.

Byron, R. (1950) The Road to Oxiana, London: John Lehmann.

Caroe, Olaf Sir (2000) *The Pathans*, London: Kegan Paul International.

Carrington, Charles (1974) *The Complete Barrack-Room Ballads of Rudyard Kipling*, London: Methuen and Co. Ltd.

Chatwin, B. (1998) *What Am I Doing Here*, London: Vintage Press.

Cornell, L. L. (ed.) (1987) Rudyard Kipling. The Man Who Would Be King and Other Stories, Oxford: Oxford University Press.

Danziger, N., ([1987] 1988) *Danziger's Travels. Beyond Forbidden Frontiers*, London: Paladin.

Doubleday, V. (1988) Three Women of Herat, London: Jonathan Cape.

Dupree, L. (1973) Afghanistan, Princeton: Princeton University Press.

Elliot, J. ([1999]2000) *An Unexpected Light. Travels in Afghanistan*, London: Picador.

Elphinstone, M. ([1815]1972) *An Account of the Kingdom of Caubul*, Karachi: Oxford University Press.

Finlay, V. (2002) *Colour. Travels Through the Paintbox*, London: Hodder and Stoughton.

Gall, S. (1988) *Afghanistan: Agony of a Nation. Foreword by the Right Honorable Margaret Thatcher*, London: The Bodley Head Press Ltd.

Kaplan, R. D., (2001) *Soldiers of God. With Islamic Warriors in Afghanistan and Pakistan*, New York: Vintage.

Kaye, Sir J. (1851) *History of The War in Afghanistan From The Unpublished Letters and Journals of Police and Military Officers Employed in Afghanistan Throughout The Entire Period of British Connexion* [sic] *With That Country*, London: Richard Bentley.

Kipling, R. (1901) *Kim*, London: Macmillan.

Kremmer, C. (2002) *The Carpet Wars. 10 Years in Afghanistan, Pakistan and Iraq*, London: Harper Collins.

Levi, P. ([1972] 1984) *In the Light Garden of the Angel King. Journeys in Afghanistan*, London: Penguin Books.

Lamb, C. (2002) *The Sewing Circles of Herat. My Afghan Years*, London: Harper Collins.

Lindisfarne, N. (1991) *Bartered Brides: politics, gender and marriage in an Afghan tribal society*, Cambridge and New York: Cambridge University Press.

Mills, M. (1991) *Rhetorics and Politics in Afghan Traaditional Storytelling*, Pensylvannia: University of Pensylvannia Press.

Murphy, D., ([1965] 1995) *Full Tilt. Dunkirk to Delhi by Bicycle*, London: Flamingo.

Newby, E. ([1958]1974) *A Short Walk in the Hindu Kush*, London: Picador.

Paine, S. ([1994]1995) *The Afghan Amulet. Travels from the Hindu Kush to Razgrad*, London: Penguin Books.

Raverty, G. H., Major (1873) *Notes on Afghanistan and Baluchistan*, London: Ridgeway.

Ridley, Y., (2001) *In the Hands of the Taliban. Her extraordinary Story*, London: Robson Books.

Sale, Lady F. ([1842]2002) *A Journal of the First Afghan War*, Oxford: Oxford University Press.

Shah, S., (2004) *The Storyteller's Daughter: Return to a Lost Homeland*, London: Penguin Books Ltd.

Shahrani, N. M., ([1979]2002) *The Kirghiz and Wakhi of Afghanistan. Adaptation to Closed Frontiers and War*, Washington: University of Washington Press.

Sierstad Asne (2004) *The Bookseller of Kabul*, translated by Ingrid Christophersen, London: Virago.

Somerville-Large, P. (1991) *A Shaggy Yak Story. Forty Years of Unfinished Journeys*, London: Sinclair-Stephenson Ltd.

Stark, F. ([1970]1974) *The Minaret of Djam. An Excursion in Afghanistan*, London: John Murray.

Stewart, R., (2004) *The Places in Between*, London: Picador.

Tapper, N. (1991) *Bartered Brides. Politics, Gender and Marriage in an Afghan Tribal Society*, Seattle: University of Washington Press.

Yule, Sir H. (1881) 'Kafirstan', *Encyclopaedia Britannica. 9th Edition, INF-KAN*, Volume XIII, Edinburgh:Adam and Charles Black.

Wood, Capt. J. (1872) *A Journey To The Source of The River Oxus. With An Essay On The Valley of the Oxus by Sir Henry Yule, C. B. With Maps. Second Edition, edited by his son*, London: John Murray.

Bibliography of Secondary Texts

Ahearn L. M. (2001) 'Language and Agency', *Annual Review of Anthropology* 30, 109-137.

Ajami F. (2002) 'What the Muslim World is Watching', *TBS* 8:1.

Ali T. (2003) *The Clash of Fundamentalisms. Crusades, Jihads and Modernity*, London: Verso.

Allan, S. (2004) *News Culture*, Maidenhead: Open University Press.

Allen G. (2000) *Intertextuality*, London and New York: Routledge.

Allen S. (2003) *News Culture. Second edition.*, Maidenhead: Open University Press.

Anderson, L. (2001) *Autobiography*, London and New York: Routledge.

Arac, J. (1988) *After Foucault. Humanistic Knowledge, Postmodern Challenges*, London: Rutgers University Press.

Asad, T. (1973) *Anthropology and the Colonial Encounter*, London: Ithaca Press.

Ashcroft, B., Griffiths, G. and Tiffin, H. (1998) *Key Concepts in Post-Colonial Literature*, London and New York: Routledge.

Aziz, C. (1998) 'Defiance and oppression: the situation of women' in E. Girardet and J. Walter (eds.) *Essential Field Guides to humanitarian and conflict zones. Afghanistan*, Geneva: Crosslines Communications Ltd.

Azoy W. (2001) 'Afghanistan's "Goat Game" and American Foreign Policy', *Wabash Magazine* Winter/Fall, 2-3.

Baker K. (2003) 'Conflict and Control: The War in Afghanistan and the 24-Hour News Cycle' in D. Kishan Thussu and D. Freedman (eds.) *War and the Media. Reporting Conflict 24/7*, London: Sage

Bartolovich, C. (2003) 'The Eleventh September of George Bush. Fortress U.S. and the Global Politics of Consumption', *Interventions* 5:2, 177-198.

Barrie, J. M. (1891) 'Mr. Kipling's Stories', *Contemporary Review* LIX, 364-372.

Basset J. (1995) *Great Southern Landings. An Anthology of Antipodean Travel*, Melbourne: Oxford University Press

Beecham R. (2003) 'Our Woman in Kabul and The Sewing Circles of Herat' 17. www.smh.com.au/articles/2003/05/16/1052885399997.-html?oneclick =true. Accessed 19 Jun. 2003.

Behar R. and Gordon D. (1996) *Women Writing Culture*. Berkeley: University of California Press.

Bell A. (1999) 'News Stories as Narratives' in A. Jaworsky and N. Coupland (eds.) *The Discourse Reader*, London: Routledge.

Besant, Sir W. (1900) 'Is it the Voice of the Hooligan?', *Contemporary Review*, LXXVII, 27-39.

Bhabha, H. (1997) 'Minority Maneuvers and Unsettled Negotiations', *Critical Inquiry*, Spring 23:3, 431-459

Bhabha, H. (1994) *The Location of Culture*, London and New York: Routledge.

Birkett, D. and Wheeler, S. (1998) *Amazonian*, London: Penguin Books Ltd.

Boehmer E. (1995) *Colonial and Postcolonial Literature. Migrant Metaphors*, Oxford: Oxford University Press.

Boehmer, E. (1998) *Empire Writing. An Anthology of Colonial Literature. 1870 - 1918*, Oxford: Oxford University Press.

Brightman R. (1995) 'Forget Culture: Replacement, Transcendence, Relexification', *Cultural Anthropology* 10, 509-546.

Brothers B. and Gergits J. (1997) *British Travel Writers, 1876-1909*, Detroit and Michigan: Gale Research.

Bulbeck C. (1998) *Re-Orientating Western Feminisms. Women's Diversity in a Postcolonial World*, Melbourne: Cambridge University Press.

Bumatay M. and Hupprich L. (2002) 'Global Internet Population Grows An Average of Four Percent Year-Over-Year,' www.nielsen-netratings.com/pr/pr_030220.pdf. Accessed 10 Feb. 2005.

Burdett C. and Duncan D. (eds.) (2002) *Cultural Encounters. Travel Writing in the 1930's*, Oxford: Berghahn Books.

Butt J. (1998) 'The Taliban Phenomenon' in E. Giradet and J. Walter, (eds.) *Essential Field Guides to humanitarian and conflict zones. Afghanistan*, Geneva: Crosslines Communications Ltd.

Buzard J. (1993) *The Beaten Track. European Tourism, Literature, and the Ways to Culture, 1800-1918*, Oxford: Clarendon Press.

Buzard J. and Childers J. (1997) 'Introduction: Victorian Ethnographies', *Victorian Studies* 41, 350-

Caine B. (1997) *English Feminism 1780 - 1890*, Oxford: Oxford University Press.

Carey J. W. (2002) 'American Journalism On, Before and After Septem-ber 11th' in B. Zelizer and S. Allan (eds.). *Journalism After September 11*, London and New York: Routledge

Carruthers S. L. (1999) *The Media at War: Communication and Conflict in the Twentieth Century*, London: Palgrave Macmillan.

Carter P. (1987) *The Road to Botany Bay. An Essay in Spacial History*, London: Faber and Faber.

Chilton, P. (2002) 'Do Something!', *Journal of Language and Politics* 1:2, 365-366.

Clammer P. (2004) 'Kabul and Tourism: Kabul Caravan', www.kabulcaravan.com. Accessed 8 Jun. 2004.

Clark S. (1999) *Travel Writing and Empire: Postcolonial Theory in Transit*, London: Zed Books.

Clifford J. (1983) 'On Ethnographic Authority', *Representations* 1, 118-146.

Clifford J. (1997) *Routes. Travel and Translation in the Late Twentieth Century*, Cambridge: Harvard University Press.

Clifford J and Marcus G.E. (1986) *Writing Culture. The Poetics and Politics of Ethnography*. Berkley, New York and London: University of California Press.

Cooper S. (2000) *Relating to Queer Theory. Rereading Sexual Self-Definition with Irigaray, Kristeva, Wittig and Ciuox*, Bern: Peter Lang.

266 *Chasing Tales*

Cormack M. (1992) *Ideology*, Michigan: University of Michigan Press.

Cornwall A. and Lindisfarne N. (1994) *Dislocating Masculinity. Comparative Ethnographies*, London and New York: Routledge.

Cronin, M. (2002) 'The Empire Talks Back: Orality, Heteronomy and the Cultural Turn in Interpreting Studies' in E. Gentzler and M. Tymoczko (eds.) *Translation and Power*, Boston and Amherst: University of Massachusetts Press, 45-62.

Dawood, N. J. (transl.) (1954), *Tales from the Thousand and One Nights*, London: Penguin.

Davidson, R. (2000) 'Against Travel Writing', *Granta* 72, Winter, 34-38.

De Kretser Michelle (1998) *Brief Encounters. Stories of love, sex and travel*, London: Lonely Planet Publications.

DelZotto A. C. (2002) 'Weeping Women, Wringing Hands: How the Mainstream Media Stereotyped Women's Experiences in Kosovo', *Journal of Gender Studies* 11, 91-108.

Dening G. (1980) *Islands and Beaches: discourse on a silent land, Marquesas 1774-1880*, Honolulu: University Press of Hawaii.

Denzin N. K. (2002) 'Confronting Ethnography's Crisis of Representation', *Journal of Contemporary Ethnography* 31, 483-494.

Donnell A. 'The Veil: Postcolonialism and the Politics of Dress', *Interventions* 1:4, London 1-6

Downey J. and Murdock G. (2003) 'The Counter-Revolution in Military Affairs: The Globalisation of Guerilla Warfare' in D. Kishan Thussu and D. Freedman (eds.) *War and the Media. Reporting Conflict 24/7*, London: Sage

Duncan J. and Gregory D. (1999) *Writes of Passage. Reading Travel Writing*, London and New York: Routledge.

Edmond R. (1997) *Representing the South Pacific. Colonial Discourse from Cook to Gaugin*. Cambridge: Cambridge University Press.

El-Nawawy, M. and Iskandar, A. (2002) *Al-Jazeera. How the Free Arab News Network Scooped the World and Changed the Middle East*, Cambridge MA: Westview Press.

Esposito J. L. (2002) *Unholy War. Terror in the Name of Islam*, Oxford: Oxford University Press.

Evans B. J. and Mannur A. (2003) *Theorizing Diaspora. A Reader*. Oxford: Blackwell.

Fawley M.H. (1994) *A Wider Range. Travel Writing by Women in Victorian England*, London and Ontario: Associated University Presses.

Fisk, R. (2001) 'Blood, Tears, Terror and Tragedy', *Counterpunch*, www.counterpunch.org/fiskblood/html. Accessed 26 Nov. 2004.

Fitzgerald T. (2000) *The Ideology of Religious Studies*, Oxford: Oxford University Press.

Flagherty M. G. (2002) 'The "Crisis" in Representation: Reflections and Assessments', *Journal of Contemporary Ethnography* 31, 509-512.

Flaherty M. G. (2002) 'The Crisis in Representation: A Brief History and Some Questions', *Journal of Contemporary Ethnography* 31, 479-481.

Foster, S., and Mills, S., (2002) *An anthology of women's travel writing*, Manchester: Manchester University Press.

Forsdick, C. (2004) Paper on Edouard Glissant at the ESSE conference, Zaragoza, Spain, 9th September.

Fortunati V., Monticelli R. and Ascari M. (2001) *Travel Writing and the Female Imaginary*, Bologna: Patron

Fowler, C. (2003) 'Introduction. Travel Writing and Cultural *Terrae Incognitae*: Ongoing Ethical and Theoretical Dilemmas', *Journeys* 4:1, 1-5.

Fowler, C. (2004) 'The Problem of Narrative Authority. Kate Karko and Catherine Oddie' in K. Siegel (ed.) *Gender, Genre and Identity in Women's Travel Writing*, New York: Peter Lang Publishing.

Frawley, M. H. (1994) *A Wider Range. Travel Writing by Women in Victorian England*, New Jersey: Associated University Presses.

'BBC Radio 4 From Our Own Correspondent Homepage', www.bbc.co.uk/1/hi/programmes/from_our_own_correspondent/3 143512.stm. Accessed 10 Nov. 2004.

Ghose I. (2000) 'Joseph Conrad's *Heart of Darkness* and the Anxiety of Empire' in L. Glage (ed.) *B/eings in Transit. Travelling. Migration. Dislocation*, Amsterdam: Rodopi.

Giradet E., and Walter, J., (1998) *Essential Field Guides to humanitarian and conflict zones. Afghanistan*, Geneva: Crosslines Communications Ltd.

Gokay B. (2002) 'Introduction:oil, war and geopolitics from Kosovo to Afghanistan', *Journal of Southern Europe and the Balkans* 4, 10-17.

Goldie, T. (1989) *Fear and Temptation: The Image of the Indigene in Canadian, Australian and New Zealand Literatures*, Montreal: McGill-Queen's

Gosse, E. (1891) 'Rudyard Kipling', *Century Magazine*, XLII, 901-910.

Greenblatt S. (1994) 'Invisible bullets: Renaissance authority and its subversion, *HenryIV* and *Henry V*.' in J. Dollimore and A. Sinfield (eds.) *Political Shakespeare. Essays in Cultural Materialism.*, Manchester: Manchester University Press.

Gregory D. (2004) *The Colonial Present. Afghanistan. Palestine. Iraq*, Oxford: Blackwell.

Grey J. (2003) *Al Qaeda and what it means to be modern*, London: Faber and Faber.

Hannerz, U. (2004) *Foreign News. Exploring the World of Foreign Correspondents*, Chicago: University of Chicago Press.

Hassan R. 'Muslim Women's Rights: A Contemporary Debate' in S. Mehta (ed.) *Women for Afghan Women. Shattering Myths and Claiming the Future*, New York: Palgrave Macmillan.

Heathcote, T.A. (1980) *The Afghan Wars 1839-1919* London: Osprey Publishing.

Hickley, N. (2002) 'Access Denied. The Pentagon's War Reporting Rules are the Toughest Ever', *Columbia Journalism Review* online, January/February.

Hickman K. (2001) *Illustrated Daughters of Britannia*, London: Flamingo.

Hill, F. and Aboitiz, M. (2002) 'Women Are Opening Doors. Security Council Resolution 1325 in Afghanistan' in S. Mehta, (ed.) *Women for Afghan Women. Shattering Myths and Claiming the Future*, New York: Palgrave Macmillan.

Hine C. (2000) *Virtual Ethnography*, London: Sage.

Hogle, J. (ed.) (2002) *The Cambridge Companion to Gothic Fiction*, Cambridge: Cambridge University Press.

Holland, P. and Huggan, G. (1998) *Tourists With Typewriters. Critical Reflections on Contemporary travel Writing*, Michigan: University of Michigan Press.

Hopkirk, P. (1996) *Quest for Kim. In Search of Kipling's Great Game*, London: John Murray.

Horannisian, R. and Sabagh, G. (eds.) (1989) *The 1001 Nights in Arabic Literature and Society*, Cambridge: Cambridge University Press.

Huggan G. (2000) 'Counter-Travel Writing and Post-Coloniality' in Glage L. (ed.) *Being/s in Transit. Travelling. Migration. Disorientation*, Amsterdam: Rodopi.

Hulme P. and Youngs, T. (eds.) (2002) *The Cambridge Companion to Travel Writing*, Cambridge: Cambridge University Press.

Humm, M. (ed.) (1992) *Feminisms. A Reader*, Hemel Hempstead: Harvester Wheatsheaf.

Hunt Krista (2002) 'The Strategic Co-optation of Women's Rights. Discourse in the "War on Terrorism"', *International Feminist Journal of Politics*, 4, 27-39.

Jayawardena K. (1995) *The white woman's other burden: Western women and south Asia during British colonial rule*, London and New York: Routledge.

Juschka, D. (ed.) (2001) *Feminism in the Study of Religion*, London and New York: Continuum.

Karasac H. (2002) 'Actors of the new "Great Game". Caspian oil politics', *Journal of Southern Europe and the Balkans* 4, 38-49.

Karim H. K. (2002) 'Making sense of the "Islamic Peril". Journalism as cultural practice' in B. Zelizer and S. Allan, (eds.) *Journalism After September 11*, London and New York: Routledge.

Keller M. (2003) *New Perspectives on Race and Gender in the Study of Religions*, London: Zed Press.

Khan A. (2003) 'Gendering War Talk. 'We are scattered like seeds and the world is full of us', *International Feminist Journal of Politics* 5, 32-40.

Kipling, R. (1920) *Letters of Travel 1892-1913* London: Macmillan.

Kipling, R. ([1937]1964) *Something of Myself, For My Friends Known and Unknown*, London: MacMillan and Company Limited.

Kishan Thussu, D. (2003) 'Live TV and Bloodless Deaths: War, Infotainment and 24/7 News' in D. Kishan Thussu and D. Freedman (eds.) *War and the Media. Reporting Conflict 24/7*, London: Sage.

Knapman C. (1997) 'Western Women's Travel Writing About the Pacific Islands', *Pacific Studies* 20, 31-46.

Knowles, C. (2003) 'Postcolonial Urban Landscapes and Narratives of Travel: The Global/Local Journeys of British Lifestyle Migrants in Hong Kong', conference paper, 'Writing the City', Oxford Symposium, University of Oxford.

Kremmer, C. (1997) *Stalking the Elephant Kings. In Search of Laos*, London: Silkworm Books.

Lancylyn-Green, R. (ed.) (1971) *Kipling. The Critical Heritage*, London: Routledge and Kegan Paul.

Lawrence K. R. (1994) *Penelope Voyages. Women and Travel in the British Literary Tradition*, London: Cornell University Press.

Lederman, A. (2002) 'The Zan of Afghanistan. A 35 Year Perspective on Women in Afghanistan' in S. Mehta (ed.) *Women for Afghan Women. Shattering Myths and Claiming the Future*, New York: Palgrave Macmillan.

Loomba, A. (1998) *Colonialism/Postcolonialism*, London and New York: Routledge.

Lowenhaupt Tsing A. (1993) *In the Realm of the Diamond Queen*, Princeton: Princeton University Press.

Lugo, J. (2004) 'Democratic practices and Information & Communication Technologies: A cross-national study', unpublished thesis, University of Sussex.

Lynch, J. (2000) *Reporting the World*, www.Reportingtheworld.org. Accessed 10 Nov. 2004.

MacNair, B. (2003) 'What a difference a decade makes', *British Journalism Review*, 14:1, 42-48.

Macrory P. (2002) *Kabul Catastrophe. The invasion and retreat 1839-1842*, London: Prion Books Ltd.

Magder T. (2003) 'Watching What We Say: Global Communication in a Time of Fear', in D. Kishan Thussu and D. Freedman (eds), *War and the Media. Reporting Conflict 24/7*, London: Sage.

Marx, E. (1999) 'How We Lost Kafirstan', *Representations* 67, Summer, 44-66.

Massing, M. (2002) 'Afghanistan Journal. A Run with the Pack. What our fast-moving press passes by', *Columbia Journalism Review,* archives.cjr.org./ year/02/5/ massing.asp. Accessed May 19 2004.

McLaughlin G. (2002) *The War Correspondent*, London: Pluto Press.

Manning P. (2002) 'The Sky is Not Falling', *Journal of Contemporary Ethnography* 31, 490-500.

Marcus G. E. (1999) *Critical Anthropology Now. Unexpected Contexts, Shifting Constituencies, Changing Agendas*, Santa Fe: School of American Research Press.

McNay L. (2000) *Gender and Agency. Reconfiguring the Subject in Feminist and Social Theory*, Oxford: Polity Press.

Melman B. *(1992) Women's Orients: English Women and the Middle East, 1718-1918*, London: Macmillan.

Melton J. A. (2002) *Mark Twain, Travel Books, and Tourism: The Tide of a Great Popular Movement*, Alabama: University of Alabama Press

Mercer, W. (1999) 'Gender and Genre in nineteenth-century travel writing: Leonie d'Aunet and Xavier Marmier' in S. Clarke (ed.) *Travel Writing and Empire: Postcolonial Theory in Transit*, London: Zed.

Miller, J. (2004) 'First Lady', www.channel4.com/news/2004/week_1/03_afghanistan.html. Accessed 01 Dec. 2004.

Mirza H. S. (1997) *Black British Feminism. A Reader*, London: Routledge.

Monaghan, J. and Just, P. (2000) *Social and Cultural Anthropology. A Very Short Introduction*, Oxford: Oxford University Press.

Monbiot, G. (2001) 'Blasting our way to peace', *Counterpunch*, www.counterpunch.org/fiskblood/html. Accessed 15 Nov 2004.

Moore-Gilbert Bart (2002) '"I am going to rewrire Kipling's *Kim*": Kipling and Postcolonialism'. *Journal of Commonwealth Literature* 37, 39-54.

Moore-Gilbert B. (1996) *Writing India 1757-1990. The literature of British India*, Manchester: Manchester University Press.

Moore Henrietta (1988) *Feminism and Anthropology*, Cambridge: Polity Press.

Moore, Henrietta, (ed.) (1999) *Anthropological Theory Today*, Cambridge: Polity.

Morris, J. ([1968]1980) *Pax Britannica. The Climax of An Empire*, London: Faber and Faber in Association with Hallmark.

Morris M. and O'Connor L. (1996) *The Virago Book of Women Travellers*, New York: Virago Press.

Nicholson, R.A. ([1907]1969) *A Literary History of the Arabs*, Cambridge: Cambridge University Press.

Oyewumi O. (1997) *The Invention of Women. Making An African Sense of Western Gender Discourses*, London and Minneapolis: University of Minnesota Press.

Orel, H. (1990) *A Kipling Chronology*, London: Macmillan.

Parsons, M., (1992) 'The facts cannot speak for themselves: the example of press coverage of the sinking of the *Belgrano*', Unpublished paper, privately communicated by the author.

Pedelty, M. (1995) *War Stories. The Culture of Foreign Correspondents*, London and New York, Routledge.

Penguin Publishing Group, (2000) *Women Travel. First Hand Accounts of More than 60 Countries*, London: Rough Guides Limited.

Pesman R., Walker, D., and White, R., (1996) *The Oxford Book of Australian Travel Writing*, Melbourne: Oxford University Press.

Philo, G., and Berry, M., (2004) *Bad News From Israel*, Pluto Press, London: Pluto.

Philo G. (2004) 'What you get in 20 seconds', *The Guardian*, July 14th.

Pratt M. L., (1986) 'Scratches on the Face of the Country; or, What Mr. Barrow Saw in the Land of the Bushmen' in Gates H.L. jnr. (ed.) *Race, Writing and Difference*, Chicago: University of Chicago Press.

Puwar, N., (2002) 'Multi-cultural fashion...stirrings of another sense of aesthetics and memory', *Feminist Review* 71, 56-70.

Rashid, A. (2000) *Taliban. Islam, Oil and the New Great Game in Central Asia*, London and New York, I.B. Taurus Publishers.

Richardson, A. (2002) *Three Oriental Tales. Complete Texts with Introduction, Historical Contexts, Critical Essays. Frances Sheridan, 'History of Nourjahad', William Beckford, 'Vathek' and Lord Byron, The Giaour*, Boston and New York: Houghton Mifflin Company.

Rice, P. and Waugh, P., (ed.) *Modern Literary Theory. A Reader. Third Edition*, London: Arnold.

Richards D. (1994) *Masks of Difference. Cultural representations in anthropology, literature and art*, Cambridge: Cambridge University Press.

Richter William L. (1984) Book review, *International Journal of Middle Eastern Studies* 16, 270-272.

Ridley, Y. (2003) 'In the Fog of War' in D. Kishan Thussu and D. Freedman (eds.) *War and the Media. Reporting Conflict 24/7*, London: Sage.

Rogers, J. (2003) 'Icons and Invisibility: Gender, Myth, 9/11' in D. Kishan Thussu and D. Freedman (eds.) *War and the Media. Reporting Conflict 24/7*, London: Sage.

Roy A. (2002) 'Not Again', *The Guardian*, September 27th.

Rubin, M., and Benjamin, D., (2000) 'Policywatch. Special Forum Report. The Taliban and Terrorism: Report from Afghanistan', *Washington Institute for Near East Policy*, April.

Russell, M. (1994) *The Blessings of a Good Thick Skirt. Women Travellers and their World*, London: Flamingo.

Rutherford, A. (ed.) (1987) *Rudyard Kipling. Plain Tales From The Hills*, Oxford: Oxford University Press.

Ryan, S. (1996) *The Cartographic Eye. How Explorers Saw Australia*, Cambridge: Cambridge University Press.

Said, E.W., (1978) *Orientalism. Western Conceptions of the Orient*, London and New York: Routledge Kegan Paul.

Said, E. W. (1996) *Covering Islam. How the Media and the Experts Determine How We See the Rest of the World* , New York: Vintage.

Sallis, E. (1999) *Scherazade through the Looking Glass. The Metamorphosis of the 1001 Nights*, London: Curzon.

Schiffer, R (1999) *Oriental Panorama: British Travellers in 19th Century Turkey*, Amsterdam: Rodopi.

Seaton, J. (2003) 'Understanding not empathy' in D. Kishan Thussu and D. Freedman, (eds.) *War and the Media. Reporting Conflict 24/7*, London: Sage

Shah, S. (2001) www.CNN.com/chat/shah/01/24/asp. Accessed 19 Nov. 2003.

Shaw, M. (2002) 'Risk-transfer militarism, small massacres and the historic legitimacy of war', *International Relations*, 16:3, 343-360.

Shostak, M. (2000) *Nisa. The Life and Words of a !Kung Woman*, London: Earthscan publications. .

Smith, B.G. (2000) *Global Feminisms since 1945*, London: Routledge.

Snow D. (2002) 'On the Presumed Crisis in Ethnography: Observations from a Sociological and Interactionist Standpoint', *Journal
of Contemporary Ethnography* 31, 501-505.

Spurr, D., (1993) *The Rhetoric of Empire. Colonial Discourse in
Journalism, Travel Writing and Imperial Administration*, London:
Duke University Press.

Steele J. E. (1995) 'Experts and Operational Bias of Television News:
The Case of the Persian Gulf War', *J & MC Quarterly* 72, 799-
811.

Stein, Sir A. (1921) *Serindia. Detailed Report of Explorations in
Central Asia and Westernmost China. Carried Out and Described
Under the Orders of H.M. Indian Government By Aurel Stein,
K.C.I.E. Indian Archeological Survey*, Oxford: Clarendon Press.

Stein, Sir A. (1928) *Innermost Asia. Detailed Report of Explorations
in Central Asia, Kan-su and Eastern Iran. Carried Out and
Described Under the Orders of H.M. Indian Government by Sir
Aurel Stein, K.C.I.E Indian Archeologica Survey*, Oxford:
Clarendon Press.

Stewart, J. P. (2000) 'The Looking Glass of Empire: Early Feminist
Interrogation of the Colonial Patriarchy, 1850-1950', unpublished
doctoral thesis, University of Stirling.

Stoezler, M., and Yuval-Davis, N. (2002) 'Standpoint theory, situated
knowledge and the situated imagination' *Feminist Theory* 3, 23-39.

Stoller P. and Olkes, C. (1987) *In Sorcery's Shadow. A Memoir of
Apprenticeship Among the Songhay of Niger*, Chicago: University
of Chicago Press.

Stratton, M. L. (2002) *Guests in the Land of Buzkashi. Afghanistan
Revisited*, First Books Library.

Tapper, N. (1985) Book review of Azoy's *Buzkashi. Game and
Power. Man* 18:1, 213.

Talpande Mohanty, C. (2001) 'Under Western Eyes: Feminist
Scholarship and Colonial Discourse' in M. Gigi Durham and D. M.
Kellner (eds.) *Media and Cultural Studies. Key Works*, Oxford:
Blackwell.

Townsend, D. (2004) 'Enjoying the gothic', privately communicated
by the author.

Tumbler, H. and Palmer, J. (2004) *Media at War. The Iraq Crisis*,
London: Sage.

Turner, G. (2002) *The Film Cultures Reader*, London and New York: Routledge.

Urry, J. (1990) *The Tourist Gaze. Leisure and Travel in Contemporary Societies*, London: Sage.

Vorgetts, F. (2002) 'A Vision of Justice, Equality and Peace' in S. Mehta, (ed.) *Women for Afghan Women. Shattering Myths and Claiming the Future*, New York: Palgrave MacMillan.

Voselsang, W. (2002) *The Afghans*, Oxford: Blackwell.

Wali, S. (2002) 'Afghanistan: Truth and Mythology' in S. Mehta, (ed.) *Women for Afghan Women. Shattering Myths and Claiming the Future*, New York: Palgrave Macmillan.

Wassef N. (2001) 'On Selective Consumerism: Egyptian Women and Ethnographic Representations'. *Feminist Review* 69, 45-57.

Watson, G. (1987) 'Make Me Reflexive - But not Yet: Strategies for Managing Essential Reflexivity in Ethnographic Discourse', *Journal of Anthropological Research* 43, 29-39.

Webster, F. (2003) 'Information Warfare in an Age of Globalization' in D. Kishan Thussu and D. Freedman (eds.) *War and the Media. Reporting Conflict 24/7*, London: Sage.

Wetherell, M. and Edley, N. (1999) *Negotiating Hegemonic Masculinity: Imaginary Positions and Psycho-Discursive Practices*, London: Sage.

Wilson, A. (1979) *The Strange Ride of Rudyard Kipling. His Life and Works*, Manchester: Granada Publishing Limited in Panther Books.

Winter, S. (1998) 'Mental Culture: Liberal Pedagogy and the Emergence of Ethnographic Knowledge'. *Victorian Studies* 41, 427-454.

Yanagisako, S. and Delaney, C. (1995) *Naturalizing Power. Essays in Feminist Cultural Analysis*, New York and London: Routledge.

Young R. (ed.) (1981) *Untying the Text: A Post-Structuralist Reader*, Boston: Routledge and Kegan Paul Ltd.

Young R. (2001) *Postcolonialism. An Historical Introduction*, Oxford: Blackwell.

Youngs T. (2004) 'Auden's travel writings' in S. Smith, (ed.) Cambridge: Cambridge University Press.

Newspaper Articles

Atwood M. (2001) 'Taking the Veil', the *Guardian*, November 17.

Beaumont, P. (2001) 'Tyranny of veil is slow to lift', the *Observer*, 30 December.

Bellamy, C. (2001) 'The proud warriors yet to be defeated', the *Daily Mail*, 17 September.

Benson, R. (2001) 'The city of the damned', the *Daily Mail*, 19 September.

Benson, R. (2001) 'Into the War Zone', the *Daily Mail*, 1 October.

Boyce, Sir M. (2001) 'Bayonet to bayonet fighting', the *Mirror*, 27 October.

Carew, T. (2001) 'My life with the mujahideen', the *Sunday Times News Review*, 23 September.

Clark, J. (2001) 'Poised to fight', the *Sunday Times News Review*, 31 September.

Colvin, M. (2001) 'Living with the sins', the *Sunday Times News Review*, 23 September.

De Courcy, A. (2001) 'Horsemen of the apocalypse', the *Daily Mail*, 22 September.

(2002) 'Fearless trekker follows in the footsteps of Mogul emperor', the *Observer*, 12 February.

Fisk, R. (2001) 'What Will the Northern Alliance Do in Our Name Now? I Dread to Think…', the *Independent*, 14 November.

Franchetti, M. (2001) 'Our bloodthirsty friends in the north', the *Sunday Times*, 29 September.

Franchetti, M. (2001) 'Defection of key men', the *Sunday Times*, 14 October.

Gall, S. (2001) 'Some believe that defeat by Afghanistan led to the collapse of the Soviet Union – a lesson US and its allies should not forget', the *Mirror*, 19 September.

Levy, G. (2001) 'The Taliban Tough it Out', the *Daily Mail*, 19 September.

Lycett, A. (2001) 'How Kipling created the Afghan myth', the *Sunday Times News Review*, 30 September.

Shah, S. (2001) 'Land of my father', the *Guardian*, 26 June.

Shah, S. (2001) 'Back beneath the veil', the *Guardian*, 8 November.

Swain, J. (2001) 'Starving Afghans set for Biblical exodus', the *Sunday Times*, 30 September.

Toolis, K. (2001) 'Inside the Taliban', the *Mirror*, 15 September.

Williams, D. (2001) 'The brutal regime that makes its women non-people', the *Daily Mail*, 29 September.

Radio Programmes and Television Documentaries

Arney, G. (2001) 'Talking, Afghan style', 'From Our Own Correspondent', BBC *Radio 4*, 30 November.

Bennet-Jones, O. (2001) 'I want to be a hostage', 'From Our Own Correspondent', BBC *Radio 4*, 12 February.

Bennet-Jones, O. (2001) 'Afghanistan's scholarly soldiers', 'From Our Own Correspondent', BBC *Radio 4*, 13 October.

Channel Four (2002), 'The House of War' for *True Stories*, broadcast 4 July.

Clark, K. (2001) 'Afghan dream comes true', 'From Our Own Correspondent', BBC *Radio 4*, 20 November.

Cuff, J. (2004) 'File on Four', special report on the Afghan elections, broadcast 29 June 2004.

Davis, C. (2001) 'Life plods on in opposition Afghanistan', 'From Our Own Correspondent', BBC *Radio 4*, 26 September.

Doucet, L. (2001) 'That's nice, I'm prime minister!', 'From Our Own Correspondent', BBC *Radio 4*, 11 December.

Gara, C. (2002) 'Dispatches: Lifting the Veil', Channel Four, 10 November.

Greste, P. (2001) 'An Afghan odyssey', 'From Our Own Correspondent', BBC *Radio 4*, 17 November.

Harding, A. (2002) 'Amorous advances in Afghanistan', 'From Our Own Correspondent', BBC *Radio 4*, 27 April.

Johnston, A. (2001) 'An encounter with General Dostum', 'From Our Own Correspondent', BBC *Radio 4*, 26 October.

Langhan, S. (2001) 'Langhan Behind the Lines: Tea with the Taliban', BBC2, 27 February.

Lomax, D. (2002) 'Panorama with the Paras', BBC1, 24 February.

Milligan, R. (2000) 'Afghanistan: through veiled eyes', 'From Our Own Correspondent', BBC *Radio 4*, 8 January.

Morris, K. (2002) 'Caught in the Crossfire', 'From Our Own Correspondent', BBC *Radio 4*, 7 September.

Miron, R. (2002) 'Fierce battles over dead goats', 'From Our Own Correspondent', BBC *Radio 4*, 7 January.

North, A. (2004) 'Following the Afghan drugs trail', 'From Our Own Correspondent', BBC *Radio 4*, 4 June.

Osbourne, P. (2003) 'Here's One We Invaded Earlier', Channel Four, May 31.

Price, S. (2001) 'Kandahar's musical revival', 'From Our Own Correspondent', BBC *Radio 4*, 23 February.

Rees, P. (2001) 'Correspondent: The Afghan Trap', BBC2, 2 December.

Reeve, W. (2001), 'Return to Kabul', 'From Our Own Correspondent', BBC *Radio 4*, 12 November.

Samura, S. (2002) '21st Century War:1 (the Good Guys)', Channel Four, 15 December.

Simpson, J. (2001) 'Afghanistan – The Dark Ages', BBC1, 7 October.

Wooldridge, M. (2003) 'Breaking the Silence: Music in Afghanistan', BBC4, 18 June.

Wyatt, C. (2001) 'Afghan women's life in the shadows', 'From Our Own Correspondent', BBC *Radio 4*, 16 October.

Index